BEYOND CONSOLATION

By the same author and available from Continuum:
Lapsed Agnostic

Beyond Consolation

JOHN WATERS

continuum
LONDON • NEW YORK

Published by the Continuum International Publishing Group Ltd

The Tower Building   80 Maiden Lane
11 York Road   Suite 704
London   New York
SE1 7NX   NY 10038

www.continuumbooks.com

First published 2010

British Library Cataloguing-in-Publication Data
A catalogue record for this book is available from the British Library.

ISBN 978-1-44111-421-1

Typeset in Janson by Tony Lansbury, Tonbridge, Kent.
Printed and bound by the MPG Books Group.

Contents

— 1 —
Give Me Back Yesterday

The headline just below the masthead of the *Sunday Independent* reads now as if directed at someone who already knew the news. There was a colour photograph of the author Nuala O'Faolain and, underneath her name, in orange type, a headline in white: 'I'm dying … Give me back yesterday.'

I was standing inside the door of a newsagent's shop in Longford, scanning the front pages of the Sunday newspaper to see if anything significant had happened while we were out of town. I was, that April Sunday, coming back from Sligo with my daughter. We had been away since Friday afternoon and, as usual, had been avoiding despatches from the outside world.

It is a strange sensation to miss something so important, like sleeping through the moon landings or returning from holidays to find that a government has collapsed and the country is halfway into an election campaign, though, for Ireland in the precise moment at which this interview occurred, what we had missed was far more significant than either.

No single event in Irish culture in my lifetime has quite equalled the impact of the interview Nuala O'Faolain gave to her longtime friend Marian Finucane shortly after Nuala was diagnosed with terminal cancer in the spring of 2008. No book I can think of, no painting, no movie, no speech, no television programme, no newspaper article, no poem or song, has touched the places this interview touched. Nothing that occurred or was said in the Irish public square in the previous generation had, in one piercing moment, so comprehensively summoned up, and in a manner that allowed eveyone an opportunity to examine it, the condition of human existence at a frozen moment in Irish life. There was no

1

escaping the embrace of this intervention, whether you were among those who heard it as it happened or who learned about it afterwards.

Give me back yesterday. At first sight it seemed like the title of a book, perhaps a philosophical reflection. If you knew what it was about, of course, it would not strike you in this way, but my first response managed to avoid entirely its literal and almost unambiguous meaning. The last thing I thought about, strangely enough, was that Nuala O'Faolain might be dying. In retrospect, the 'I'm dying' seemed to state the situation starkly. But, without the precise knowledge of what it alluded to, the second part of the headline seemed, at first sight, to undo the explicitness of the declaration. It might have been a philosophical observation on the nature of human existence: we are all dying. But, 'Give me back yesterday'. There was something ominous about these words, and yet, beside the photograph of the smiling author, they managed to conspire with something in the culture to nudge me away from immediate comprehension. I picked up a copy of the newspaper and turned, as instructed, to page four. There, the headline read: 'I don't want more time. As soon as I heard I was going to die, the goodness went from life.' Above this, in smaller type: 'Nuala O'Faolain tells of her anger and upset as she faces her last weeks on earth.'

I bought the newspaper in a daze and tried to find a coffee shop to read it in, but, this being Longford on a Sunday, had to give up and go on to Kinnegad.

On the way I thought how strange it was that nobody had told me about the interview, which (I learned) had been all but the sole topic of conversation in the country for the previous 30 hours. Afterwards, I came to see this as a piece with the generality of responses. The interview was, in a sense, big news, becoming a talking point in Ireland for many weeks afterwards and again following Nuala O'Faolain's death, almost exactly four weeks later. The interview itself was widely reproduced, almost all the newspaper carrying lengthy transcripts of long sections of it. People talked about the 'honesty', the 'courage' of it. And yet, somehow, it seemed that nobody was interested in getting to the core of what Nuala O'Faolain had said.

2

In Irish society, the dying are largely invisible and to an even greater extent inaudible. They do not advertise themselves. We talk about them sometimes, as though they were a different species. We feel sympathy for them dying like this, but no empathy. Our culture may once have sustained human beings up until the point of death itself, but it no longer does so. Nowadays, our culture is carefully constructed to filter discussion about death, and each of us has a very clear vested interest in colluding with this. When someone within the community is visited by the prospect of imminent death, he or she undergoes an immediate transformation in the eyes of the culture. At the announcement of terminal illness, something trips in the collective mind to cast the dying into another category, as though bad luck has rendered them different from the rest of us. It is not that they have entered another phase of the natural human cycle, but that they have already moved outside the culture's definition of the human entity. They become objects of pity and sympathy, but not of identification. In the coming days and weeks, this condition would be reflected in the commentary that followed the interview and subsequent death of Nuala O'Faolain.

As often happens when one gets such news, my response was edged with regret. Nuala O'Faolain and I had had a brittle relationship over much of the previous 17 or 18 years in which we had known each other. We had never been friends, but had been, at the outset, quite friendly. My first contact with her occurred just after I joined the *Irish Times* as a feature writer in the summer of 1990. She was by then a well-established columnist with the paper and also undertook occasional feature writing and reporting assignments. Although she was about 15 years older than me, we belonged to the same cultural generation, the one defined by the opening-up of Irish society to the wider world in the 1960s.

When I first joined the *Irish Times* I worked from home and rarely went into the office, but, on my occasional visits, I would sometimes encounter Nuala, who always seemed to have a perspective on whatever it was I would be writing about, or what was going on in a more general way, and was never shy about letting me know what she felt. In the beginning our conversations were brief and infrequent, but more and more I found myself being willingly diverted by her bubbling enthusiasm, occasionally disquieting forthrightness and tendency towards indiscretion.

In 1991, I became a columnist myself and we suddenly found ourselves with something more in common. From then on, for a while, she began ringing me once or twice a week to discuss events and what she believed were our mutual interests within the newspaper. She thought we columnists should stick together more, perhaps meet once a month to discuss what we were doing and how we felt we were being deployed and treated within the newspaper. She had this idea that we were all involved in some common endeavour, perhaps to do with societal progress or raising consciousness or something, whereas I saw us as separate, discrete entities in a flux of perspectives that might, at most, indicate some direction by accident or osmosis.

Her idea about creating a fellowship of *Irish Times* columnists did not come to anything: there was never as much as an inaugural meeting. Nobody except Nuala seemed greatly taken by the idea. But I liked her, and enjoyed meeting her, most of the time. Her desk was a couple of rows behind mine, and sometimes she would wander down to ask me what I thought about this or that or to deliver herself of some unprompted declaration about someone or something in the news. I found her engaging and good-humoured, most of the time, and we would occasionally become diverted into longer conversations over by the photocopier or on the flaking stairwell that connected the newsroom with the features department.

She wasn't one for small talk, but had a habit of launching into her point. After reading an interview I did with the U2 singer Bono one day, she walked over and asked, 'So, this rock music thing – it has its own language, like modern art, that you need to learn before you can tune into it at all?' Then we were off for an hour or perhaps two, while the newsroom cranked up through its gears behind us.

Sometimes she could seem offhand, even rude. If she was distracted by something or had no particular bone to pick that day, she could pass by my desk without a word, or, if preoccupied with something she was working on, would terminate an approach in a word or two. Sometimes she would ring me at home and talk for hours, but the next day I might call her back and encounter, for no particular reason that I could fathom, a terse and businesslike Nuala who sought to terminate the conversation as quickly as possible. I learned not to take this personally. The next time I met her, she would be in a different mood and we would behave as if the previous episode had never occurred.

I remember one laughter-filled afternoon we spent at a seminar organised by the *Irish Times* management to induct us into a new method of 'communication' and people management, whereby each journalist would be allocated a personal file, a kind of report card, which would be updated once a year in a process of consultation between the journalist and his or her line manager. It was an idea imported from America and was patently ill-suited to the purposes of an Irish newspaper. Nuala and I ended up sitting together at the seminar and making our tutor miserable in our attempts to outdo one another in satirising the idea. We spent most of the day laughing like schoolchildren.

Later on, our relationship entered a different phase, one of mutual, albeit 'professional', hostility. We found ourselves on opposite sides of an ideological battle in which feelings had a tendency to run high. Nuala was a convinced feminist and I, as the 1990s gave way to the new millennium, found myself writing more and more about the hidden discriminations affecting men, largely as a result of discovering the way family courts were treating fathers whose relationships with their children's mothers had run into conflict. Once or twice, Nuala wrote scathing pieces about my contributions on these subjects and and on one occasion I replied in kind.

In December 2000, I responded to a column written by Nuala from the United States, where she was then living, in which she criticised me and another *Irish Times* colleague, Kevin Myers, for what she termed our 'self-indulgent abusiveness' towards feminists. She criticised the way we wrote about 'an imaginary race called women'; it was not what we said, but the way we said it. She had been 'sharply hurt', she wrote, by the way Myers and I had written about issues in relation to what used to be called 'the sexes' but are nowadays called 'the genders'. 'The rancour and even venom behind their generalisations and the way they use "feminist" as a curse-word, is terribly upsetting', she wrote. Neither of us, she asserted, would 'last long' in a reputable newspaper in the United States.

I responded by challenging Nuala to cite examples of the kinds of things she was talking about. I had never used 'feminist' as a curse-word, never made generalised statements about women and had not been guilty of self-indulgent abusiveness. I quoted a number of her own statements about men, which might well be described as ticking several of the boxes she had mentioned in her indictment of Myers and myself. ('The evil of machismo is driving the suffering of the planet'; 'Many men avoid, as best they can, the ennui of caring for their children.')

I had immediately recognised in the response a typical feminist strategy: project onto your opponent things you yourself are trying to get away with, and bury their arguments under a mess of personalised and unsubstantiated insinuation. Nuala had not cited one line of anything either I or Kevin Myers had written. In fact, my articles had, in the main, been attempts to draw attention to the way society, with the assistance of the feminist cohort, had been burying the claims of men to have relationships with their own children. In her article, Nuala had graciously acknowledged that I had been 'a truly important voice for unmarried fathers', but I recalled in response that, when I first began to speak about this issue, Nuala O'Faolain had been among those who had attacked me.

I went on: 'But Ms O'Faolain's article was useful in that it exhibited the intellectually dishonest nature of feminist responses to criticism, and revealed why they are really "offended". Feminists feel no obligation to obey the courtesies of public discourse because until recently they have been beyond criticism. Having created a massive victimology out of the alleged oppression of women, they arrogated to themselves the entitlement to speak for all women and created an eleventh Commandment: "Thou shalt not criticise women." Feminism was the first of what is now a lengthening line of societal sub-groups and ideological platforms which can claim immunity from criticism by the simple expedient of accusing their critics of hating half the human race.

'What "offends" feminists about what Kevin Myers and I write about gender is not "the way they say it", but that our arguments are unanswerable.

'I have witten about fatherhood, male health, homelessnes and suicide, the abuse of men in the family courts and the Big Lie concerning domestic violence. Always I have written as an advocate of men and their human rights, my references to women being largely incidental. Essentially, I have suggested that men are in certain ways oppressed. Feminists, claiming a monopoly on suffering for women, do not like this. Nor do they like the fact that, by advancing a plausible case, people like myself and Kevin Myers have had an effect on public consciousness. It is imperative that we be shamed into silence. And this is why no feminist has ever responded to an article of mine with a coherent refutation or critique, but always with *ad hominem* abuse and the childish assertion that I am "anti-women".'

Nuala's article employed the full feminist armoury, implying, *inter alia*, that Myers and I were probably not getting enough sex. 'Ninety per cent of the woman-haters in the world don't hate women at all', wrote Nuala. 'They just want more and better sex for themselves.'

One of the most extraordinary aspects of her article was the way she presented Kevin and me as on one side of a line, with herself and womenfolk in general on the other. If women ruled the world, she declared, the world would be a better place than it was. 'Ireland would not be like it is. The desks of opinion columnists would not be tidied while they sleep by women who are doing night-cleaning work so as to be at home to give their kids their breakfasts before getting them off to school.'

This was too much for me to take. In response, I noted the 'staggering condescension of a privileged Oxbridge scholar sniping from behind the skirts of working women who have more in common with most working men than with her'. I pointed out that I no longer had a desk in the *Irish Times*, and also that, as a single parent who works from home, I very often worked in the early hours at my desk in the attic, and then went downstairs to prepare my child's breakfast and get her ready for school. In this I was responding implicitly to something Nuala had written before: that children 'belong' to mothers in a way they could never belong to fathers, and it seemed to me that, in this recent contribution she had gone a little further and implied that all women were entitled to consider children as 'belonging' to them in a way they could never be considered to 'belong' to men, even to their own fathers. It was, I felt, as these things go, a pretty comprehensive deconstruction of something that, in the absence of a response, might have had the culture nodding in pious agreement with Nuala O'Faolain.

When the anger of the moment died down, as often happens with such exchanges, I regretted the occasionally personalised tone of what I had written, so much so in fact that, although she tried to reopen the discussion a couple of times with subsequent criticisms of things I had written, I did not respond.

My settled feeling about all this ideological battling is that really it is all a convoluted adversarial process by which a society eventually comes to see what is obvious. Each side becomes entrenched in a partial view, and prosecutes this to the absolute boundary of sense, sometimes beyond. But really, everyone is involved in the same process of discovery, while seeing things from varying perspectives on the argument. My settled, and I hope not sentimental, feeling about Nuala O'Faolain is the same as my feeling about many other feminists I have done battle with. Rather than opponents, I see us like the two guys in a poem by Rumi: 'And watch two men washing clothes. One makes dry clothes wet, the other makes wet clothes dry. They seem to be thwarting each other, but their work is a perfect harmony.'

Of course, if I could say this now to Nuala, I know what she would say: 'When did you ever see two men washing clothes?'

We never met again, so I have no way of knowing how personally she took these somewhat peevish and rancorous exchanges, or how she responded to the underlying knot of difference they indicated. At the time, I was in the frame of mind to take them quite personally, but these things somehow nearly always blow over and there is no way of knowing how we might have dealt with the matter had we met. One of the pitfalls of being a public commentator is that you must occasionally run into those whom you have criticised or locked horns with in print. Another is that such people sometimes die before you do, leaving you unable, fearing accusations of hypocrisy, to join in the public ourpouring of tributes and regret.

I was torn between these feelings as, in the Hilamar Hotel in Kinnegad I read the lengthy transcript of the previous day's interview. The facts were stark and bleak. Nuala O'Faolain was dying of cancer and expected to be dead in a matter of weeks. She had been diagnosed six weeks previously in New York. There was nothing philosophical about the notion of her dying. 'Now I am actually dying', she said, 'and I have metastatic cancer in three different parts of my body.' The disease, which began in her lungs, had spread to her brain and liver. It was incurable. She had turned down the option of chemotherapy.

It was as if I had been dealt a blow. It is not that I felt a sense of loss in any sentimental sense, for I had not known Nuala well enough or recently enough to have that kind of response based on friendship or attachment. I had liked her and, in a particular way, loathed her, in different situations and at different times. There was some of the usual feeling you get when you hear such news about anyone you have been acquainted with, even vaguely or incidentally. There is a certain element of curiosity, of fascination with the remorseless action of the force that creates and destroys us. But underneath that there was a complex of feelings: shock at the lucidity with which she expressed her condition; a sense of loss on her behalf for what had been a somewhat autumnal but nevertheless successful literary career; some guilt about the way we had become estranged in public; some regret about the fact that this situation was now placed beyond mending. It seemed clear to me that I could not, after all that had been said and done between us, approach her in these final weeks of her life. What would I say? What would she say? What if she had been deeply hurt and offended by our remote exchanges? I think now that this was cowardly of me, but at the time it seemed unthinkable that I could seek to make contact with her.

Beyond that, I got to the feelings I soon realised everyone was getting to as a result of her interview. There was a numbness at the thought of death, any death. There was sorrow for the loss of such an exuberant spirit, but combined with a wish that, if the outcome was as certain as she seemed to believe, it would be over for her sooner rather than later. And there was a kind of wonderment and even a perverse kind of envy that someone finding herself in this dizzying, once-in-a-lifetime situation, could attain such presence-of-mind in describing her feelings.

Reading the transcript, I felt myself torn between a morbid fascination and a kind of despair. There was an unfairness about the idea that someone still relatively young, and in the prime of her professional life, could be struck down. I had seen this before, a number of times, with close friends. But always such people had retreated behind a veil of ambiguity, denying death, defying death, making jokes about death, but never spelling out how they saw what was happening to them.

Situations involving imminent, premature death invariably acquire a strange triangularity, whereby the dying person and those who know and love him or her are separated behind Chinese walls. You might expect that, armed with the same information about the prognosis, both parties would, with whatever difficulty and sorrow, enter into a dialogue based on these facts, but this rarely happens. The doctors, very often, will outline the position directly and truthfully to both the patient and those close to the patient, but separately and on the basis of a confidential charter. Thus, nobody is freed up to state the situation plainly. Often, what seems to happen is that the person facing death bends over backwards to spare those loved ones, who themselves wish to spare the patient having to speak about something that they themselves do not want to talk about and assume he or she doesn't want to either. There then follows a pretence, punctuated by occasional outbreaks of gallows humour, followed by denials and further pretence.

— 2 —
Where Every Tear Will Be Wiped Away

In a previous book, *Lapsed Agnostic*, I described how, as a child of nine or ten, I started going to funerals on my father's behalf, as his kind of aide-de-camp. He had an unusual attitude towards funerals, in that he seemed to want to mark the passing of any member of the community, no matter how slight their relationship had been. So whenever word of a death came through, sometimes once or several times a week at particular times of the year, he would give me a pound note and a mass card and send me down to the priest to have it signed in return for this not inconsiderable consideration. And because he was invariably working while the funeral was happening, I began to take on the responsibility of going along to the funeral mass as well, placing the signed card in the wooden box at the foot of the coffin in front of the altar, lining up with all the other locals and sympathising with the bereaved family members.

What I did not write in that book was that I had, many years later, revisited these experiences with the help of Ivor Browne, a psychiatrist who used to organise group therapies in a disused church in the grounds of Grangegorman mental hospital, in Dublin, in which people could undergo a therapy based on holotrophic breathing in order to 're-experience' any traumatic experiences that lurked in their pasts. The therapy involves deep abdominal breathing and loud music of varying styles spliced together to create different moods, each mood being allowed to assert itself briefly and then be broken suddenly to deflect the patient into a different level of consciousness. Ivor, who had been a friend of mine for some years, invited me to come along and take part in one of his occasional weekends devoted to helping people get in touch with their 'inexperienced experiences'. I was curious but sceptical about the capacity of any such therapy to take me to any part of my mind I wasn't already familiar with. Moreover, I was suspicious of the concept of recovered memory, having read about innumerable cases in Britain in which the memories thus excavated had turned out to be unreliable, some resulting in false charges of sexual abuse. But Ivor was persuasive, so one Friday afternoon in November 1994 I turned up at the church in Grangegorman along with about 30 other seekers after whatever it was we were seeking.

The weekend started with a little dancing, and then some exercises in free association. As we were dancing around, I was reminded of the film *One Flew Over the Cuckoo's Nest*, my all-time favourite movie, in which Jack Nicholson plays McMurphy, a small-time criminal who ends up in a psychiatric hospital and causes mayhem among the long-stay inmates. Late on Friday afternoon, Ivor asked us to pair off for the therapy, the idea being that, while one of us was undergoing it, the other partner would keep a watch. I was paired with a man from Cork, who had done the therapy before. He wasn't hugely forthcoming about his experience, but I gathered that he had encountered some kind of block that had caused him to stop responding at a certain point. I was to be his guardian angel during the first session, and we would swap positions for the second session later in the evening.

I was, as I say, sceptical. I did not find the idea reasonable, in the sense that its logic was beyond my experience. That you could induce regression in yourself by the simple expedient of breathing faster seemed to me to be insane. I was pretty convinced that I was among a bunch of neurotic narcissists who had nothing better to do than fantasise about the possible reasons why life had sometimes given them a rough ride.

My scepticism was jolted somewhat when the therapy started. In less than a minute the whole place was bedlam. The people undergoing the therapy were lying on mattresses on the floor, and some of them began to writhe and scream and cry, while others jumped up and had to be restrained by the nurses who were supervising. My partner immediately launched into the repetition of a mantra, with which he persisted for the duration of the therapy: 'I'm a stone, I'm a stone, I'm a stone, I'm a stone ...'

It was wondrous and frightening, but I remained unconvinced that it had anything much to tell me. I suspected that most of those present were probably recidivist fantasists who indulged in regression therapies in the way other people played golf. At the same time, I was becoming more curious and intrigued.

Beforehand, I had tried to elicit from Professor Browne, with little success, some sense of how the process of 'remembering' might register. Would I suddenly re-enter a past time and find myself aware of a three-dimensional reality that I recognised? Would the memories come flooding back, as though a reservoir of repressed memories had burst its walls? Would I see the faces of people from my childhood, as in a movie, and would they look as they had looked then, rather than the way they looked now?

None of these things happened. I lay on the mattress, listened to the music build up, and followed the taped instructions issuing over a tannoy system. I began to breathe rapidly from my abdomen. In truth I remained sceptical, thinking that, at the very least, Ivor was going to be disappointed with this particular patient. This prospect worried me somewhat also, because I was anxious to please and did not want to be the odd man out. Nothing seemed to be happening. Then, suddenly, I felt cold. I asked my partner to get me an extra blanket and hoped that Ivor would come along soon because my teeth were beginning to chatter. This would keep Ivor happy, I reflected. I then noticed that something appeared to be happening to my legs, which had gone numb and seemed to be tensed as though comprising single unjointed limbs.

At that moment, Ivor did come along and asked, 'So what's going on here?' as if he was certain, in spite of all my reservations, that something would be going on. Delighted to be able to make a contribution to things, I said, 'I can't feel my feet'. He bent down, grabbed my two feet and slid them up towards my body. It was as if he had thrown a switch. Instantly I began to cry, not a sobbing or a weeping but a full-blown wailing that drowned out all the other noises in the church. I had no idea what I was crying about, but I appeared to be experiencing a grief greater than I had ever imagined. I remained conscious of the space around me, of my partner The Stone, now himself sobbing inconsolably while kneeling by my mattress. I cried for perhaps two hours, until I was weary of crying as I had never been weary of anything. But still no memory came, no movie, no faces from the past.

Ivor was delighted. 'I knew you fellas from the West always have dark secrets stored away', he declared. 'We're going to have to get you out of that blackness.' This, I knew, was a code for Ketamine, an hullucinogenic drug he sometimes used to speed up the therapy. Some of my fellow patients had already succumbed to the promise of the needle, wielded by a nurse known as Ketamine Carmel. One guy, when the nurse pulled down his shorts to administer the injection, was observed to have adorned his backside with the inscription, 'Hi Carmel!'

I was adamant that I would not take the drug. I had given up alcohol four years previously and was nervous about the possibility of discovering a new outlet for my infinite desires. When, in the wake of my wailing session, Ivor again broached the idea of taking the drug, I determinedly declined.

The next day we did it all over again. My partner had reverted to stoniness and his session was uneventful. When mine began, I once more found myself sliding into a sea of grief, this time almost immediately. Ivor came along. 'We'll have to put a stop to this', he said. Once more I refused to take the Ketamine. The crying went on. But this time something happened. There was no movie, no flashback as such, but suddenly there was a slight change of awareness, like stumbling across a memory in the course of a daydream. It came to me in the form of a moving image, but not in any insistent way, not as an irruption of something unknown, but merely as the sudden encroachment of a fleeting and at first unexceptional thought. I pulled it back and looked at it. I remembered what it was. I could recall a coffin being carried aloft on the shoulders of several men, up the steps of a church, which I took to be my local church at home. It was the colour of the coffin that struck me. It was almost yellow, much brighter than the usual coffin or casket, a light coat of varnish on a box of white deal, the cheapest timber you could buy. I knew immediately that it was a 'County Council coffin', the kind you used to get if your family could not afford to bury you and had to ask the local authority for assistance.

I knew, too, that the coffin contained the remains of a man called Jack McLoughlin, who used to sometimes come to our house to 'throw in' the turf or tidy up the garden. To me he had always been elderly. I used to help him throw in the turf and he would enthral me with stories of his life, going back to the War of Independence. Many years after his death, I had now registered, for the first time since the event, that this noble and beautiful man had been buried in a County Council coffin.

But this was not the whole of my grief. Within moments, by whatever process of the mind's appetite for connections, I found myself revisiting the scenes of a hundred funerals, including my granny's, 30 years before. I had never cried at a funeral, except at my maternal grandmother's, when I was nine years old, and someone had immediately asked me, 'What's wrong with you, young fella, did someone hurt ya?'

All the sadness I had never expressed at encountering the griefs of all these neighbours suddenly came to the surface. For several years in my childhood I had zoomed in close to this sorrow but had never allowed myself to share in it. I had watched from a distance as wives sobbed over the coffins of husbands taken suddenly by heart attacks, and mothers having to be lifted out of the graves of their children whom they did not want to leave behind in the cold earth. I had watched it all unblinkingly. I had not shed a single tear. Now I was shedding them all at once, in a way that seemed to defy all understandings of the body's capacity to retain water.

Then, weakened from crying and longing to stop, I almost pulled the arm off Ivor when he came along and suggested again that I take a shot of Ketamine to jolt me out of this dark place. We agreed on half the normal dose, but it was enough.

Immediately I began to shiver again. I thought I was about to re-enter the grief with a renewed vigour, but the opposite happened. I started to laugh. I laughed as long and as loud as I had cried. The mood of the church seemed immediately transformed. I was able to hear the voices of people whispering at the far end of the church and soon began to engage in conversations with them. I repeated lines I remembered from *One Flew Over the Cuckoo's Nest* – 'Give me my fucking cigarettes, Nurse Ratched. I want my fucking cigarettes.' Afterwards I learned that this caused a woman whose abusive father had made her go out to the shops to buy his fags, to jump up and make to throttle me. At the time I noticed a flurry of peripheral activity but hadn't really registered what it was about.

The Ketamine experience reminded me of being on the piss, of drinking to escape, and drinking, as I had done, as if to jump out of my skin. The connection between this and the grief seemed inescapable. Ivor told me later that there appeared to be an extraordinary degree of separation between the dark and light sides of my personality, like a corridor in which all the light was at one end, though I didn't really need him to tell me this. I also became aware, without his prompting, that this separation had been some-where close to the root of my problematic drinking, that I had used drink to achieve something of the effect achieved by Ketamine Carmel and her needle full of hope.

I had never given a moment's conscious thought to the fact that I had been to so many funerals at such a young age, and that this might not be the most natural thing in the world for a child to be doing. It was a curiosity, a light-hearted anecdote to tell in the pub, but no more than that. Looking back, it seemed clear that what I had done was shut myself off from the sorrow of others, and then to mimic their sadness as a way of conveying sympathy, striking the right note and fitting in. I had, literally, dissociated myself from their grief, but had drawn it to myself also, in a horrified and yet fascinated kind of way.

We know about death, and sometimes get to observe it up close, but our sense of things is that it is something that happens to other people. And when it does happen to other people, we tend to look at it less than squarely, for fear of allowing into our vision the prospect that it will one day happen to each of us.

Nearly 20 years ago, a friend of mine, Derek Dunne, a fellow journalist then in his thirties, died painfully of cancer of the pancreas. Everyone knew he was dying, including himself. And yet neither he nor any of his friends could find words to talk with him about this. I visited him right up to the night before he died. Each time, we talked about nothing but the future, the books we might write, the mischief we would cause, the many things we had yet to experience of life's glorious possibilities. At the end of each of these encounters, we found ourselves doing something we had never done before, in all our years of friendship. When parting, we would shake hands, with a nonchalant 'See you tomorrow'. As Derek grew weaker, I noticed that, each evening, his handshake grew stronger until one evening his grip was so strong that I thought he would break my hand. 'See you tomorrow', he said. He died a few hours later.

Human societies have always had a fear of death, but what we call 'traditional' societies had ways of dealing with this. Mostly, such mechanisms came in the guise of religion, a communal conscious-ness of mankind's relationship to the infinite mysteries of the universe and creation, which deals with the fundamentals of human life in ways that we have disastrously come to regard as optional extras of human culture.

In a country town, the death of a local is followed by an intensely ritualised few days, during which each member of the community becomes, to a greater or lesser extent, bound up in the emotion of the event. From the spreading of the news to the filling of the grave, and even beyond, there is a time-honoured process by which the death is absorbed and accommodated by the community.

To facilitate the engagement of the community with the loss of one of its members, the remains of the dead person will be laid out either at home or (a relatively recent development) in a local funeral home. The removal to the local church, usually at evening time, will be attended by the vast majority of local people, who will stand in line to sympathise with the bereaved, a process sometimes lasting four or five hours. Next day, the mass and burial will attract even more people, and afterwards it is common for everyone to be invited to a local hotel for lunch or refreshments. At the end of what is usually a three-day period, the ritual will have made on the consciousness of the community an impression that, while remind-ing every member of his or her mortality, also functions to dissipate some of the natural dread that the idea of death strikes in the unprotected human heart.

When I left my home town to go and live in Dublin, one of the things I welcomed was the liberation from these almost weekly rituals. But then, gradually, I became aware that this freedom came at a price. Going home for weekends, and reading in the local paper of the deaths of people I had casually known, I became aware of a feeling in myself of what I will call stagnant sorrow. The deaths were affecting me in the way they had always done, but, without the opportunity to participate in the extended rituals of quasi-official mourning, I was left with unresolved feelings of loss and sadness that my reason and sense of reality had not led me to anticipate.

A similar feeling would overcome me sometimes in Dublin, when occasionally, driving along, I would be obliged to pull in to allow a funeral to go by. I would sit there and bless myself, glancing into the back seat of the limousine following the hearse. There would be nothing new in any of it, but still it never failed to unsettle me, and afterwards I would note in myself a feeling of gnawing desolation which might sometimes last for a day or more. I have no doubt that it was this avoided, postponed grief, this stagnant sorrow, that became unleashed on that mattress in Grangegorman.

My tears, in a sense, had been a measure of the loss of something unacknowledged in myself: one of the taken-for-granted benefits of an essentially religious society. Nowadays we tend to reduce religion to the idea of an enforced system of controls on our happiness, allegedly in preparation for the perfection of the Hereafter, and many of us have long since jettisoned this idea of curtailing the pleasures of this life in favour of an uncertain reward in the next. Oblivious of the deeper consequences, we have chosen what we think of as freedom and rejected this enforcement of what we had come to see as an imposed system of fear-driven control.

One of the collateral consequences of this shift has been the destruction of those elements in our culture which previously dealt deftly with death. Once the ritual brought the community to a moment of hope, and anticipation of the place where every tear would be wiped away. Now, implicitly, when we look to the end, we see not choirs of angels clustered around pearly gates, but a yawning abyss of nothingness from which we look rapidly away. To put it succinctly, we have condemened ourselves to years of terror because of a reluctance to bend the knee to an authoritarian God.

And this means that, at certain moments which await each of us, we have no words to say to one another. We cannot even look one another evenly in the eye. We must speak in code, in lame jokes, in patronising lies and embarrassed circumlocutions. We have lost the codes by which we communicated about one of the most fundamental aspects of our humanity.

We all know we are going to die. Well, actually we don't, not really. We understand, in a general kind of way, that humans are mortal, and that other people seem to die all the time; but our culture is constructed to remove from each of us, for much of our lives, the awareness that mortality is part of the condition that defines us. What was most arresting about the Nuala O'Faolain interview was that it provoked a moment in which this denial was not sustainable. But afterwards we returned to the denial, perhaps because the kind of society we have created gives us no other option. We have, surely, a responsibility to confront this, if only for our own selfish purposes.

I have noticed some odd phenomena in myself since I turned fifty. One is that, for the first time, I have become aware, to a degree that transcends the abstract, that I will die one day. When I find myself in or near a graveyard, I invariably nowadays reflect that, one day, what is left of my earthly self will end up in a place like this. For many years, thanks to the denial mechanism of the prevailing culture, I did not feel this.

I don't think I am unusual in the way I have thought, or have declined to think, about death. For most of my life, death has been a concept associated with other people. I have watched people die, have heard about people dying, have talked about death to people much like myself. But until I reached fifty I never thought about death as something that might happen to me. Of course, I knew in some abstract way that I would die one day, but I didn't think about the idea of my own death as something that came to bear on my existence, which comprised the present and the immediate future, a future so imaginatively elongated as to be all but infinite. Even when close friends died, sometimes friends who were younger than me, I didn't think of death as a risk to myself. These people, I seemed to tell myself, had contracted diseases, had been unlucky, had smoked too much. It wasn't that I thought myself particularly lucky in this regard or necessarily immune to the conditions that struck down others, but that I had some deep sense of a narrative thread to my own life that could be satisfied or resolved only in a very long, perhaps an infinitely long, life.

Then, almost literally one day, all this changed. I don't suggest it changed abruptly on my fiftieth birthday, but a process seems to have started on that day that has continued and grown stronger since then. I still think but rarely of death in a morbid, fearful way, but I certainly think of it a great deal more frequently than I used to. Perhaps it is still a little abstract. Sometimes my thoughts will turn to death when I am ill, which so far has been with something unserious, perhaps some flu or virus that drives me to bed in spite of myself. There, weakened and at a loose end, my thoughts will float morbidly towards the idea that, sooner or perhaps later, I may lie like this in a terminal condition. Such moments are merely depressing in a minor and somewhat abstract sort of way, and can usually be banished by the simple expedient of thinking about something else.

But my most vivid feelings about death, once I started to have them, happened not in episodes of downheartedness but as an aftertaste of some moment of pure joy arising from an engagement with the reality of life in the world. I would be walking along a country path in sunlight, the birds raising Cain all around me, a bee stuck in some obsessive clinch with a buttercup and buzzing as though trying to drown out the birdsong, when suddenly I would be struck by a feeling of inconsolable regret about the inevitable, permanent loss of such moments. No promise of eternity could hope to comfort me.

Such epiphanies seem to strike with increasing frequency as I grow older. Walking through the countryside, I come across a derelict cottage with most of the slates gone, the windows broken and the door off its hinges. I sneak inside and look around. The place is a mess into which nobody has entered for some time. The floor is strewn with old newspapers, boxes of books, crockery, bottles, a crumbling settee. But there is something more here than merely things – there is a feeling here that at first eludes any attempt to name it. I go from room to room and encounter the same feeling. There are bits and pieces of furniture about the rooms, an old iron bed with a rotting mattress, a wardrobe with a couple of old shirts still hanging there. A chest of drawers with a jumble of decaying rags of garments, and underneath some trinkets, an old watch and perhaps a bundle of what might be love letters. There is a smell of damp and must, but also of something else. Then it comes to me what the feeling is: terror. A terror of this place. A terror of the lives that were lived here and have left their traces. A terror of the meaning, the emotions, the joys and sorrows still attached to the objects around. A terror associated with the smell. The smell of decomposition. It comes at last: a terror of death, of the lives that were lived here but are now, what?, extinct? I leave, no, I run away. I seek out noise, bustle and cleanliness. I go to a coffee shop or a shopping mall, where there is shouting and laughter and spilling of drink. I go where there is life.

— 3 —

Winking at the Milky Way

'I think there's a wonderful rule of life,' Nuala O'Faolain told Marian Finucane, 'that means that we do not consider our own mortality. I know we seem to, and remember, "man thou art but dust", but I don't believe we do. I think there's an absolute difference between knowing that you are likely to die, let's say within the next year, and not knowing when you are going to die – an absolute difference.'

Yet, there was an odd disproportionality between the interview's content and the reaction it provoked. People talked about the interview being 'refreshing'. They said it was good to hear a terminally ill person talking so openly about death. Nobody said why it was refreshing or good to hear this. People said they were frightened by the interview, that they felt for Nuala O'Faolain, that they cried listening to the interview, but rarely went much beyond such declarations. It was as though the implication of such observations was agreed to be obvious, but most obvious of all was the phenomenon of avoidance.

People praised Nuala O'Faolain for her 'courage' and 'honesty', but I do not think they are the dominant elements of her contribution to public awareness in this interview. Most of what was said afterwards was remarkable only for its platitudinous characteristics. By general agreement, the importance of the interview was that this nationally known and beloved woman was prepared to talk at all about the fact that she would soon be dead, to look at some aspects of this situation and utter sentences about what she felt or thought. Most of the reactions conveyed a sense that, though death had placed its hand on the shoulder of Nuala O'Faolain, it was for the rest of us something to be briefly scrutinised and then allowed to slide back into the irrelevancy to which it belonged.

The interview seemed to be more than the sum of its parts. What marked it out was more the idea that someone was sharing such thoughts at all than that there was anything original or enlightening being said, or indeed that there was any great courage or honesty involved in saying it. Indeed, it seemed implicit in the exercise and in some of the things Nuala said at the outset that she was speaking out like this in search of some kind of comfort, reaching out to those whose lives she had touched before, perhaps in the hope that someone, somewhere, might be able to extend her some convincing form of consolation.

But it is difficult to say anything with certainty about the meaning of this, unless you were listening to the interview as it happened; only this could be said to constitute a total encounter with the experience. Reading the interview transcript a day later, I was aware that, having missed the event as it unfolded, I could never reach in myself for the intensity with which those who heard it would have responded. Reading it was enough to fill me with sorrow. I could only imagine what it might have been like to be hearing it as it happened. Still less could I imagine what it might have been like to be Nuala O'Faolain talking as she did about this most fundamental experience of her life.

I subsequently listened repeatedly to the interview, and was moved each time to a new degree – both by the content, which sounded infinitely more intense than I had imagined it from print, and the hushed and tearful tone of Nuala's voice. But by the time I came to hear it, I already knew what it contained, what it was about, and pretty much what it meant. I knew from the beginning where it was going. For those listening as it happened, it would have represented an entirely different experience, the kind of experience that even live radio rarely delivers, closer to a great play than a real-life episode, but lacking the deep-set knowledge you retain when witnessing a great play: that what you are hearing is fiction.

Nuala O'Faolain spoke of her situation before receiving the news. She had been happy. She had been in a relationship with a man who had a fourteen-year-old daughter, but had moved out to her own little room, which she loved, because she realised that she 'wasn't going to be any good as a stepmother'. She had been writing a book and had applied for a fellowship. But then, one day after fitness class about six weeks previously, she had felt a dragging in her right side and had gone to the A&E department of a New York hospital. She said: 'I was sitting there waiting to hear what was wrong with my right leg when the guy came past and said that "your CAT scan shows that you've got two brain tumours and we're going to do X-rays to see where they're from; they're not primaries". And that is the first ever, ever I knew.'

For a time she had been in shock. Then she decided to come home to Ireland. She had declined the offer of further treatment. 'Even if I gained time through the chemotherapy, it isn't time I want. Because as soon as I knew I was going to die soon, the goodness went out of life.

'It amazed me, Marian, how quickly life turned black, immediately almost. For example, I lived somewhere beautiful, but it means nothing to me any more – the beauty. For example, twice in my life I have read the whole of Proust. I know it sounds pretentious, but it's not a bit. It's like a huge soap opera. I tried again the week before last and it was gone, all the magic was gone from it.'

She had decided on dying sooner rather than later. She did not want to prolong the agony for the same thing to happen anyway at the end of an even lengthier period of misery than she knew she was facing now. 'You see, the cancer is a very ingenious enemy and when you ask somebody how will I actually die? How do you actually die of cancer? ... You know? I don't get an answer because it could be anything. It can move from one organ to the other, it can do this or the other. It's already in my liver, for example. So I don't know how it's going to be. And that overshadows everything. And I don't want six months or a year like that. It's not worth it.'

Marian Finucane put it to her: 'If there are people who have cancer or loved ones who have cancer and passionately believe that the treatments are going to work for them, there is the possibility that this could cast a despair over them.'

'My despair', Nuala replied, 'is my own. Their hope is their own. Their spirituality is their own. My way of looking at the world is my own. We each end up differently facing this common fate. I wish everybody out there a miracle cure.'

Much of the rest of the interview was about her family and how good they have been to her, about her email reconciliation with her former lover Nell McCafferty, one of the pioneers of Irish feminism, and about her recent trips, since the diagnosis, to Paris and New York, trying to rediscover the joy of living, even though she had so little time remaining. She talked about the loneliness at the core of the experience of dying. Sometimes, she said, she prayed for her friends to go away, 'for the very essence of this experience is aloneness'.

'So it is two in the morning or four in the morning and you're walking around and all you know is that whatever it is you are feeling or thinking is yours and nobody else's. And there is nobody else to lay it off on and that aloneness is the centre and the thing that you never know when you are well ...'

At times she brought to the interview the kind of detached clarity about her own feelings that had characterised her two volumes of autobiography. Compared to many others, she said, she was dying 'comfortably', compared to the many who had died in Auschwitz and Darfur, or in the Congo, or like her two brothers who had died of drink, exiled and alone. 'I have friends and family, I am in this wonderful country, I have money, there is nothing much wrong with me except dying.'

Asked by Marian Finucane if she believed in an afterlife, she replied in a whisper but emphatically: 'No, I do not.' Asked if she believed in a God, she said, laughing a little at some deep but perhaps inexpressible irony: 'Well that's a different matter somehow. I actually don't know how we all get away with our unthinkingness. Often last thing at night I've walked the dog down the lane and you look up at the sky illuminated by the moon and behind the moon the Milky Way and the Milky Way and the Milky Way, you know – you are nothing on the edge of one planet compared to this universe unimaginably vast up there and unimaginably mysterious.

'And I've done that for years, looked up at it and kind of given it a wink and thought "I don't know what's going on". And I still don't know what's going on, but I can't be consoled by ... by ... mention of God. I can't.'

Would she like to be so consoled?

'No.' In print it might have been anything, but when you heard it, there was no doubt. It was an emphatic 'No'.

'Oh no, I wouldn't. If I start doing that, something really bad is happening to my brain, though I was baptised and I remember my First Communion and I went to Catholic schools and I was in the Legion of Mary and I tried to stick to my pledge. And though I respect and adore the art that arises from the love of God and though nearly everybody I love and respect themselves believe in God, it is meaningless to me, really meaningless.'

At first glance this seems conclusive. But is it? It is interesting that, in response to two questions that the layperson might think of as amounting to the same idea, Nuala O'Faolain gave what might be seen as two conflicting answers. On the one hand, she emphatically dismissed the idea of an afterlife, but, on the other, thought that the issue of God was 'a different matter somehow'.

And I am greatly struck by her construction, which appears to have gone unnoticed by Marian Finucane at the time and was overlooked in all the discussion afterwards, that she didn't know 'how we all get away with our unthinkingness'. Perhaps she meant in relation to the image she invoked immediately afterwards, about the night sky and the vastness of the universe. Or perhaps she meant something else. If so, what? Our unthinkingness in respect of what? Of God? Although slightly later on she seemed to imply that she had no belief in God, her observation that 'that's a different matter somehow' implied that she was answering 'Yes', or a kind of yes to the question about God. Her next sentence, 'I actually don't know how we all get away with our unthinkingness', seems to hint at a much deeper set of perceptions, but it is left unexplored. But, then, going on, she seems to harden again, to close down what appeared to be an openness, perhaps even a plea for reassurance to the people listening. No, if she started to think of the consolation offered by the idea of God, something really bad would be happening to her brain. She wished people of belief every comfort, but she didn't think about it. She never believed in the Christian idea of an individual creator. How could she, knowing, as she did, so many 'Buddhists and atheists and every kind of thing'. Let 'poor human beings' believe what they want, but for her it was meaningless.

A strange thing is that the transcript of the interview as published in the newspapers on the day after the interview does not contain the phrase 'give me back yesterday'. Neither does the recording of the interview, although it does show that she said something subtly but critically different. Until I heard the interview, that phrase haunted me. Nothing else she said seemed to capture her desperation so comprehensively.

In the *Sunday Independent* version – and every other written transcript I was able to locate, by Googling and otherwise – her words in this section had been ever so slightly but oddly mis-transcribed. She had been talking about a song she wanted Marian Finucane to play at the end of the programme: 'And yet I want to mention one thing you might play at the end, particularly for dying people', the transcripts have her saying, 'but I picked up little bits here and there about Ireland, largely at the Merriman Summer School, which is one of the great things in my life, a song I heard a few years ago, "Thíos i Lár an Ghleanna" – a kind of modern song, 1929 I believe – and it's sung by Albert Fry and I think other Donegal singers. And the last two lines are two things, asking God up there in the heavens, even though you don't believe in him, to send you back, even though you know it can't happen. Those two things sum up where I am now.'

What Nuala O'Faolain said was exactly this: 'I know you don't go playing records, particularly for dying people, but still … I picked up little bits here and there about Ireland, largely at the Merriman Summer School, which has been one of the great things in my life, a song I heard a few years ago, that everyone else knows except me, and it's called "Thíos i Lár an Ghleanna" – a kind of modern song, 1929 I believe – and it's sung by Albert Fry and I think other Donegal singers.' She mentioned the final lines of the song, making a stab at the Irish but getting it clumsily wrong, and then trans-lating: 'And it's two things: asking God up there in the heavens, even though you don't believe in him, to send you back yesterday, even though you know it can't happen. Those two things sum up where I am now.' At this point she began to weep.

In fact the song is called not 'Thíos i Lár an Ghleanna' – these being the opening words, meaning 'down in the middle of the glen' – but 'Tráthnóna Beag Aréir': 'Late yesterday evening'.

The strange thing is that Nuala was mistaken about the meaning of the song. The lyric is ambiguous but appears to be written from the viewpoint of a man who has emigrated, on the day after encountering, 'late yesterday evening', a maiden who had 'the prettiest face and personality' and 'made good sense go astray'. The idea that he is departed, in whatever sense, is buried deep within the lyric, which to the casual ear might pass for a conventional love song. He describes the white drops of dew on the grass as he courted his new-found love. The way the song translates into English is odd, because the use of the word 'God', introduced in the first line of the second verse, might be a casual taking of the deity's name in vain: 'And God, how pleasant our behaviour was …' But in the Irish version, this interpretation is impossible. The protagonist addresses God as 'A Rí', 'Oh King', and asks Him to acknowledge the beauty of the encounter.

He speaks also to the 'love of my heart', lamenting the brevity of their 'heart-playing'. It is strange: far from not believing in God, the man seems to believe equally in God and his beloved. Only in the third verse is there the insinuation that something drastic has happened to separate him from his beloved, though exactly what is never specified. There is a sense of exile and separation, suggesting an emigration song, a commonplace convention in Irish music through the ages. If he got permission to return and speak to his love, the protagonist laments, or if he could overcome destiny, what would he care about this life? He would walk with his love 'through the cotton grass and through the dunes by the edge of the sea'. And he would lose God's kingdom if he could kiss her mouth.

In the final verse he speaks to his beloved and remarks on how short their lovemaking was. Then, turning to God, he asks the 'King of the bright glory' to 'bring back last night'.

Among the remarkable things about this lyric is that it is based not merely on a belief in God but on a relationship with God that enables the protagonist to speak in almost equally familiar terms to God as to his beloved and to draw God into the intrigue of his romantic adventure of the evening before. The mode of addressing God is reverent but also friendly, and yet there is this provocative assertion that even God's kingdom might be sacrificed for the opportunity to kiss again the lips of the beloved. The song is a celebration of the heaven-on-earth that romantic love can sometimes seem to deliver. And, recognising God as the architect of this 'bright glory', he asks God to use His powers to return them to the night before. Were this to happen, he freely concedes, he would be prepared to lose both Heaven and Earth, in exchange for the bliss of one kiss with his beloved.

It is, in fact, a deeply religious song, in the broadest possible sense. There is no suggestion whatever of a disbelief in God, or of a calling upon a God whose existence is doubted. And yet Nuala O'Faolain, in remembering the song, was convinced that this is what she had heard. Neither is there a sense that the song's protagonist does not believe it is possible for God to do what he asks. On the contrary, the point of the song seems to be that the protagonist, in whatever exile he now finds himself, finds access to the meaning of the events in question by speaking to a God through Whom he understands reality. His communication with God is affectionate and quite forward. There may even be a sense in the song that the love in question may have been some kind of fleeting, illicit affair, now placed out of reach by life and its circumstances, or perhaps by death. The protagonist seems to play with a sense of God as both friendly and judgemental, a force that might help him to reclaim his love and yet might be obliged to exact the proscribed punishment on account of the sinful nature of the enterprise.

It is an intricate, profound and beautiful song, laden with a complex comfort accessible only through paradox and an intuitive sense of rightness that transcends normal understandings. Clearly, at some level, the song had once touched Nuala deeply. Through the prism of a culture that refuses to nurture belief, she had heard its sentiment as the culture might have rendered it, if given the opportunity to remake it. Searching now in her desperation for an image to describe her own feelings, she chose this song while seeming to miss both its mischief and the consolation it offers: that there is a loving and loveable God, and that He and his Kingdom exist in a place that seems perched high on the paradox of human-kind's capacity to imagine a meaning that is tender and indulgent and understanding of human weakness.

'Unthinkingness', that word Nuala O'Faolain employed, is a good description of our culture in relation to God, the origin of mankind, the related question of creation and all the associated fundamental issues of existence. She included herself in her implicit condemnation of that unthinkingness, but also seemed to be stuck, if not indeed determined to remain stuck, in a mind-set that almost perversely refuses to look at these essential questions for fear of what this gaze might require one to conclude. Marian Finucane at one point asked her about something she had written some time before: that what matters in life is passion. No, she replies, passion 'can go and take a running jump at itself'. That seemed a bit silly to her now. 'What matters now in life is health and reflectiveness. I just shot around. I would like it if I had been a better thinker.' She was glad now she didn't have a child to whom she would have to explain and say goodbye. She regretted that she had spent so much time drinking. She had come from a family of drinkers. 'I drank too much 'til I was forty, which was a waste of my one and only life.'

The cultures of present-day societies appear to construct them-selves or be constructed so as to avoid contemplation of the great questions. This is certainly the case with Irish society. In our public square today, there seems to be more open discussion than ever before about how reality is structured, where human beings emerged from and why we are here. But this discussion exists almost entirely at the level of abstraction, removed from the fundamental reality of the individual human being. It is as if each of us owes his or her existence to something that is somehow unmoored from our human desires and needs. There is much talk about evolution and the fact that we know, up to a point, how mankind developed from an uncertain moment of initiation. But most of us have no more than a crude grasp of this story. The culture we inhabit seems to regard these matters as settled, to feel no need for each of its inhabitants to share this knowledge, even though it relates to the sense any of us has of the essential meaning of existence. Behind the easily trotted-out 'rational' assumptions are the ineffable mysteries: where the first spark of life came from; where the first speck of matter came from; where there might be to 'come from'; what happened in the aeons of time before everything we know about?

The fundamental error of this increasingly secular/agnostic age is that religion is something imposed – that it is comes from outside and moulds, oppresses, brainwashes. But my religious belief is my very being, my relationship with the entire order of reality. I am connected to everything that ever was and ever will be. I am alive in infinite time and space, which eventually converge in what cosmology calls space-time. This incomprehensible reality is what keeps me alive, keeps me connected, keeps me charged with the human appetites – for hope, beauty, truth, justice, happiness, love, good – for what is called God. This condition pre-exists me. I cannot shake it off. I can deny it, but that won't change my fundamental structure in nature, which is dependent, which is created, which is charged with a unique destiny, and which is fundamentally mysterious, perhaps most of all to myself.

Among the characteristics of this condition are dependence and mendicity – begging. But the fact that I am a beggar strangely makes me less fearful, more balanced, more serene. Knowing that, in a demeanour of humility, it is possible to remain connected to the force that created me, enables me to greet every day as an adventure. I cannot wait to awake and see what happens!

But out in the world I am propositioned by a different and seductive idea: that the hope that drives me can be uprooted from the tradition from which I emerged and replanted in the material world, in my earthly existence only – and that this will make me more free. This is the great lie of our times. It can seem plausible in the joyful, happy moments, but when I encounter sorrow, or age, or sickness, or death, I see that it is a fragile kind of hope that relies on the capricious and erratic capacities of humanity.

Religion relates to the fundamental nature of human beings, having grown out of the inescapable facts of reality: humankind, mysterious to itself, seeking to understand its own essential structure and comprehend its place in the universe. The human structure, which remains in spite of all our alleged progress as a species, comprises three ineluctable elements: we have been created, we are dependent, we are mortal. And yet our culture seems to tell us, moment to moment, that we can defy these facts, or ignore them, or hold them in abeyance, to be confronted at some vaguely defined future time, perhaps by other people who are somehow less fortunate than we are in being weighed down by these unpalatable limitations.

Perhaps this is what Nuala O'Faolain meant about our unthinkingness. And yet she did not, even in these final weeks and days, seem to wish to go beyond what she had assumed, or what had been assumed on her behalf and with which she had unthinkingly slipped into acquiesence. Even now, gazing at this unthinkingness, she was not disposed to think about it. Though the strands of comfort she might have grasped at were of a different nature to what she had declared herself to believe, she was aware of their existence and yet declined to think about them beyond the level of a certain sentimental engagement. It was as if, even now, she was more concerned with seeming to be consistent in the eyes of the culture than in looking at what she herself might have been feeling deeper down. There would be something really bad happening to her brain, she said, with a apparently unconscious irony and a certitude that seemed to understand itself only in one way. The thing is: there was something bad happening to her brain, but even this did not seem to bring her face-to-face with the ultimate questions. She went right up to the front door of the truth but did not knock.

Our societies seem to think and talk about religion a great deal: the damage it has wrought; the sometime dubiousness of its claims; the restrictiveness of its diktats. But, truth to tell, there is hardly any thought, *per se*, about religion, about God and about the larger mysteries with which religion, for all the shortcomings of organised religions, seeks to engage. The main objective of most public-square discussions about God and religion is either to denounce the influence of religion as an impediment to freedom, or, in response to this impulse, to reinforce existing beliefs as a protection against such heretical endeavours. This constant argument is presented as a struggle between reason and irrationality. Whereas those who question the claims of religion are extended the courtesy of being deemed to operate from the solid ground of reason, those on the other side are at best patronisingly congratulated for the tenacity with which they hold to irrational beliefs. Believers are not regarded as approaching their beliefs through the discipline of thought. The word 'faith' is used on both sides of the argument to put an end to the idea that such concepts can be approached by means of human reason.

This is why Nuala O'Faolain's use of the word 'unthinkingness' was interesting: as though she had belatedly come to the idea that there might have been a way into these matters through thought, through reason. It is also perhaps why her odd interjection of the word 'unthinkingness' did not result in a discussion. Even to pursue the idea that we do not think about religion would have required a breaking of the pattern of unthinkingness.

To pursue the point would have involved a process of public thinking out loud. Marian Finucane was interested only in 'beliefs', the standard reductionism employed to initiate whatever limited discussions are enabled to occur about the totality of what reality presents us with. The thing about 'beliefs' as conventionally understood in contemporaty mass media culture is that there is no reasonable way of getting into them. They may be thinking or unthinking, but the presumption tends to place them closer to the latter than the former, and this requires them to be treated with the courtesy of avoidance. Increasingly, the logic of our 'rational' public discussion is that beliefs must be respected, tolerated, accommodated, but not really taken seriously. They are not thoughts, after all, but inherited notions that have more to do with defining a person's identity than reflecting their conscious engagement with reality.

From the loose way she expressed herself, it is possible to conclude that Nuala O'Faolain appeared to be talking not of the individual private thoughts of human beings, herself included, but of the public thought process of a society talking to itself. If so, she was undoubtedly onto something. The idea of God is not permitted as a response to the unimaginable mystery. It has become too bogged down in ideas of superstition and tribalism and platitude and hypocrisy and manipulation and abuse. Our societies are prepared to concede in public that belief in a deity is something some people hold to, but there is an unspoken understanding that, while there is an obligation on the liberal mind-set to be tolerant of such simple-mindedness, this holding to God is an outmoded and rather reaction-ary outlook on reality and life. All these assumptions, prejudices, ideas, anti-ideas and certainties become live in virtually every public discussion, almost regardless of the 'beliefs' of the participants. Even though these subjects relate to the most fundamental aspects of our existence, all the time we allow ourselves to be bullied by the culture, the background radiation of thought that governs us without us even realising, seeking to limit our curiosity, or sidetrack us into what seem like important issues but are really just constructions designed to avoid the fathomless nature of reality.

Indeed, it is not necessarily possible to tell the beliefs of any individual from what they might say in public – not because some-one will necessarily dissemble or consciously evade the issues, but because, without some resolve to break through the culture, we inevitably fall into a use of language which adopts all the 'established' assumptions and prejudices. Is it possible for me to reach any reliable, truthful conclusion about myself if, to arrive at any conclusion at all, I must utilise the tools provided by a culture with a vested interest in directing me towards a conclusion that is already decided in the language I use?

All these subtexts were 'live' in the inteview between Nuala O'Faolain and Marian Finucane. I do not know what Marian Finucane thinks about God, and can decide nothing about her personal beliefs from this or any other interview she has conducted. What I can conclude, however, is that, unconsciously or otherwise, she backed away from the provocation implicit in Nuala O'Faolain's ambiguous responses, perhaps because she wished to steer clear of controversy in the circumstances in which she found herself; or perhaps because she believes these matters to be clear and already settled; or even perhaps because she was mindful of the possible insensitivities of pursuing her friend on these matters at such a fragile and emotional moment for them both.

There was, in other words, a third participant in this interview, an entity inaudible and invisible, but nonetheless ever-present throughout. I am thinking of the culture, that ever-present phenonemon of media-saturated societies, which imposes its will on us every moment. Forty of fifty years before, an interview on Irish radio between a radio interviewer and an Irish writer knowingly close to the point of death would have been governed by an entirely different of assumptions. The writer would most likely have been a believer, or presented him- or herself as such. The interviewer, likewise, would have been a believer or would have been sufficiently conscious of the monolith of public piety to remain within a set of assumptions readily triggered by a series of ritualistic invocations and platitudes. Now, however, almost regardless of the private beliefs of the participants, the culture was insinuating a different, close to opposite, logic.

Why is this? It is not, surely, that human beings have in the meantime fundamentally altered in structure or needs, or that we have discovered so much more about the universe that we can now look back at these supposedly simplistic positions and smile indulgently, if a little irritatedly, at the things we once believed.

In truth we 'know' almost nothing we did not know before, but have fallen prey to cultural developments that circumscribe our capacity to articulate our deepest needs just as surely as, in a different way, did the simple verities of old.

— 4 —

The Silent Melody

Some words we might depend on at certain ineluctable moments in a human life are no longer usable, even in moments of the most extreme need. In the wider culture, the words our very lives or sanity might depend on are booby-trapped with prejudice and contaminated with disappointment. There is no common language in which to speak of the most vital things to someone who does not conform to a narrow cultural classification. And even the old, culturally booby-trapped words, when used within the borders of a specific belief-group, are likely to reveal themselves as hollowed-out shells from which the meaning has been removed.

It is as if the words to hope with have been stolen from under our noses. There are other things you could say: that we have lost some or all of our faith, or innocence, or gullibility; that we have freed ourselves from the tyranny of imposed superstition; that we are more realistic than our ancestors were. But you would also have to conclude that we have become limited in ways our ancestors were not, that our capacity to think of ourselves and our total relationships with time and space has been reduced in ways that render us less happy, less peaceful and, oddly enough or perhaps not, less free.

While we pick away at the fabric of the religious traditions we have inherited, delighted with our cleverness and our resulting freedom, we seem not to have understood that the same process that we glory in is also throttling something vital in our humanity. We retreat from the piety and devotion which has disquieted us by its simplicity and prescriptiveness, but have not been able to find new words anywhere else.

Only in the totality of our lives do we reveal our fullest nature. I am not just the person I am now but also the person I have been and the one I may become, the one who will grow older and eventually die. But our culture seeks to push this truth out of sight, to pretend that reality is defined by youth and its sense of knowingness and omnipotence. It is as though we see ourselves only in the forms we imagine we have created for ourselves, in which our powers are maximised and relatively unbounded by limits, denying the unavoidable reality that we are dependent beings in an infinite order.

But there are certain characteristics of the human mechanism that are objectively undeniable, and that each of us, before the mirror or the executioner, must at some level concede. One is that, to put it in the least controversial manner possible, we do not make ourselves. Another is that our continued existence is to a high degree contingent on factors beyond our, or anyone's, control. A third factor is that we are mortal. This means not merely that we will die but that we are prone to degenerative conditions that steal away elements of what we think of as our humanity. We age. We become less attractive in a sexual sense. Our minds go. Together, these factors define us in a way that requires us to arrive at some fundamental understanding of ourselves and our situation. If we are not simply to exist for a time on the surface of the earth, cast about by the terrors within and the elements without, we need a larger understanding of what it is we are doing and where it is we are going.

Religion once offered this understanding to everyone. Whatever else you may say about it, it at least enabled the individual to arrive at some comprehension of his situation which enabled him to function, after a fashion at least, and thus to focus on the moment of being, having resolved, to some extent, the larger questions of existence.

It is not that these questions have been resolved or that they have gone away. It is not even that, in a general sense, they are acknowledged in our culture. Vaguely we remain aware of them. But because of a growing cultural rejection of specific manifestations of mankind's attempts to deal with these questions, i.e. specific religions and institutionalised religion, the questions lack a structure upon which we might continue to look at them. The only words we have seem to 'belong' to one or other tradition, and so are useless to any attempted approach from another direction. It is not possible to say or write any reasonably extended series of words – more than a couple of sentences – without setting off the cultural tripwires that lead immediately to a short-circuiting of the conversation.

Take the following paragraph, as an attempt to outline, in what is, by tradition and social practice, a Christian culture:

> As human beings we have within us a question, a need, a longing, a plea – about our lives, our origins and our destinies. This question demands an answer. Indeed, we are this question, and like all questions, we have an answer. We do not know what, ultimately, we desire, but we know that, like Nuala O'Faolain, we are filled by a desire that life go on, that our loved ones not be lost or forgotten, that love, beauty, knowledge go on and never die. We know in the deepest part of our hearts that we cannot be redeemed by science or ideology or what is termed progress in any of its manifestations. In recent generations we have started to close ourselves off to the consciousness, two thousand years old in its most shimmering condition, that only in the knowledge of transcendence can we achieve the optimal conditions for human survival. Only such an awareness matches our most fundamental need. This is the deepest hope of the human heart, the one that stands behind all others. It is what drives us, protects us, motivates us and, by keeping our gaze fixed on the horizon, enables us to move through moments of the most extreme difficulty and pain.

In this passage, from a newspaper article I wrote in the immediate aftermath of the death of Nuala O'Faolain, the line of thought seemed to be going alright until the mention of the culture in question being two thousand years old. For the committed Christian, of course, this is not a problem. For those actively antagonistic to religion, it is an immediate turn-off (although to be realistic about it, these are likely to have tuned out long before, at the first indication that the passage does not comprise a denunciation of religion). My point, however, is that, for the vast majority who are of neither the initiated nor the alienated, the wider cultural context causes these words, the simple reference to a two-thousand-year-old tradition, to send out a signal that there is nothing here to be explored. Although the rest of the words are directed at seeking some kind of exploration of the absolute dimension of the human entity, this clear and contextually uncritical mention of Christianity sends off cultural alarm bells and causes most of those likely to come across it to switch off.

Our cultures, therefore, no longer afford us a way, in the conventional public arena in which we spend so much of our time, of seeing ourselves as we really are. Religion, the means by which we once achieved a semantic accommodation with total reality, has been discredited, by a pincer movement between the reductions and abuses perpetrated in the name of religion and the opposing reaction from outside. One side claims the franchise on redemption, the other victory over unreason; but the vast bulk of modern populations are, as a consequence, left unable to claim either. Stripped of their language of absolute reality, our cultures begin to squeeze and oppress us in ways we are incapable even of perceiving. What we have lost has been a loss to ourselves, to our essential humanity, and yet we have been persuaded to read it as liberation. We respond to invitations to celebrate our victory over tradition as though oblivious that we have half-sawn through the branch we are sitting on.

Because we have created for ourselves a culture that in many ways denies our humanity, we have, each of us separately, become trapped in a terrifying avoidance of the most unavoidable fact of life: that death is certain and not necessarily irrelevantly distant. A culture that denies this reality is, to say the least, unkind to those who inhabit it.

I was talking to a television researcher not long ago who told me that he had been trying, without much success, to get some well-known Irishmen to come on television and talk about having turned sixty. I was not surprised at his lack of success. Admitting to being sixty in our current culture would be to resign from relevance, announce the end of sexual expectation, opt for invisibility and marginalisation and put your hand up to being close to a spent force.

Ireland now suffers from a condition that infects every political culture in the West. Its symptoms have been rather scarifyingly outlined by Robert Bly in his remarkable book *The Sibling Society*, in which he paints a devastating portrait of cultures obsessed by youth, suspicious of forms of authority that might seek to deprive youth of its 'freedoms', intent upon destroying the heritage of what Bly calls 'vertical' culture, in favour of the 'horizontal' culture of the present. Nobody likes to think about old people any more, and when we do, we think of them as a different species, never of the fact that we, too, are growing old and will one day die. It is not just ordinary thoughtlessness, but active avoidance of the issue, because of the connotations of age in a culture that values youth so highly and seeks therefore to airbrush out all evidence of ageing.

When I was a boy, older people were at the centre of Irish society. In fact, the country was run by old people, who, to be strictly truthful, did not have much time for the young. Most young people took the first boat out, emogration being, in the phrase of the time, the 'safety valve' of Irish society, and those who stayed learned to keep their mouths shut. Today, the exact reverse is true: youth is venerated and age dismissed and ignored.

Like everybody in Western society, we live in a culture that celebrates youth and, as a corollary, repudiates age. Largely unconsciously, sometimes subtly, through media, pop music, advertising and sport, the culture communicates to us a sense of the ideal human state and the meaning of life in general, and this unwritten description includes an ideal human age. There is a tyranny at the heart of present-day culture that oppresses each one of us from the fulcrum of a certain tipping point in our existence. It derives from the fact that the culture we have constructed tends to hold out, to each one of us, a moment in the human lifespan that is routinely lionised, elevated by everything our public belief system holds precious about being alive. This moment is not the same for everyone, but generally speaking it comes sometime in one's late twenties or early thirties, a moment of pseudo-perfection in the human lifespan.

Most of us are not yet, or no longer, that ideal age. But those who are younger are already being conditioned for this brief flowering of cultural perfection, and those who have passed it by are so tyrannised by the power of the idea that they cling to its values even though the reality of their lives moves exponentially in the other direction. Because we have created a culture that stays young, even though its inhabitants grow old, the culture inflicts on each of us a growing sense of alienation, which we respond to either by withdrawing to a private space or standing our ground and trying to extend our grasp on youth for as long as possible. The option of remaining resolutely where we are on the human cycle and celebrating each stage of the journey as a new and precious experience is achievable only against the grain of the culture.

The culture, that consensual monster that nobody operates but everyone is governed by, nags us all the time and taunts our very natures. The daily insinuation of advertising, pop music, chicklit, soap opera, reality TV, and the casual small-talk that borrows its life from all the above, drums the idea of the ideal moment into the subconscious of every attentive consumer. When the moment passes each of us by, there isn't even a 'ping' in the consciousness to mark this passing. But, gradually, a new awareness seeps in, a sense that someting vital has slipped by, that nothing will ever be the same again.

A word by way of clarification of what I mean in this context by 'culture'. We tend to think of what we call 'culture' in fragmented sets of ways. Sometimes, hearing the word in a particular context, we think of high culture – music, art, philosophy, literature. Other times we hear the word differently, perhaps as a term for what makes a particular society what it is, the idiocyncrasies of a discrete tribe or community. But really, the concept of culture in its purest sense denotes the content of the social environment in which we live.

Understanding culture is like listening to what we call silence. If you sit in the (alleged) silence of a room and listen to this thing called silence, you soon find that, even when there is no obvious sound like wind or rain to be heard from outside, the aural topography comprises a silky cacophony of sounds that are everpresent but somehow discounted from our crude sense that we are hearing nothing. There may be the low hiss of central heating, the faraway drone of traffic, the creaking of doors and furniture, the distant roar of the sea. When you tune out of your search for normative sounds, and listen to the subtext, you begin to hear this deafening clamour of activity that exists just beyond the edge of the lived experience, constantly pushing inwards.

Culture is like that. Up near are the things that are agreed, by and large, by the majority. Beyond that, we imagine there is just the exotica of the minorities, the extremisms of the disgruntled and excluded, the redundant beliefs of the ageing and the as yet unacknowledged perspectives of the next generation. But there is much more than this at play in the everyday brain of society.

Culture is really thought, expressed in various concrete forms – visual, written, spoken – but also in more subtle ways, or in combinations of the above happening at many times the speed of lightning, to the point of invisibility. Culture is a set of beliefs, driven like nails into the heads of the members of a community, guiding them in their waking moments to behave in certain approved ways.

The effect on us of the culture in which we live are not obvious. The elements in our cultures which make us think in certain ways when we might just as readily, with another set of stimuli, think in different ways, are invisible to us because they have become so normalised as to appear to be natural elements of the reality around us. They are beyond obvious, because of their invisibility. In a sense they do not exist, except as neutral, organic elements. They blend into what we understand as reality so as to become unremarkable. We do not remark on them, and it would start to seem strange if we did. The gift that poets and artists have is to see these elements in reality and draw attention to them, but most of us regard such engagements as a kind of imaginative game whereby the 'creative' personality indulges a tendency to see things that are not there, but uses these flights of fancy to create combinations of words and sounds and forms that look and sound interesting or agreeable.

We look at reality, at the three dimensions around us, and we think that we understand what this is and how it affects our minds and our lives. We think that the culture is the sum of all the parts which the people who live in it have built into it, and therefore that it accommodates to their common life in the manner that the rules of a board game are suited to the requirements of the players. But culture is more than this.

Think of culture as being like a furnished room, but one you encounter only in the dark. There are chairs in there, and tables, and other items, but you cannot see them. You are blind. But you learn to walk about the room, without knocking into things, finding your way through, sometimes taking your bearings from use of the table and chairs, but never seeing what it is you're making use of.

And in this room there is a music that guides your movement. But it is a silent music, a silent melody that speaks to you in ways you do not consciously understand but which nevertheless you obey, but without knowing you are obeying. You do not hear the music, would deny its existence. And yet something makes you behave in the same way, day after day. Perhaps it isn't a music, but something else, something that cannot be heard or seen or smelt or felt, but which governs you nonetheless. This is culture.

The silent melody accompanies me every waking moment, and into my sleep as well. It suggests what I may say, and what I may not say. It intimates to me what I may say at a price, what that price will be, and whether or not the risk is worthwhile. When I speak, the culture answers. Always. Sometimes it answers with silence, rendered articulate in other ways, in the meaning attached to such silence by experience. Sometimes it will nod sadly. Sometimes it will shake its head. Sometimes it will laugh out loud. Sometimes it will agree with me and congratulate me on my honesty and courage, having deliberately misunderstood what I have said. The culture is like a human being, but the most capricious and mysterious human being I have ever come across. She is with me all the time, except that I am mostly unaware of her presence. If, for some reason, I were to become aware of her presence and betray it in the company of other people, they would begin to think me insane.

The culture we live in now is complex and devious. It defines us in ways we do not think about and therefore cannot even hope to understand. Any attempt to make visible the culture is partly doomed to failure, because it moves and shifts all the time, being governed by the desires and prejudices and terrors of all its members and what they want each other and the world in general to believe about them. I give my tithe to the culture every living moment, feeding into it what I want it to know about me, what I would like it to relate about me, but also much that I do not intend to betray. I blush, an involuntary function, and the culture understands this far more than anything I have said. And the same is true of everyone else, in their relationships with the culture, so the result is something we cannot even begin to describe but at best can acquire an intuitive sense of. And yet the culture is ever-present, policing me without my knowledge or consent, as surely as the presence of a parent conditions the behaviour of a child.

This parent, though, is a vast presence, hugely intelligent and yet neurotic, irrational, emotional, aggressive, sly, bossy, manipulative and deceptive. In any given situation, the culture has a view of what the best outcome might be, but it is much less certain about why it thinks what it does. It finds all kinds of ways of telling me what it wants, mostly through the banks of messages already implanted, but also through a constant process of updating. Every word I hear, every image I see, every sigh released in my presence, every whisper I cannot make out, is telling me something the culture wants me to understand. More than that, every hat someone wears, every car someone drives, every pair of white socks with black shoes someone has put on in the dark tells me something to feed my sense of things. I am never allowed to rest even for a sleeping second, without some kind of information being conveyed to me by my constant companion, the culture.

Cultures think. They don't think as humans think, nor do they think as the sum of the humans who inhabit them. They have their own thought processes, which bear down on the individual member and, if anything, cause him or her to think differently, which is to say more acceptably, more 'correctly'. This helps to explain why, sometimes, the human heart does not seem to be represented in the thinking of a mob or an institution or even a movement. It also helps to explain why it might be the case that the very same words, used by different people, can have different meanings, sometimes even close to opposite meanings.

Who runs this entity we think of – or don't think of – as culture? Nobody. Or everybody. We all run it, together and separately. It is a subtle tyranny, which allows for dissent, for the refusal, for the contrarian perspective – but always within limits, always indeed as a necessary safety valve which in the end serves to protect the dominant thinking. The silent melody draws the community into a shared hymn. It has scope for dissonance, but not too much. And even the dissenters are much more defined by the culture than they are by their dissent from it.

The very words that come to my tongue, or whisper to me from inside my head, are given to me, and therefore cause me, within my very self, to describe to myself what I see in particular ways, excluding other ways of seeing the same things and, in sharing with others these subjective perspectives, finding affirmation in the impression that everyone else sees the same things in the same way. But how do I know they share my impressions of anything? And even where they appear to, is this not merely the culture acting within two discrete beings, causing them to appear to come to the same conclusions when really they have simply been dragged along on the same tramlines of language?

Such questions have taxed philosophers, poets and adolescents since the beginning of time, but seem in the main to exclude themselves from the dominant cultures of which I speak, perhaps because their very existence might create a kind of dissolution, causing the culture to lose its purchase on reality and suffer from a kind of rolling process of collapse in which the meaning of everything would enter a perpetual flux and the meaning of anything would become, at any given moment, unclear.

How, then, do I know myself? What is there to know? Can I learn anything from others? Do they share my reality or simply my language? Are the conclusions we come to in our interchanges of experience some kind of approximately definitive version of who we are, or are such conclusions so contaminated by the culture that they cannot be relied upon?

How we see ourselves depends on, is mediated through, culture. We don't 'own' our sense of ourselves. My sense of myself is separate from me, being imposed on what is already there. And yet the imposition tends to become, in the human imagination, the whole. I walk around thinking of myself as John Waters, as the father of Roisin, as the son of Tom and Ita. But what this means depends on the place these facts find in the stuff of the culture. Without culture, I would not know myself as I do, and therefore would not be who I am, or think I am. Who I am seems clear and obvious, but it is only as clear and obvious as the stuff that makes up the culture that defines me, and this is not clear and obvious at all. Sometimes I suspect that, in my heart, in the deeper me, I do not even have a name.

The sense I have of myself, moment to moment in my conscious mind, is not absolutely subjective. It is, in part at least, given to me. I am, therefore, more than myself. I am the essence of myself and other elements that have been added from outside, by other people, by the culture, and before that by the force that created me. How I see myself is defined differently now than it might have been defined had I lived a hundred or a thousand years ago. There are immutable elements that define my humanity, but there is no absolute sense of human existence, no constant idea of the human mechanism that enables me to look out, day after day, as the human species has looked out millennium after millennium, on a changing landscape and reflect in a coherently developing manner on the meaning of existence. We colour ourselves, moment to moment, and mistake that colouring for the essence of ourselves. But deeper down there is a different reality: the child who cried on the way to his baptism, the awestruck boy who gazed at the moon, the man who held his first child and wept.

There is, in our culture now, a strange sense that the structural limitation of mankind as dependent on something mysterious has been overcome. This is not explicitly stated, but it is nonetheless believed in the culture at some level – not literally, not even consciously, but still in a way that is real. Each of us picks this up, day after day, as we live through a time in which we are being communicated with on a constant basis by forces we take for granted in a particular, singular way, but which have more far-reaching influence on our sense of ourselves than we can imagine.

It may or may not seem obvious, but there is a difference between private thought and public thought. Inside ourselves we have a capacity to think in a certain way, but in the public arena we must discuss things in a different way. Generally, though, we do this using similar words, the same language inside and out, and generally, too, we are unaware of the consequences of this phenomenon. The language we use, because it appears to grow organically out of a simple need to communicate, suggests itself as being a neutral instrument capable of enabling a completely objective witness. Of course, as Orwell intimated, it is not neutral at all. But it is neutral least of all in the most fundamental questions confronting man. Here, more than anywhere else, the language we use has evolved to support particular mind-sets. In religious societies, language is broadly constructed to support the idea of an absolute reality. In material societies, the language is constructed to support the idea that mankind is the author of his own destiny.

Another unnoticed element is the way our culture separates reality into disconnected elements. Think of the newspaper as a metaphor for society. On page one it has the news stories, the main events of yesterday; on the back it has the sports; in the middle somewhere it has an arts page, a features page, a letters page, an opinion page, a business page, an economics column, and so on. All discrete entities, all separate elements of the newspaper, very often supplied by different people working in different departments. Although this is something we take for granted, it is not a natural phenomenon. It does not reflect the realities of the life of the person who reads the newspaper. I don't have different departments. I just have me. I have one mind, one body. I am one.

More and more the world takes on certain characteristics of a newspaper, the public sphere of thought automatically dividing things into various sections. This is business, this is entertainment, this is religion, this is art. We take this process of division for granted and assume it to be a natural state of affairs. It is not.

Imagine yourself at a moment before mass media were invented or created. If one had speculated back then about what kind of a world would be brought into being by technologies providing instant communication right across the globe – by means of which all kinds of opinions and information could be spread instantaneously – you would probably anticipate that this would greatly improve the capacity of the human species to discuss, to express innermost desires, aspirations, dreams, feelings, attitudes. You would imagine that the public conversation would be characterised by a multiplicity of ideas, all enjoying similar levels of democratic accessibility, available to everybody.

But this has not happened, and we are unaware that it has not. We assume, because we hear this babble all the time, that there is a great variety of opinions. But more and more what we seem to have is dominant ideologies constantly asserting and reinforcing themselves, fighting off any form of dissent or using dissent as a form of defence to enhance and protect themselves.

The idea that what we read in the newspaper is some kind of objective representation of spontaneous reality is a fiction. Instead, the newspaper offers an ideological presentation of reality, a partial representation, which emerges in a relentless though subtle and complex way. We need to think about this beyond the banal level of conspiracy theory. It is not as if every day at three o'clock a bunch of people go into a room and plan how they are going to manipulate public opinion. Actually, they do go into rooms at three o'clock, and in those rooms appear simply to decide on lists of news stories and how they are to be presented. Nevertheless at the very heart of such processes is a spontaneous cultural collusion which feeds off all kinds of interests, fears, prejudices, desires, ambitions, and all these converge to create what you will see on the front page the next morning. What is presented there as a version of reality is not, objectively speaking, 'the important things that happened yesterday', but rather what a certain group of people, coming from a certain kind of cultural and ideological and professional background, thought was important enough to present to the public of what occurred in the teeming life of the world the day before.

Newspapers, in other words, present an ideological version of reality. So what is the nature of that ideology? What is its fundamental essence?

The process in question has many aspects and often all kinds of directions and strands. If you peer closely enough, you can see all kinds of strange phenomena swimming about, many of which you cannot even name, and some you can all too readily name. But the most important thing to be said is that, by virtue of being ideological, the version of reality a newspaper, any newspaper, offers is not truthful, because ideology by definition is a partial explanation of reality.

— 5 —

Human Beings or
Human Beans?

In a letter to the *Irish Times* some years ago, Professor Brendan Walsh, of the Department of Economics at University College Dublin asked: what is the problem with ideology. 'My dictionary', he wrote, 'defines "ideology" as "the set of beliefs by which a group or society orders reality so as to render it intelligible". Why, then, has it become a term of abuse in Ireland?'

The question was an intriguing one because it stated something generally unacknowledged, but also because it is an old and much-ventilated question in the academic circles within which Professor Walsh moved. There are libraries filled with deconstructions of ideology, and barely a significant modern philosopher, from Marx to Barthes, who has not contributed. Considering that the chief conduits of ideology into the stream of everyday life are media and academia, it struck me that the question, asked by a leading academic in a leading newspaper, was either disingenuous or naive.

Of course it is true that 'ideology' has indeed become a term of abuse. I use it so myself – ideologically – to place opponents beyond the Pale of common sense, whenever I want to paint myself out of a corner and am too lazy to argue any more. As Terry Eagleton put it, ideology, like halitosis, is what someone else has. The word, of course, has multiple meanings. Professor Walsh proffered one, but any dictionary offers several others, including: 'an idea that is false or held for the wrong reasons but is believed with such conviction as to be irrefutable.' Generally, when we accuse someone of being ideo-logical, we suggest that they are seeing the world though the gauze of a fixed system of thought, whereas we, of course, deal in 'reality'.

In defending the innocence of ideology, Brendan Walsh chose a definition that presented reality as a natural and readily apprehensible state of affairs, which ideology simply seeks to 'order'. He was not so much suggesting that his own world-view remained uncontaminated by ideology, as that ideology is a neutral tool in the description of 'reality'. But this 'reality' may well be the progeny, if not the accumulation, of the prevailing ideologies. Walsh was therefore arguing from within an 'ideology of objectivity' – implying that the systems of thought employed by him, and others like him, were simply aids to the comprehension of an objective actuality, whereas they were actually, so to speak, its very substance.

We all, similarly, believe that our arguments derive from a state of nature, uncontaminated by systemic thought – an impossibility in a world whose very essence resides in its colonisation by thought-forms trapped in prisms of language. Daily, our newspapers and broadcast news programmes repeat and affirm the dominant ideological themes that hold our society in its present shape. If you object to this being called 'ideological', it is because you support these ideologies to the point of perceiving them as the natural order. Most 'news', for example, tells us nothing truly new, but serves up a slightly different version of the same diet, much as a hotel offers the same breakfast menu every day. The core of our newspapers are interchangeable from day to day, repeating and reinforcing what we already 'know' to be 'true', renewing our sense of the absoluteness of what is, in truth, a highly selective version of reality.

Professor Walsh was correct in implying that ideology is not necessarily pernicious. The problem is not that we adopt constructs with which to assist our apprehension or articulation, but that we 'order' these into hermetically sealed positions, opposed to incoherence.

The best answer to the professor's question I have come across is to be found in Václav Havel's *Letters to Olga*, the collection of letters he wrote to his late wife during the years he was imprisoned in his native Czechoslovakia for refusing an ideological prescription.

Havel wrote that he had always rejected the idea of a complete, unified, integrated and self-contained belief system, because 'I simply don't have the internal capacity for it'. What he had, he said, was faith: 'a state of persistent and productive openness, of persistent questioning, a need to "experience the world" again and again.' He explained that what he called 'the Order of Being' is multiform and elusive, and 'simply cannot be grasped and described by a consistent system of knowledge'.

His solution? '[A] kind of "parallelism" or "pluralism" in knowledge … Of eclecticism I have no fear whatever; such fears can only bother someone who is unsure of himself, who does not believe in the steadfastness of his standards of plausibility or precision, in his own reason and its natural continuity, quite simply, in his own identity.

'The more slavishly and dogmatically a person falls for a ready-made ideological system or "worldview", the more certainly he will bury all chances of thinking, of freedom, of being clear about what he knows, the more certainly he will deaden the adventure of the mind and the more certainly – in practice – he will begin to serve the "order of death".'

Mainstream media in our mass media society generally offer a clear ideological view of reality, the fundamental essence of which could be defined as an ideology of progress. Everything, or almost everything, is presented according to an underlying idea to do with man's omnipotence. Everything, or almost everything, suggests that human needs will eventually be met entirely by progress, that we are being driven forward by a project of self-improvement that one day will answer all our questions.

It is possible to dissent from this ideology and still be included in the discussion, but, if you volunteer for such participation, you after a while begin to realise that the function of such contributions is not to offer an alternative version of reality but rather to provide a gracing pseudo-democratic aspect to the dominant message. You can go against the cultural grain, but, unless you are particularly obtuse, must recognise that what comes across from such contributions is simply that the outlet in question is sufficiently tolerant to allow for the publication of clearly wrong-headed views – in this case views that question the very central essence of progress and its commitment to confer on humankind all that is humanly desirable. Clearly any such views are not merely wrong, but dangerously wrong.

The result is that the public sphere is presented with, in existential terms, a choice that could not be starker. We are invited to believe absolutely in the idea of progress or to tend towards the despair that flows from the suspicion that anything else is redundant and doomed.

We like to think that the changes undergone by the human species are characteristic of a progressive journey through time, but really this much-vaunted 'change' just serves to accentuate the fixed elements of our humanity – the fact that we are created, dependent and mortal beings. These dimensions remain constant, and loom much larger in us than anything that is imposed from outside, but this does not convey itself above the babble of the culture.

There was a time when mankind's sense of itself was defined by what I will call The Mystery. Man awoke to himself, to his shape and feelings, to his limbs and responses to reality and began to comprehend that he was the creature of something far greater than himself. He, one such man, was inside this body, or inseparably part of this body, which had been constructed, forged and moulded someplace else. He hadn't done it himself. He looked at his hands in wonder and they had not yet become hands. He had no name for them, nor much sense of their purpose. He became aware, by instinct, hunger, cold, of the need to sustain himself. He found food and fed himself. He noted that it was already there, that the answer to this need in him had already been provided. He constructed shelter for himself, and noted, too, that the means to do this were present also. He observed, then, certain essential things about himself: that he had not made himself, that he was dependent on the existence of the means to sustain himself, and that these means were, by and large, present in his environment. This, of course, is a simplification of events, but it remains useful as a crude sketch of the position.

But this is not how man has ended up, and to convey this it is necessary to effect a similarly crude but functional sketch of things. Over time, man began to fend for himself. He came to expect the means of his survival to be available. He had some measure of control in this regard, as he learned to husband the Earth's resources in his own interests. He fashioned tools to help him in this endeavour. Soon the tools became as though parts of himself, additional to his limbs and his mind. Soon, too, he began to take these for granted.

Some of these tools were created by man as sturdier replicas of elements of himself. A hoe or a spade, for example, and even more so a graip, came out resembling the hand of its inventor. It was sturdier, sharper and had no feeling. It made life easier, less painful, and also made man's work faster and more efficient. Soon, man began not only to take his tools for granted but to find them indispensable. His hands, which used to work the clay, became softer, but he had these new 'hands', so this did not matter. He began to see his tools as extensions of himself. He made weapons he could throw from himself, projecting his power into the space around him.

He had become aware of something in himself he called a 'spirit' or 'soul'. It is said that primitive man first began to conceive of this spirit as like a fire within himself, creating the life and energy to make him function, but more than that, the intelligence and feelings that set him apart from the other living entities he encountered around him. He saw these things, like his hands, as given to him. The life in him had been put there by something much greater than he could dream of, something mysterious and seemingly immensely powerful.

But his intelligence soon seemed to him to be capable of much more than he had imagined. To save time and reduce his work, he set his mind to thinking more and more about tools, how he might create new limbs for himself, more efficient weapons and instruments to make his life easier. But the more complex and refined these instruments became, the more man thought of himself as their creator. He ceased to see the things around him as given and started to see them as the raw material of his own creativity. By then, man was really in the throes of a fundamantal reappraisal of his understanding of himself. He named all the parts of himself and observed how they worked together. Operating from this model, he was able to produce more and more efficient instruments to enable him to work faster and better. Soon, he discovered ways of creating tools with 'spirits' of their own, internalised systems which converted energy into action just as the man's body seemed to do. He called these tools 'machines'.

At first, awestruck by his success in creating these tools with spirits of their own, man soon began to take them for granted. It was logical and simple. All you had to do was understand the principles on which they were constructed. Yes, it showed that man's intelligence was capable of achieving much more than he might have imagined, but still it was simply using things that he had discovered to be true in order to extend that intelligence into the world.

Still, man remained conscious of the mysterious elements of himself, and had yet to locate some kind of solid basis within the mystery to build his own creation. There was no bedrock here for his reason to build on. The mystery was like a bog which sank back under the weight of man's desire to comprehend it. But he built on it still, floating a foundation of sorts across its span, and the balance of the edifice became its means of support. Then man forgot that he had simply floated his understanding of things on the great marsh of the mystery and started to imagine that he had built his empire on the solid rock of his own knowledge and understanding.

But then a strange thing happened. Man, while remaining conscious that he had created the machines, began to think of himself as a kind of machine as well. It was as if the image of the machine as a reflection of himself was playing tricks on his imagination. Was the machine a reflection of him or was he an anticipation of the machine? After all, if he had created the machines as extensions of himself, didn't that suggest that he himself had been like a machine in the first place? And if the 'spirit' he had put into the machine could be understood in terms of the mechanical principles he had divined as he went along, did that not also mean that, somehow or other, the 'spirit' within man himself could be understood in something like the same way? The spirit, in other words, was like the engine of a machine, marvellous to behold but actually, for all its complexity, amenable to human comprehension. The spirit of the machine is separate from the machine, but intrinsic to it. It makes it move and function but not by any supernatural force. So why should man himself be any different? The spirit and the body worked together in harmony, and neither had a life without the other. Man might not understand everything to do with himself, but he had a functional working knowledge that explained most of what he needed to sustain himself day by day.

Gradually man realised that the idea of himself as a kind of machine appealed more to his pride than to the sense of dependency that came with believing himself created and contingent upon factors beyond his control. Man never actually articulated this, not out loud. Perhaps he never even thought it. But in the depths of himself he began to feel that it was so.

More and more the machine seemed to define him. Then he became aware of how the machine had changed him. Once, interacting with reality through his body, he had become muscular and strong. But now, since he had created all these tools with spirits of their own, he had grown weak again. The solution, however, was simple: he would create more machines to make him strong again. And while one set of machines was working away to do the things man once did to sustain himself and keep himself strong and muscular, he would engage in hand-to-hand combat with another set of machines in order to restore his body to the shape it had once had.

His work finished, he looked at his new machines and saw that they were good. He decided to put them in a room together. He called it a 'gym', this room full of machines with the power to change the shape of man's body. And, since these machines were of man's own creation, did this not mean that man was now himself at least the part-author of himself? If the machines he had created could themselves create muscle and dissolve fat, then, even if man had not yet reached the stage of being able to say that he was his own creator, he could at least say that the whole business of creation was somewhat different to what he had once imagined.

For as long as man has sought to make his work easier for himself, one of the most insistent impositions of human culture on the individual sense of self has the been analogy of the machine. It is one of the things the culture whispers to us incessantly as we go about, overruling any sense in ourselves as created beings, dependent on a force greater than ourselves, and defined not by considerations to do with maintenance and wear-and-tear but by something mysterious with which we interact without knowing very much beyond the immediate circumstances.

This consciousness is real but invisible and therefore not merely deniable but actually, to all intents and purposes, non-existent. It persists but is unnamed, unspoken, unacknowledged, and therefore has no existence except in the deep fabric of reality. We do not talk as if we are machines. We do not think, at least not in any conscious, concrete sense, that we are machines. But, somewhere deep within ourselves, we have come to regard ourselves in this way, as reflections of the technological world we have created for our ease and pleasure.

Man sees his own reflection and is changed by this. He sees himself as an object outside of himself. With that simple technology, the mirror, we have the means of seeing the totality of the problem. Mike Cooley, an Irishman and a philosopher of technology and its consequences, wrote in a book called *Architect or Bee?* about technology and what it does to the human soul, how man creates technology which then steals part of his humanity and reduces him at least as much as it increases his power. Cooley has also been concerned about the necessity to create new forms of technology, more in tune with human-centred aspirations, stealing back from the machine and the system the parts of man which have unwittingly been given away.

Mankind has followed a pattern of creating technologies in his own likeness, and then proceeded to see in such creations a precise mirror image of the human condition. There have, according to Cooley, been three broad stages in this evolution: machines that walk, machines that feed and machines that think. The first machines worked by clockwork: man, by winding up a spring, gave life to something outside of himself. Art and culture began to mirror this, depicting human beings as machines, all sinews, cables and joints. The second stage was machines requiring an energy form like coal or wood: the steam engine for instance, which, once 'fed', became active and independent. We again, according to Cooley's analysis, began to see ourselves as such a machine. The third, perhaps final, stage is the 'thinking' machine, which seeks to supplant the intelligence that created it.

Having created each new phase of machine in his own image, man then, perversely, began to see himself as an image of the machine, disregarding the fragile, intuitive, creative and emotional elements as forms of eradicable flaws. In an interview for my 1994 book *Race of Angels*, Mike Cooley told me: 'We are at a stage now where we can only accept something as rational and scientific if it displays three predominant characteristics: predictability, repeatability and mathematical quantifiability. And, by definition, this precludes intuition, subjective judgement, passive knowledge, dreams, imagination and purpose.'

Our language, itself a technology, mutates to match our mechanised view of the world, locking us into our potentially fatal condition. The disintegration of public language, as used in politics, economics and other domains of civic discourse, is narrowing in its capacity to express what we really feel. Even our poets, as we shall see, are not immune. 'As a scientist and an engineer, I've always found', Mike Cooley reflected, 'that the things you can state explicitly constitute only a tiny part of that which is the human experience. How do you state explicitly: love? How do you state explicitly: fear? How do you state explicitly: affinity? Such things are processes as well as definitions. And therefore they are things which we have to possess. To really describe love for something or somebody, we must demonstrate it rather than simply define it, and they haven't found any way of doing that. So what they tend to say is that if you can't state something explicitly, it isn't real knowledge in the modern sense.'

There are many examples of how technology affects us in ways we now take for granted. Consider the question of opinion polling, taken for granted in modern societies as representing an almost infallible method of divining what large numbers of people think about a given subject. On a weekly or sometimes a daily basis, we accept as unquestionably 'scientific' the idea that by obtaining the opinions of maybe 500 or 1,000 people, we can tell what everybody thinks. This provides an example of how the mechanisation of society has rendered 'self-evident' a view of the human being that arises not from an objective view of the human condition but of the observed effects of a technological interpretation.

In the 1930s, when George Gallup discovered the patterns that gave rise to modern opinion polling, it was as if he had tumbled onto something new about mankind that had always been and would always be true: that the opinion of the many could be divined by a scientific analysis of the opinions of the few. But perhaps it is only true because we are already fashioned by the technology and the ideology of the society?

Gallup summarised his theory as follows: 'Suppose there are 7,000 white beans and 3,000 black beans well churned in a barrel. If you scoop out 100 of them, you'll get approximately 70 white beans and 30 black in your hand, and the range of your possible error can be computed mathematically.'

We take on trust that opinion polls do what the media witch-doctors say they do, and only their previous accuracy convinces us to maintain this faith. What, though, if the reliability of opinion polling is a product of their use in societies already primed by exposure to limited menus of ideological options? Can it really be true that, as human beings, with all the imaginative capacities and variabilities of that condition, we have, in our political lives, tended to function more and more in such a manner that our capacity for individuality and original thought has become as predictable as the behaviour of inert objects in a barrel?

This question opens up an entirely different view of opinion polls. We tend unquestioningly to assume that the widely accepted relative accuracy of polls has to do with the integrity of the scientific methodology alone. But what if the reliability of opinion polls in anticipating human behaviour is the consequence of the emergence of a particular form of political culture, of which opinion polling is a central and vital element? In other words, perhaps opinion polls are reliable not because human beings are naturally no more interesting than beans, but because the kind of societies we have created tend to make us speak and behave in a beanlike way, at least while in the public domain. Having debased our politico-intellectual stock to a thin gruel, perhaps we have diluted our collective thought capacities to a dwindling pool of possibilities. Is it possible that the public discourse that preoccupies us to the extent it does is the result not of the spontaneous public articulation of the cumulative concerns, aspirations and perspectives of the population, but a debased, reduced, recycled and jaded agenda, driven from an invisible centre and legitimised by opinion polls?

Perhaps it is possible to create an altogether different kind of society, in which the viewpoint of an electorate comprising millions of people could not be ascertained by reference to a tiny sample of 1,000 people or fewer. Such a society, were it possible, would certainly be infinitely more interesting, but also – and perhaps this is germane – a lot less manageable than our present one.

Perhaps the culture we have created, and are reinforcing all the while with the constant insinuation of a digested popular view, is not the best possible form of freedom at all but a circumscribed social existence bound by unseen yet nonetheless firm boundaries. And perhaps, therefore, the meaning of democratic freedom amounts to something a little more complex than the notions championed by media cheerleaders in our time. Perhaps, in other words, the natural state of things is that, if I want to find out what a million people really think about things that matter, I must ask each one of them.

Nowadays, we imagine we know better than those who preceded us or those who live in 'primitive' societies where reason has yet to awaken. The weather, for example, is subject to meteorological patterns that can be studied and understood. Jumping about to a tom-tom beat makes no difference. We, therefore, are more rational than the savages who believe in the power of ritualised rain-dances. But the 'modern' belief that the weather can be divined by watching a blonde woman point to a chart on television is actually no more 'rational' than the rain-dancer's belief that the matter was governed by what he deems to be magical. The person watching the weather forecast is not therefore more 'intelligent' than the rain-dancer. They are essentially the same, except that they each tend to behave in accordance with the diktats of culture at the time and place in which they happen to live. There is nothing intrinsically 'rational' about the idea that weather is the result of natural causes. Very few people understand much about these natural processes, but simply accept the assumptions they have been assured are correct. They therefore 'trust' the weather forecast in much the same way as the ancient tribe trusted the rain-dance. They take for granted that the communal knowledge of the culture is reliable. They may, scientifically speaking, be more 'correct' in their understanding of things, but they are not necessarily more intelligent. They have just absorbed the agreed meaning of an inherited 'bundle' of knowledge which had been counted and bound perhaps before they were born. There is no need to open it and count it again. The essential mental process of the television viewer watching the weather forecast and the witch-doctor leading the rain-dance is pretty much the same. Both are acting on inherited knowledge. Both are acting in accordance with agreed cultural assumptions.

But there is extraordinary social and cultural pressure on each of us to accept what is agreed. In the context of the unquestionable scientific foundations of the modern science of opinion polling, for example, doubts about the basis of this technique will always be seen as 'irrational'. But it all depends on what you think rationality is. You might say that opinion polls are a form of voodoo, because they operate according to a theory and methodology that lie beyond the ken of most of those whose opinions they claim to apprehend.

How many of those whose view of the world is created and defined by the consensus of the public view as expressed in opinion polls could tell you that the margin of error in any given poll is calculated by multiplying by two the square root of the result obtained when the figure in question is multiplied by 100 minus itself and the answer divided by the sample? Does the fact that, notwithstanding our ignorance of the process, we all accept at face value the reliability of the methodology make us more or less 'rational'? Is a refusal to accept this logic as self-evidently capable of intuiting the deeper sensibility of a society necessarily a symptom of an unscientific viewpoint?

How can someone who simply accepts one set of assumptions reserve the right to sneer at someone else who has used essentially the same mechanism to arrive at a different perspective?

Opinion polls provide a way of seeing that there is a necessary distinction to be made between logic and science. Something may be scientifically established because it provides a method or an explanation for something that is, or appears to be, in accordance with reality. This method or explanation may be widely accepted, without necessarily being popularly understood. It is difficult, if not impossible, to disprove the validity of the logic of opinion polling in our societies, but in a different kind of society, one not governed by mass media influence and ideological programming, it is likely that opinion polling would not work at all. It is reasonable to deduce, therefore, that the allegedly scientific basis of opinion polling offers merely an appearance of coherence in circumstances where certain conditions are consistently met. The precise same thing can be said of rain-dances.

One of the obstacles between us and an understanding about this kind of thing is the fact that the words we might use in an attempt to unpick ourselves from the grip of the culture are themselves intrinsic elements of the culture. We tend to think of words as neutral representations of reality, as natural phenomena. We assume that language is natural – what else would it be? We choose words, don't we, to say what we please? But language really works as a kind of tramline that takes us each time along a preordained course. Language, supplied to us from some central repository, comes replete with definitions of reality, and perspectives on reality, which do not make themselves visible in the words they infect, but nevertheless condition the result: the thought conceived in the words.

The human thought process is not, therefore, the kind of neutralised deductive mechanism that our culture has nowadays come to believe in. It is a fragile process, governed by external factors, which influence its calculations far more than any internal mechanism.

One way of seeing this more clearly is to fix on the way a phrase can suddenly erupt into the language and become commonplace without anyone seeming to decide that this is a good idea. It is interesting to note how, occasionally, a phrase appears apparently from nowhere, and becomes ubiquitous as both a new way of saying and seeing.

When we hear the term 'going forward', which has crept into common usage in recent years as a synonym for 'the future', we tend to smile, perhaps grit our teeth, perhaps snort briefly in contempt for something we cannot quite name. But our response to this term is not merely an expression of linguistic or semantic orthodoxy: it is a primal response born of a fundamental repugnance. For the term 'going forward' is no ordinary cliché, no mere further evidence of the limitless capacity of suited humanity to coin clichés of mind-bending inanity. 'Going forward' is a special case, because it encapsulates within itself an entire ideology, a whole way of seeing the world differently than it was seen in the past.

In the past there was 'the future'. This, however, was implicitly unhelpful to the creation of an engine of endless human aspiration. Talk of 'the future' necessarily implied that what lies ahead is unknowable, mysterious, outside mankind's control. This was problematic for the logic of an ideology which promised that progress held all the answers to mankind's needs and longings. For those in charge of priming and fuelling the machine of progress, 'the future' was like some island paradise waiting to be colonised. And yet the very idea of 'the future' was a kind of taunt, implying a limit to human dominion, and insinuating a boundary between this and the unacknowledgeable realm of unknowability.

Hence 'going forward'. Isn't it obvious? What if the future could be abolished and replaced with something else, something more malleable, more suggestive of human control? The phrase 'going forward' does not do this, not quite, but only because this objective is, in truth, impossible. What it does achieve, however, is the idea that the future has been claimed, colonised, landscaped and controlled. The phrase 'going forward' implies the abolition of the idea of uncertainty concerning what lies ahead. It implies that what was once 'the future' has been mastered and tamed, and that we are now invited to proceed into something prepared in advance. The term is no mere quirk of the linguistic idiosyncrasy of professionals seeking new words with which to signal their professional distinctiveness. No, it is, rather, the encapsulation of their entire manifesto, conveying the hubris that defines their project. And one of the important things about this phrase is that it does not simply enable us to stride confidently into the future as into an already landscaped space, but that it actively prevents us from seeing this aspect of reality, the time lying ahead, in any other way.

This phrase is especially interesting, then, because it is not, as it appears, merely a trite attempt to jargonise the everyday as corporate culture instinctively seeks to do, but an unintentional rendering-visible of the underbelly of the ideological programme from which it emerged.

Our culture, for related reasons, is deeply suspicious of the word 'belief', certainly in the context of what is known as religious faith. If you closely observe the constructions of opinion columnists in today's newspapers, you will very soon perceive that they rarely if ever employ the words 'I believe' but invariably opt for form-ulations like 'I understand', 'I sense', or 'It seems to me'. To say 'I believe' might seem unexceptionable, in the same way as 'I do not believe' might seem equally unproblematic, and this construction, as it happens, is commonplace. On the face of it, both are simply expressions of particular world-views. But in the culture we have constructed, the phrase 'I believe' is infinitely less convincing than the phrase 'I do not believe'.

For someone to say 'I believe', in anything resembling a 'religious' context, is immediately to pigeonhole himself in a way that the culture implicitly recognises as suspect. His 'belief', by implication of the culture, is not founded on anything but some leap of faith, some inherited notion, some superstition. 'I do not believe' in this context, however, is not regarded in the same way. Although the unbelief of one may have no more solid basis than the other's belief, it does not have to justify itself in the same way. It can invoke the scepticism of the culture to its argument and therefore avoid both the necessity of justifying itself and also any condemnation on account of being a position not based on facts, knowledge or science. Scepticism is enough. If the phrase is accompanied by a snort or a smirk, so much the better. Then it becomes even more obvious, in the 'logic' of the culture, that the unbelief is a highly rational form of response to reality.

Nearly all supposed serious discussion of the existence or non-existence of God is conducted in a language manifesting this con-dition, whereby arguments on one side become, purely by virtue of the language employed, self-evidently implausible and naive, and arguments on the other side, through objectively speaking no more supported by substantiating argument, are deemed self-evidently rational and intelligent. The machine that is the culture does all the work, and is almost impossible to answer in words that are free of its logic.

— 6 —

The Sabotage of Hope

Each of us has two lives: the public and the inner, and each of these lives has its own tongue, which we might call, respectively, the tongue of the public square and the tongue of the heart. In one sense, the two are coterminous – each usually comprises, for example, vocabulary drawn from a single language, in this case English. But in another sense, they are utterly dissimilar. The tongue of the public square speaks of 'rational' things, things we 'know about', things we can 'prove', but above all things we feel confident about articulating in a public space that becomes more and more limiting in what it allows us to say in its jurisdiction. The tongue of the heart is loosed only in our private spaces and realms: in our most intimate relationships, in a diary, in a moment of recognition or rapture or indiscretion to a fellow in the gallery or the theatre bar during the interval, perhaps to our gods before the altar, but mostly in silence to ourselves.

With each expansion of the reach of public communications, the quality of communication has been reduced. As the scope for consensus becomes more limited, the scope for saying, in public, profound personal things is more and more diluted: we feel able to say only things that 'everyone' will be bound to see as reasonable. Anything tentative, vaguely irrational or truly heartfelt is reserved for the personal sphere. We no longer, in the great Irish poet Patrick Kavanagh's word, 'blab' about the things that might enable us to alert each other to the griefs we thought our special own. Even as the balm of the poetic and transcendent becomes more urgently required, we are losing the public means of telling each other that we are not alone in our loneliness.

It mainly comes down to money. The word 'consumerism' is one of those dead words, like 'materialism', or 'spirituality', which intrudes on our public conversation only as platitudinous weapons of mass destruction, short-circuiting true comprehension. But, when you think about it, it is obvious that global commodity-markets would tend to maximise their potential in a culture where all beliefs concerning the satisfaction of human craving are directed towards the purchase and consumption of material things. This would almost certainly imply an imperative to close down competition from things of the spirit.

Media are creatures of the market, and so must do its bidding. The injunctions of the market are conveyed in a complex way, and really cannot be perceived other than in their effects, which are remarkable. They include: the media compartmentalisation of the world into, for example, what is 'rational' and what is not; the policing of these compartments with cynicism and scorn; and the public humiliation and/or marginalisation of those who do not follow the rules.

The poet has been banished to the arts pages, where his eccentric meanderings could cause but the minimum of confusion, even if he were disposed to trouble-making, which increasingly he, or indeed she, is not. Religion is still reported on the front pages, but in a manner largely confined to its political aspects. In our everyday speech, we have replaced religious invocations like 'Please God' and 'Thank God' with secularisms like 'hopefully' and 'thankfully', a change that reflects our shifting sense of ourselves from creatures to pseudo-creators of reality.

God, when He makes the headlines now, has been consigned to quotation marks, or some such distancing device, which simultaneously invokes the concept of a deity and questions His existence, disposing of Him with an irony He now shares with mythical figures and invented soap characters. This last sentence would never be published, as it is, by a secular newspaper, because the sub-editor would automatically replace the upper-case 'H's with the more acceptable lower case 'h'.

The internal culture of media in relation to religion might, with the merest hint of parody, be depicted as follows: 'Some of you seem still to believe all this hogwash about "God", and, because you are our customers, we continue to accord these superstitions due prominence. But really … !!!'

This is not necessarily the honest personal response of individual journalists, or even a majority of them. Journalists, mostly, have hearts that speak, as much as the hearts of non-journalists, in the tongue that dare not betray itself. But in their public role, journalists must obey the rules of the marketplace, which dictate that, whereas things of the spirit may be mentioned in passing, and to this extent treated with respect, they must not be accorded the same importance as the rational business of pursuing the version of happiness suggested by the strange processes of modern society. If people were allowed to glimpse, in an atmosphere of seriousness, that the feelings in their deepest beings were shared by perhaps a majority of their fellows, the whole consumerist edifice might begin to crumble.

Writing in a foreword to the annual report of the Irish Catholic Communications Office some years ago, Archbishop Seán Brady of Armagh, and Primate of All-Ireland, strongly criticised, without naming names, several Irish Sunday newspapers, and urged Catholics to use consumer power to effect change in the media. Catholics, he said, should be careful about buying newspapers that continually offend their moral and religious values, and should in particular review their purchase of certain Sunday newspapers if these continued to ridicule and undermine religious belief. Such acts of discretion, he urged, might lead to 'a fairer and more representative secular Sunday media in Ireland'.

He remarked also on the unrepresentative nature of journalism and on the particular scarcity of opinion writing from a religious perspective. It was 'peculiar', he said, that more people in the media do not reflect the generally held values of the population in relation to family, faith, religious practice and community. In this regard he again turned his focus on Sunday newspapers which, he noted, were utterly out of kilter with the lives of their readers, many of whom will have attended some form of religious worship before picking up the Sunday paper.

The Archbishop had raised an interesting question but did not extend his argument sufficiently. Perhaps he wished to emphasise his perception of a particular anomaly in relation to the Sabbath, but the phenomena he described are by no means confined to

Sunday newspapers. They affect all Irish media, including broadcast media and the so-called quality daily newspapers.

One of the reasons is fairly simple: the media are not democratic. I don't mean only that the internal operation of the media is not a democratic process – it isn't, of course, because democracy would render the media unworkable – but that the media, for all journalism's claims to act as a bulwark of democracy, are not really all that bothered about democratic values. In Western societies, the media are businesses, of course, but that is a secondary issue, since it should be possible for them to operate to commercial principles and still manage to approximately reach the basic democratic requirement. The real problem has to do with the culture of journalism, which is a far more monolithic entity than is ever acknowledged by journalists. Journalism is a kind of cultural club, in which the members respond to an unwritten set of prescriptions relating to the purpose and character of the profession. Thus, journalism tends more towards the support of prevailing ideologies than it does towards truth-telling.

Journalism prides itself, for example, on being a 'progressive' profession, which means that it is governed by a fundamental, indeed fundamentalist, opposition to traditional ideas. To call oneself a journalist and not to subscribe to 'progressive' principles is to invite suspicion and hostility from other journalists. In Ireland, this culture is especially virulent because of the historical role of Catholicism as moral police force, which brings all the 'progressive' instincts of journalists to the fore. There are, of course, journalists who regularly deviate from the orthodoxies, but they are a minority and generally must operate from outside the cultural heart of the profession. They work from home, rarely socialise with other journalists, and often do not think of themselves as journalists at all. Moreover, many such journalists fall into the category of tokenistic counter-balance, providing a gracing aspect to the otherwise unrelenting ideological monolith that is the modern newspaper or broadcasting organisation. Every word they utter or write is, by virtue of the background radiation against which it is heard or read, imbued with an aura of wrong-headedness, and, by its very presence in the medium in question, suggests a degree of media tolerance that anticipates and implicitly defeats any claim that the media are other than open-minded.

Archbishop Brady was certainly correct in his impression that Irish journalism is deeply hostile to Catholicism, but it would be a mistake to believe that journalism is opposed to religious practice or belief. In fact, there is what might be characterised as an unacknowledged 'hierarchy of tolerance', by which journalists accord respect to believers on the basis of an assortment of factors, including historical victimhood and opposition to Christianity. Thus, Muslims are almost invariably accorded enormous respect. Jews likewise, except where they are in conflict with Muslims, in which case their historical victimhood meets a higher trump. Christians come way down, though of course in Ireland Protestants are higher than Catholics, who prop up the hierarchy of (in)tolerance. I once attended a meeting of an organisation of Irish atheists at which there was a lengthy discussion about how the group might seek common ground with 'moderate' Muslims against Christianity.

One of the difficulties besetting the capacity of religion to confront the nature of the modern world is connected to language, how it is used and who controls it. Religions have their own languages, with which they speak among themselves, though each of these has more in common with others than is often acknowledged. Believers the world over speak broadly the same language of piety, austerity and devotion, with varying degrees of insight into the core meanings of these phenomena. But their communications with the outside world are necessarily limited or doomed to be misunderstood.

The problem is not so much with secularism as with the public language that has evolved in tandem with it. The language of the public domain is not so much actively hostile to religion as simply incapable of articulating religious thoughts. This frequently causes the message of religion to be misstated and therefore misunderstood.

Of course, many of the objections to religion in the modern world are well-founded, in the sense that the records of various institutional forms of religion are chequered with abuses of power, obscurantism and authoritarianism. In my book *Lapsed Agnostic* I wrote about the influence of the 1960s' generation, the Peter Pans, who made a burst for freedom from the dark shadow of religion-dominated moralism and created for the first time in history a culture centred on the values of youth. I met more than a couple of people who told me that, in the course of reading the book, they had become irritated by my descriptions of this condition and the fact that I seemed not to acknowedge that I was myself a product of this generation and its freedom-seeking. Progressing further through the book, they found that I did indeed make such an acknowledgement, that in fact it was my membership of the freedom generation that enabled me to see where things had gone wrong with the freedom project. It is very much a characteristic of Irish public debate that denunciations almost invariably take the form of accusations, and people are therefore not attuned to the idea that sharper critical clarity is often attainable through observing your own mistakes.

What the 1960s have come to represent in our culture is the moment when societies started to look forward to the power of the young and ceased looking back to the authority of the old. This was the moment when youth first began to assert a political force, when freedom, or a particular version of it, was posited as an answer to authority and tradition. It would be ludicrous to deny that the moment was long overdue. But, like all things that are good, it was pushed too far, and the main trouble with the 1960s' revolution is that it created in European culture a rupture between youth and age, which has yet to be repaired. The moment and its symbolic assertion of individual freedom were essential, but no more essential than the preservation of tradition. As a result of the overwhelming acceptance of the values of the revolution, we are still unable even to imagine freedom and tradition being capable of happy coexistence.

I was born in 1955, which makes me approximately the same age as rock 'n' roll. This has significance for me because it provides me with a sense of having lived through a time when something coherent was happening, something with a beginning, a middle, and, not that far into the future, an end – a phantom destination that promised perfect happiness.

The rock 'n' roll element is not incidental: culturally and ideologically it gives expression to the concept of freedom which has defined Western humanity throughout my lifetime. Rock 'n' roll has about it an aura of perpetual revolution, of agelessness, of defiance of everything, including nature itself. Forty-odd years ago, the British band The Who, in their anthem of Sixties rejectionism, 'My Generation', sang 'I hope I die before I get old', articulating something that conveys still the mind-set of this age of freedom. The important thing was to remain young, because in youth it was possible to avoid the issue of ultimate meaning. Not only did the question of the Beyond not matter because it was, relatively speaking, so far away, but for the moment its logic stood between you and achieving happiness and satisfaction right here, now. Thus did youth become central to the culture we created as we emerged from that 1960s' moment of revolution. If you could freeze yourself culturally in a moment in time, there was no need to believe in anything but your own capacity to be happy on your own terms. At the age of twenty, five years seemed an eternity in which to enjoy yourself by breaking all the rules the greybeards had imposed in order to curtail your freedom. To die was not so much to go to a better place, a question the culture elided, but to be spared the humility of decay.

What is extraordinary is that the generations that entered the public realm between the mid-1950s and the late 1970s, and which today control the levers of power in our societies, have managed to perpetuate the idea of remaining young long after youth has passed them by. They have created a culture in which agelessness is paramount, even though the delusional nature of this aspiration is obvious and ineluctable.

Perhaps every generation is destined to commit a crime against the next, though the nature of these crimes appears to change through time. A grudge concerning the alleged wrongs committed by our fathers' generation, more than forty or fifty years ago, is still widely nourished in our cultures, though disingenuously, as a means of frustrating attempts to reopen the discussion about fundamental things. The alleged wrongs of the past had generally to do with the imposition of rules that were not fully or properly explained and which therefore seemed to be arbitrary and somewhat vindictive. To listen to the louder voices in our cultures, one would imagine that these wrongs still continue, when in fact they are, to the extent that they occurred at all, long in the past. Meanwhile, many of the wrongs of the present are ignored because to highlight them would be ideologically inconvenient by virtue of insinuating that not all flaws are to do with the unenlightenment of the past. Today, the generations which grabbed cultural power in a coup against the greybeard killjoys they conjured out of their desire to be free, perpetrate a wrong that is related but wholly different to the wrongs they continue to condemn: a refusal to be truthful about the experience of freedom.

I belonged to these generations, growing up at the centre of this culture, deeply immersed in it as a rock music journalist and writer. Somehow, the culture persuaded me to perceive only a narrow dimension of myself, and to promise me particular kinds of freedom for as long as I agreed to employ a narrow definition of my humanity. But, the more I became unable to remain within this mould, the less the culture seemed able or willing to meet my needs and desires. After a while, it became obvious that this limitation was intrinsic to the culture, and indeed that things could not have been otherwise. But even more interesting was the way the culture had succeeded in hushing this up, in persuading people not to talk about their sense of disappointment or the extent to which, as they grew older, or fell victim to the conditions that sooner or later afflict all human beings who do not die before what seems like their time, the promise of freedom and happiness had been surreptitiously withdrawn by the culture. Somehow, everyone to whom this happened – and it happened, sooner or later, to everyone – seemed to have been persuaded to believe that the fault lay with themselves, that they had been pursuing the promise of freedom in the wrong way or in the wrong place or with the wrong people. There was nothing wrong with the promise – they needed simply to give the wheel another spin. This time they might be luckier.

As I reached middle age, I was just beginning to find ways of authentically describing my experience of this aspect of the culture, but it was not easy. Because the culture was defined by the ethic of rebellion, and the morality of this rebellion was self-evident to everyone involved, it was difficult to describe what one had actually experienced without seeming simply to have changed sides, to have betrayed the idea of freedom, or simply to have gone mad. To attempt to describe reality outside the bubble of the culture was to acquire the appearance of a traitor, to become a reactionary – a lamentable shift, immediately presented by the culture as the consequence of a middle-age crisis.

Perhaps crisis is indeed what it is, but what might such a crisis signify, if not that the journey of the human being through earthly time is defined by, among other things, the gradual discovery of the ultimate paradox: the mortality that gives way to the eternal?

My sense of things now is that I have only recently begun to think of myself as I really am – that, until relatively recently, the culture managed to conspire with my own desires to reorientate my dream of freedom, so as to prevent me from speaking, or even seeing, the truth about myself. My sense of it is that, for most of my life so far, the culture has managed to block me, or dissuade me, from perceiving myself truthfully across the entire span of my life.

This trick works on our denial – our denial of how reality contradicts and undermines the idealised versions of ourselves that we draw from the culture. Because we have created a culture that stays young, even though we ourselves grow old, the culture inflicts on each of us a sense of alienation, which we respond to either by withdrawing to a private space or by remaining and trying to extend our grasp on youth for as long as possible.

This culture withholds a central meaning, but denies that it is doing this. In all its babble of promise, it fails to suggest an ultimate destination, but at the same time slyly implies that some such destination exists, while denying the possibility of transcendent meaning. The question of meaning is elided, not so much in the formal discussion of our societies, where the issue of human purpose is in a sense 'covered', but in the very atoms of the culture, in the assumptions and conventions that govern reality, in what is conveyed between words, in the shadows of the constructs that we take for granted in everyday life. This condition seeps into language, into the very glances we exchange with one another. Each of us, internally, remains to some degree authentic, but when we meet in the public square, we are so fearful of betraying how much our inner reality is in conflict with the culture that we affirm the culture all the louder and provoke others to do likewise.

Thus, ours is a culture that sabotages hope. It implies that hope is possible, and yet has removed from sight the only source of hope that exists beyond the baubles and sensations offered by the marketplace and the false promise of eternal youth rather than eternal life. A culture constructed over 2,000 years on the awareness of Christ has been reduced in forty years to a culture in which hope is defined merely by the prospect of some more of that which has already failed to satisfy, until, at a moment specific to each life, the whole thing becomes untenable, at which point the accumulated and postposed despair of a lifetime of false seeking enters in with a vengeance.

The culture insistently tells us that, if we have been trying out these baubles and sensations and are not satisfied, it is only because we have been doing things wrong. We have not worn the baubles correctly, or we lack the necessary skills to experience the sensations to the full. It is a matter of technique, or attitude, or perhaps a little chemical assistance. Or perhaps I need a new suit to reclaim that eroding ideal version of myself. And, strangely, no matter how many times our personal experience tells us that these promises are suspect, the power of the message continues to convince us that the failure to achieve satisfaction resides in some inadequacy within ourselves. In the more extreme cases, the unsatisfied and therefore inadequate citizens of the marketplace are defined as victims of pathologies or illnesses. They are depressed, or addicted, or simply disturbed.

And because our societies are driven by these misapprehensions about freedom, and because of the fear we share that if our illusions are laid bare we shall have nothing to live for but death, we refuse to look at the absolute horizon of reality, which has come to signify nothing in our cultures but the edge of the abyss, occasionally glimpsed out of the corner of the eye. When, from time to time, perhaps at the funeral of a friend or in the presence of the blurt of despair of another, we are brought face-to-face with reality, we turn away in terror and bewilderment.

In this culture, faith is doomed to the function of consolation for those who come to realise they cannot measure up to the ideal or anything like it. And something in the demeanour of the religious sensibility confirms that this is true. An embrace opens up which itself betrays the characteristics of disappontment, of resignation, of terror, of a kind of failure. Christ is offered as a consolation prize for those who cannot meet the standards of the culture. In other words, religious culture, in spite of itself, acquiesces in the marginalisation of religion.

Perhaps the most urgent cultural task of the coming time is to analyse how it has become possible to replace mankind's seeking after the absolute meaning of reality with a narrower ambition, and yet to claim this narrower ambition as more enlightened and progressive. Part of this exercise will be an examination of the logic calling itself 'reason' which enables this narrow version of reality to remain plausible.

The ideal conditions for healthy human progress are some kind of fluid interaction of tradition and freedom. The defenders of each need to be conscious that absolutism is the enemy of everyone. Tradition needs constantly to be tested in the crucible of the present moment, to have its dead elements discarded and the healthy core preserved. Here, freedom is essential. But freedom is a deceptive word which, in its modern meaning, conveys a pursuit of desire without limit. Because of the structural limitations of what I shall mischievously call the human mechanism, there is a point at which the pursuit of desire, in any direction, becomes destructive. One of the consequences of the disrespecting of tradition since the 1960s is that this consciousness of limits has been mislaid.

Since the 1960s, tradition and freedom have seemed to exist in separate channels, dissociated and mutually hostile. Each has had its advocates and defenders, who tend to band into warring tribes, claiming absolute virtue for a value that, in truth, can properly flourish only in a dialectical coexistence with that which is excoriated. Similarly, political culture has automatically divided its voices between traditionalists and progressives, conservatives and liberals, even though experience tells us that the only sustainable progress is arrived at when these opposing energies are combined.

In the 1960s, freedom was defined for a generation as the right to do as you please. The manifesto declared that only proscriptions and misanthrophy stood between humanity and perfect satisfaction. This revolution changed our world, but without changing human nature. Human beings are now much freer, by these criteria, than before, but still no happier, perhaps less so. In *Lapsed Agnostic*, I wrote about my experiences of this freedom, using centrally the example of alcohol. My intention was not confessional, but to describe the discovery of the limits of my humanity. Having followed the recommended path towards freedom, I reached the precipice of my own capacity for satisfaction. From there was I able to glimpse, in the distance, beyond the culture, the absolute reality to which I was structurally related. It took some years of reflection about my before and after life to persuade me there is another kind of freedom: the kind born of a truthful relationship with one's own destiny. Those of us who, three or four decades ago, promoted youth to the centre of human meaning did not realise – not really – that we would one day grow old, and that we would have created a culture dedicated to denying our own humanity. Nor did it strike us that, in elevating our sense of youthful omnipotence to the highest altar of the culture, we were denying the larger truth about ourselves even in our then condition, because youth is not just a passing phase, it is also, even as I experience it, just a dimension of my humanity, whose governance by time is purely incidental.

This revolution continues to define our cultures. For the moment, at least, we accept that there are limits on human freedoms – but only, one sometimes suspects, by virtue of our sense of the as-yet incomplete nature of the freedom project and its rational-scientific revolution. At the back of the Western public conversation for most of our lifetimes has been the amorphous idea that, at some unspecified time in the future, human progress will be capable of rendering freedom an infinite resource. Even when we acknowledge philosophical difficulties with this, we do so while citing and indicting certain reactionary ideologies which, we insist, have stymied the progress project with the residue of their backward thinking. We cannot, it seems, distinguish between the dancer and the dance: between perceiving the hurts inflicted by a fossilised traditionalism as existing separately from the content of tradition, or tell the moral difference between sinners and sin. We seek to purge everything and to insist that our new culture of freedom be uncontaminated by anything held to by the old.

Nor does our outlook on such matters seem capable of countenancing the idea of a circular pattern in the drift of human understandings. We perceive progress as linear, as emerging from the primordial fog and stretching forward into the dispersible mists of the undiscovered future. We therefore see fundamentalist ideologies, among which we include Christianity and – especially in Catholic Ireland – its Catholic manifestation, as a hangover from an ignorant past rather than as a carrier of abiding truth and wisdom.

Traditionalist arguments against, for example, abortion, euthanasia or stem-cell research, are frequently presented in modern political discourse as evidence of obscurantism, rather than as expressions of anything absolute or ineluctable in the equation of human potential. And, because the messages of traditionalists are invariably accompanied by strong dollops of human passion – rage, fear, piety and grief – our latter-day sense of rational superiority makes it easier to elide the idea that the clash between traditionalism and the cult of progress may be telling us something about the absolute nature of the human project. To suggest that there will always be a price to be paid for progress, and that the further science takes us, the higher that price will become, is to join the reactionaries. To suggest that a necessary balance between the human will and the unknowable requires us to match each new human discovery or development with its own weight in humility is to surrender to obscurantism and superstition.

Almost unbeknownst to itself, this culture, created out of the entirely understandable and in many ways correct ambition to shake off traditionalism, seeks at all times to protect its revolution. The devices aimed at achieving this are deeply embedded in the culture and its infrastructure of communication. The spectre of tradition is all the while kept at bay by a series of unconscious stratagems often not visible even to those who operate them.

A couple of years ago, I noticed on the front page of one of the Irish broadsheet newspapers a photograph that drew my attention for reasons that I could not immediately articulate. It was in August, on the day after the celebrations of the Feast of the Assumption at Knock shrine in County Mayo, showing two elderly male stewards in their robes at prayer. One was seated in a chair, his head bowed, a hand to his forehead. The other, just behind him, was kneeling at another chair, his hands covering his face. The photograph was captioned, 'Let us Pray: stewards at the Assumption service at Knock shrine'.

Photographically, it was, to be frank, no more than an mildly interesting image. But what I found most interesting was the effect created by its placement on the front of a publication priding itself on being a secular newspaper, above the fold, the chief visual 'hook' of the newspaper on the newsstands that day. On the front of a religious publication, it would have had a different meaning: a straightforward illustration marking an important religious event. But here it seemed to be saying something else.

Of course, frequently media carry images of people at prayer, though usually in group-shots in the course of a public service of some kind. But, even allowing for the possibility that the photograph was to some extent intrusive, this in itself did not account for the odd feeling it gave me.

The newspaper in question tends to carry fairly substantial amounts of coverage of certain aspects of faith and religion, but is sceptical about religion, as about all – or most – forms of political or institutional power. Generally, its editorial positions are implacably opposed to the religious outlook on issues – for example, abortion and divorce – concerning which the religious imagination tends to become ideologically exercised.

When the subject of the core meanings of religion is broached at all, it will be treated in a compartmentalised space, fenced off from the newspaper's 'rational' content, a stratagem designed to protect the ideology of the newspaper by conveying that, although it is committed to its own principles of diversity, readers should not be alarmed by these occasional ventilations of superstition. This is just one of the interesting anomalies of being a secular newspaper in a society where a majority of citizens are still, nominally at least, believers. Secular newspapers seem often to divide their readerships against themselves, rarely carrying direct acknowledgements that their readers may have spiritual or religious dimensions, and yet treating faith and religious affairs as important phenomena in which readers might be expected to show an interest. The paper in question speaks to a secularised society, which it had no small role in creating. Its readers may sometimes pray, but they will rarely find anything in this newspaper that takes for granted that this is a sensible thing for them to do.

Hence, in the context of its use, the incongruity of the photograph served to appropriate the private prayerful moment of the two elderly stewards in a manner isolating them from the readers of the newspaper and turning them into a spectacle to be studied and contemplated. Interestingly, there were several other pictures from Knock inside the newspaper, accompanying an excellent report by the paper's religious affairs correspondent. The message of the report was that Assumption Day at Knock remains a vibrant element of the Catholic calender, with attendance up on the previous year. An interesting feature, according to the report, was the numbers of young people and foreign nationals now attending, and this aspect was underlined by one of several other photographs accompanying the article inside. This showed a young girl taking a photograph of her teenage friends as they posed underneath the large outdoors crucifix, with the basilica towering in the background: a young man with a tweed cap, his arms around two girls. In the foreground of the image, an elderly man dressed in a striped sweater knelt in prayer, his back to the cameras of both the girl and the newspaper photographer. In many respects, it would have made a more effective front-page image than that selected by the relevant editors that day. It said something, even if something ambiguous, about youth and faith, but also carried an undertone of the old era of Catholicism. It spoke of young people on a day out, and contrasted their gaiety with the piety of the more orthodox pilgrim. Had it been published on the front page, however, it would have conveyed something that, in truth, is anathema to the house ideology of the newspaper in question: that Catholicism may belong to the future as much as the past.

The picture of the two elderly stewards, however, was on-message, though that alone would be insufficient grounds for objecting to its use. Additionally, through no fault on the part of the photographer, there was something voyeuristic, even condescending, about it. I struggled with this a while before it came to me that, in addition to the written caption referring to the two stewards, there was another one, invisible but still as clear, as though it had been inscribed on the unacknowledged and deniable cultural contract between the newspaper and its readers. That contract is 'rational', secular and highly ideological. It has a certain view of religious matters, which is complex but nevertheless coherent as a mutual understanding. This view is communicated in much more than words and pictures – in the surrounding radiation, the spaces and choices and priorities and omissions that comprise the material of a daily newspaper's relationship with its readers.

So what was this unwritten caption? It was, I intuited, some kind of reduction or disparagement of the two men in the photograph. If you look at things in absolute terms, these two men were engaged in a procedure as vital to themselves as eating or drawing breath. They were opening themselves up to their infinite dimensions, which is to say they were engaging in the established ritual for acknowledging and communicating on the wavelength of absolute existence. It was not any sense of a breach of privacy that bothered me, but they idea that this act, understood in a particular way by the two men engaged in it, was being presented in a context and to a waiting gallery of readers for whom it would have, or at least be expected to have, an entirely different meaning. The idea of an infinite channel would not have communicated across the cultural chasm between the moment in Knock on Assumption Day and the newspaper rolling off the presses the following morning. Deep in the subtextual messaging was the idea of an anachronistic and irrational practice, an outmoded cultural outlook and a dying belief-system. I looked at the photograph again and gradually the unwritten caption began to crystallise for me: 'Look at these guys,' it winked. 'What are they like?'

Of course the caption doesn't really exist, except perhaps in the half-grin, or barely audible titter, of the reader who looked at the photograph and was reaffirmed in his or her prejudices. I know that, if I were to name and accuse the newspaper in question, the editor and all those responsible for choosing this photograph would react with outrage, and I also know that this outrage would in a sense be justified. Nobody will have 'chosen' the photograph to create the effect I describe. The choice will have occurred, at least ostensibly, in an entirely innocent way. But it is also true that the shared understandings between all those involved made any but the most perfunctory communication unnecessary, a routine sequence of contributions setting in train a wordless process leading inexorably to the 'ping!' of recognition in the consciousness of the reader as he or she, sitting in a coffee shop or on a Luas tram, idly glanced down at the front page and instantly absorbed what the photograph was saying.

All treatment of religion by secular newspapers is subject to this syndrome. On the day after the publication of a report of abuse of children by members of religious orders, a newspaper publishes a beautiful photograph of the pope kissing a child. The subtext is clear but eminently deniable. Not a word is identifiable as indicating what this subtext might be, but almost everyone laying eyes on the photograph immediately understands that it is intended to trip off a feeling of unease in keeping with a deeper, unstated ideological agenda.

Even when they provide in-depth coverage of religious issues or occasions – as they did following the death of John Paul II and the election of Benedict XVI – secular newspapers do so with something of the style of a vegetarian waiter serving up a medium-rare steak. Behind the quality of the coverage which serves the cultural needs of those adhering to the residual belief-system is a note deliberately struck to signal unbelief, to convey the imminent obsolescence of the superstition. Religion may still have its place in society, this note communicates, but it is a declining phenomenon – outmoded but reluctant to die away, interesting for its longevity and persistence, sometimes engaging for its spectacularity, but, most of all, to those of us of a more refined outlook, a little quaint.

All the while our public culture holds implicitly to the idea that unbelief is smarter than belief. Without having to show why, advocates of disbelief (if such a committed status can be accorded them) lay claim to intelligence, reason and science in support of their scepticism and derision. And yet, if you think seriously about life and its meaning, and if you embark on a serious voyage through the accumulated bank of human knowledge, it strikes you sooner or later that this knowledge is radically limited. We don't know where we came from. We don't know where we're going. We don't know why we're here. Sure, science has come up with all kinds of partial understandings of things, but many of these are far from settled views, and many more are mere speculations couched in language that really isn't capable of conveying anything that doesn't fit within the existing paradigm of understanding. Before and after science there are question marks. Moreover, most of the discoveries of science are unknown to, or poorly understood by, most of those who rely upon the existence and rumoured achievements of science to ridicule concepts of God or the possibility of another reality existing beyond this one.

The idea that we shall enter another dimension when we depart this one is implausible only if you take the present reality totally for granted. If you assume that everything that exists is 'natural' and 'obvious', you become blind to the wonder of the world and its countless mysteries, and are therefore more likely to scoff at religious interpretations of reality. But if you can look anew at this reality in every moment, it soon strikes you that the idea of a world beyond this one is no more exceptional than what you are looking at right now. Try to imagine, if you had never seen this present reality, but had been capable of consciousness somewhere 'behind' it – could you even remotely have dreamt of the beauty and wonder of this universe?

Sneering at religion is simply lazy thinking seeking to avail of a culture created by previous lazy thinking to claim for itself an intelligence it does not deserve. Though this superciliousness lays claim to a basis in reason, there is nothing reasonable about it. It is merely the reflex action of the unthinking, huddled together in fear that admissions of human vulnerability will cause them to be laughed at. There is something seriously wrong with our culture when it allows someone to lay claim to a heightened rationality for an interpretation of reality based on nothing but scepticism, pessimism, cynicism and despair.

All this cultural noise bears daily down on the individual who seeks to find some channel of expression for his infinite dimension. Perhaps, the culture being so degraded, he is not even aware that he has such a dimension. But he knows that he lacks something, that some desire deep within him remains unsatisfied. But when he pricks up his ears to hear or peels his eyes to see, all that is there is this low-level mockery and dismissiveness of the perspectives and essences that might serve to open him up to the channel he so desperately seeks. The result is a population that hungers for something it can no longer put into words, having lost the words to hope with.

— 7 —

The Dominion of What Is

A couple of years ago, I was invited to an arts festival down Cork way to take part in a debate about God and Irish society and read from my then recently published book, *Lapsed Agnostic*. It was an interesting experience because it enabled me to see up close the cultural consequences of the way our public conversations have come to represent, or otherwise, the reality and significance of religion.

The debate involved me and a Catholic priest going head-to-head on the motion of 'Spirituality and Creativity', a catch-all topic that seemed capable of expanding in any conceivable direction. The implicit assumption that we would necessarily be at loggerheads struck me in advance as rather odd, since my sense of things would have been that, at this stage in my life and on the clear if complicated evidence of my book, we would find many more points of agreement than otherwise. The audience for our debate was about 300 middle-aged and elderly, well-heeled people, mainly from the region, and a sprinkling of younger people. In this, it seemed proportionately representative of the wider society in terms of its interest in and engagement with the concept or institutions of religion.

The priest was a likeable man, a poet who came from the locality but had been posted abroad for many years. He had not been speaking very long when I began to realise why we had been pitted against one another. He was a deeply religious man but one who seemed to find frequent occasion to apologise for the record, if not the existence, of Catholicism. He made frequent references to the dark history of Irish Catholicism, a couple of mildly disparaging mentions of the influence of Rome, and seemed in general to be seeking to talk about religion without being specific about anything.

It was clear that, in the context of Irish Catholicism in its historical sense, if not of Roman Catholicism in general, he saw himself as something of an oppositionist. I could see, too, that with this audience he seemed to be pushing an open door. They were lapping it up, nodding and clapping at his every utterance. They seemed particularly keen about his suggestion that there was a difference between 'religion' and 'spirituality', although he did not spell out precisely what he meant by this. He said he felt the church needed to apologise to the Irish people for its stewardship of their spiritual lives. It was clear to me that his main purpose in speaking was to put clear blue water between himself and the institutional church, and to ingratiate himself with an audience he sensed to be of a similar outlook.

I do not have a set spiel for these occasions. What I say very much depends on the context – not because I have different positions for different occasions, but because the context invariably insinuates the emphasis. If I am up against some smug cleric who seeks to deny there is any real issue of complaint with Irish Catholicism, I tend to beome the attorney for the prosecution and seek to set out the true history of the Irish church's descent into a destructive moralism since the Great Famine of the 1840s. If I find myself up against one or more of the two-a-penny critics of religion in general and Catholicism in particular to be encountered in ambush mode all over the culture, I tend to go back to basics, bringing the discussion around to the place of religion in the essential human structure. There is actually no inconsistency between these two positions, although conventional public discourse in Ireland holds that you must either be a 'progressive', which is to say opposed to religion in principle, or a 'conservative', which generally seems to involve defending the indefensible.

This was a slightly unusual situation, so I did neither of the above. Instead I confronted both the audience and my fellow panellist and asked them what they wanted. Did they want to be Catholics or not? Did they want to be Christians or not? I looked around the room and observed aloud that they didn't look like Hindus or Buddhists, that in general they seemed to be Irish people of a certain age, which probably meant that the vast majority of them had been born into the Catholic faith. I stressed that I was addressing them as a collective, as a cross-section of the wider culture, rather than as individuals. As individuals, I might well argue, they could believe anything they liked and get away with it for as long as they lived. As a collective, however, they faced a different problem: the perpetuation or replacement of the culture from which they, as individuals, had gleaned their spiritual nourishment but were now intent upon rejecting.

It seemed to me that their demeanour represented a kind of search for something that was other than what was, something that was not what they had been, and yet was nothing else that you might call by a specific name. I asked them again: What did they want to be? What did they want their children to be?

I pointed out that we were standing or sitting in the heart of a Christian civilisation. This is what had made us what we were, for better or worse, and most of it had been very much for the better. I explained that the systems we depended on, the economics, science and art that served as the walls and foundations of our culture were essentially of Christian construction. I read a short extract from Rodney Stark's book *The Victory of Reason: How Christianity Led to Freedom, Capitalism and Western Success*: 'Had the followers of Jesus remained an obscure Jewish sect, most of you would not have learned to read and the rest of you would be reading from hand-copied scrolls. Without a theology committed to reason, progress and moral equality, today the entire world would be about where non-European societies were in, say, 1800: A world with many astrologers and alchemists but no scientists. A world of despots, lacking universities, banks, factories, eyeglasses, chimneys and pianos. A world where most infants do not live to the age of five and many women die in childbirth – a world truly living in "dark ages".'

I praised the pope, describing him as one of the world's most progressive thinkers. I said that Benedict XVI, by then three years into his pontificate, had confounded his enemies and delighted his admirers. Benedict had been, by the secular media analysis, a stop-gap and a throwback, a 'reactionary', a 'right-winger', an obscurant-ist, but what had emerged was what had been implicit in his magesterial writings over several decades: a supreme intellect mounted in a most animated humanity, a man who in his lifetime had watched mankind lurch between great good and the greatest evil, and who as pope had sought to reconcile these observations with the truths he had inherited. I said that from the outset Pope Benedict had eyeballed the culture of the age, his first two encyclicals confronting the two most pressing issues of our time: the haemorrhaging from public language of, respectively, love and hope.

Although preceded by a reputation as a theological traditionalist, he seemed to have comprehended the post-modernist impulse towards knowing emptiness even better than many of its adherents. He had brought an intellectual rigour to the core of Christianity in the public square, expounding and illuminating the core connections, and disconnections, between Christianity and modern culture. In truth, he had been the most modern and radical of popes.

When he spoke, he did so as the head of the Roman Catholic Church, but his overriding concern seemed to be for the soul of society. He faced an age in the throes of an identity crisis and sought to show it the way out. His project was the restoration to Western culture of an integrated concept of reason, the re-separation of the metaphysical from the physical. Benedict, I said, had succeeded in bringing Catholic legalisms back to their deepest significance, reaching out, in spite of the background noise created around him by a largely hostile and mischievous media, to the educated generations of young people who hungered for something to transform the lassitude invoked in them by a culture selling sensation and freedom but nothing approaching the kind of satisfaction they craved.

This subtle pope, I said, had struggled to be heard in a media climate characterised by sabotage and diversion. Repeatedly the media sought to distort or reduce his statements, to make them fit with prejudices unfurled on his election. But Benedict had emerged as a man of courage, grace and shimmering intellect, his message undiluted, his status enhanced in the human spaces beyond the newsdesks and the studios of the international media.

All this drove the audience close to madness. A man in the front row accused me of tribalism. He said he was sick of hearing this stuff. I asked him who had been saying this stuff lately. He didn't answer. A woman at the back chimed in that she hadn't come to the event to hear 'dogma'. I said I hadn't uttered a word of dogma but I could do that as well. I asked her what she had come to hear. 'I thought we were going to have a discussion about mysticism', she replied. I said I didn't do mysticism. The priest sought to stoke the fire while seeming to spring to my defence. In fairness, he pleaded, I hadn't uttered any dogma; it was just that my tone was a little dogmatic. They loved that.

This audience was exhibiting what might be called the dominant characteristic of post-Christian Irish society: a searching for something other than what is. What is usually called 'spirituality' in our culture is mainly an evasion, an attempt to define itself by what it is not, which is to say that another term for 'spirituality' might be 'Not-Catholic'.

One of the odd little tricks that our culture has succeeded in playing on us is convincing us that our existences are attended by limitless possibilities. In fact, my existence in any given moment has no element of choice about it. It is 'what is'. What is happening in my life is what is happening in my life. I have choices, yes, but they relate to what may yet happen, to the future, to how I might exert my will to change my immediate reality. The strange thing is that this notion of future uncertainty has somehow come to be 'drawn backwards' into the present, where it serves to suggest that 'what is' might easily have been something else, that what I am is just one of a possibly infinite set of possibilities for my existence. This causes me to become paralysed by the idea of the intrinsic randomness of my existence. Where I am, who I am with, what I am doing, might, with a different throw of the dice, have turned out entirely differently. Reality, thus, is arbitrary. This idea, in its ideological incarnation, is used to attack all notions of absolute value or truth, suggesting that any single value system can be deconstructed by reference to the equal claim of any other idea.

Interestingly, those who seek to deconstruct one value system by reference to another, competing system, are almost invariably not suggesting that the one be replaced by the other. They are simply using one to eliminate the other, a different thing. They seek only a vacuum. Thus, the Muslim notion of God is used to undermine the Christian idea of God, not because there is a wish to replace God with Allah, or Jesus with Mohammad, but because the existence of a conflicting idea is convenient to the purpose of discrediting one particular idea, and ultimately all ideas, of God.

Our culture has rendered this form of thought so pervasive and semantically persuasive that it is almost impossible to argue against it. The only defence is a belief in the dominion, the absolute nature of 'what is', in the value of 'something over nothing', in attachment to the particular, the specific and the real. I am in a room now because it is the room I am in now. I am not in another room. If I were in another room, my human condition would be exactly as it is, and might well, under the influence of the culture, be fooled into hankering after being in this room instead. But experience tells me that the reality of existence, to the extent that this is defined by the present moment, has but one possibility: what is.

Reality, therefore, is not random, not arbitrary. It is definitive and clear. There is no point in my hankering after different surroundings or different beliefs as a means of discovering myself. Either I assent to what is or I choose nothing. I am a Christian, not a Muslim. If I were a Muslim, I would not be a Christian. Yes, I am free to choose between them. In a certain sense, it does not matter which I opt for: either way, I have, through my particular culture, a means of access to the divine, the infinite and the sacred. But this does not mean that the facts of 'what is' are in some way arbitrary. There are no other facts. Ultimately, unless I opt out of the question altogether – a more complicated question than merely declaring my abstention – I must choose one, the other or an endless vacillation between the two, which really amounts to making no choice and having no beliefs.

And since it is necessary to be particular, the most coherent particularity lies with what I have been until now. By changing horses mid-stream, I do not stand to improve my chances of discovering truth, but merely to drown in the fathomless depths of uncertainty that lie between the two. If I allow myself to be coaxed or inveigled into a confusion about which horse I should be on, I will be certain only of my ultimate horselessness. I am on the horse I am on now because it is the horse I am on now. This, too, is a reasonable position, but one our culture has made impossible to see in this way.

Like the society they typified, the members of my afternoon audience sought, having found Catholicism not to their liking, to tiptoe around it, marking out a new territory in those elements that appeared to be 'spiritual' or 'mystical', but preferably not Christian and most certainly not Catholic. I told them that I didn't think this would work for Irish society, that it might conceivably, once a clear choice was made and adhered to, work for any one member of the audience, for as long as he or she survived in this dimension, to create a spiritual life out of the remnants of a Catholic unbringing and the alternativism that enabled an avoidance of this. But if applied at a cultural level, it would result only in confusion and lead inexorably to despair.

'What about Celtic Spirituality?', a man asked. What about it? 'Isn't there a place for it?' I suggested that Celtic Spirituality was like having yesterday's dinner today. It was a perverse attempt to sidestep the reality of now. Faith was faith in the moment or it did not exist. Once you had it, you could adorn it with all manner of things, but if you didn't have it to begin with, the adornments were reduced to kitsch and corn.

The discussion was heated but without much sense of a common language. Anyone observing the drama of the event with an objective eye would have concluded that it was a discussion between an audience seeking a new and progressive outlook on spiritual affairs, against a rather unlikely-looking representaive of some reactionary tendency seeking to take Ireland backwards to some near obsolescent form of behaviour. I saw it differently: as a battle between a spurious ideal, represented by the poet-priest, and the possible, represented by myself. The audience, virtually to a soul, was with the priest. At the end, he approached me and asked if I wouldn't mind him giving me a bit of advice. I said to fire ahead. He mentioned the name of a well-known Irish journalist who, having been a bit of a raver when younger, had become famous for adopting reactionary positions in middle-age. He said it wasn't a question of my turning out the same, but that people might begin to see it like that. I told him he was probably right but that there was nothing much I could do about how people decided to see things.

But the next day was interesting in a quite different way. This time I would have an opportunity to present my own thoughts without having to follow anyone else's agenda or angle. I would read from my book and afterwards be interviewed by a young female novelist. Given the previous day's antagonisms, I was a little nervous, and my state was not improved by a well-known poet – not the priest of the day before – who approached me outside the venue just before the reading and muttered, 'This had better be good!' It was the kind of cryptic remark Irish poets like to make to maintain their sense of enigma: it implied a willingness to give me a fair hearing, but also suggested a diminishing reservoir of tolerance for any further heresy or error.

I was surprised to find that at least as many people had turned up as for the previous day's debate. This hinted at an openness I hadn't detected in that encounter. I noticed in the audience a number of stars of the Irish literary firmament who had not been there the day before, and who either eyed me in a steely fashion or avoided eye-contact altogether.

It is a strange thing to have 'crossed over' in one of the central cultural battlefields of modern Ireland. There is very little allow-ance made for the possibility that you have made an honest reappraisal of things. The standard assumption is invariably that you have been 'got at', or have become frightened of dying, or perhaps that you must have been prone to stupidity all the time except that this tendency had somehow escaped notice hitherto.

Remarkably, the young novelist had read my book and liked it. She was therefore in a position to tell the audience what was in it, as opposed to what they imagined might be in it, or what they had gathered from the several disingenuous, and one or two poisonous, reviews in the national newspapers. She saw it for what it was: an attempt to slide underneath the language of the con-ventional discussion about religion. She gave me a powerfully supportive introduction and after I had read for a while, asked me some questions. And, because her questions were formed out of a close reading of my book, they enabled the discussion to skirt the trampled thoroughfares and enter into the odd little cavities of thought that people think are unique to themselves and become quite astonished to discover are part of some mysterious shared consciousness.

Instead of talking about morals and sin, we talked about desire, about what it is and how it can deceive you. We talked about shopping. We talked about drink. People began to get it. I briefly revisited some of my statements of the previous day, in particular the need for religion to have some kind of a structural specificity in the cultural context. They got this too. In the end a queue of more than 100 people formed to buy my book and have it signed. Even the priest I had locked horns with the previous day was effusive. He shook my hand and said I was a mighty man.

— 8 —

The Keyhole of Reason

We think of reason as being like algebra or something: $x–y = y–2x + r^2$. Our culture teaches that unless I can demonstrate something, it cannot be true. This is a reduction of reason comparable to trying to examine reality through a keyhole. I see vague moving shapes, but most of my capacities are neutralised.

If I confine my sense of reality to what is demonstrable, I would not be able to get out of bed in the morning without first checking that the floorboards are still there. I can have no reasonable expectation that the kettle will boil or that the car will start when I turn the key. If we demand that everything be demonstrated before we begin, then nothing is possible because we know almost nothing.

Nothing about the caterpillar tells you it is going to become a butterfly. It is counter-intuitive. It is unreasonable. But it happens. Only the experience of observing the mystery of creation enables me to expect it to happen and then to take this process for granted.

Life is fundamentally mystery. How did I, an apparently discrete and self-propelled being, inseparably linked to a wider reality, suddenly erupt into being on 28 May 1955? I have a superficial explanation, but really my information goes back perhaps two or three layers before hitting the unknowable. I am mysterious to myself. I did not make myself. These words arrive on the page having come from me, and in this sense I might be called the source of them. But if I peer into what I have been encouraged to think of as 'my' intelligence, I find that it observes itself in a way that renders ineluctable the conclusion that there are elements within it that come from someplace else, from before or beyond what I think of as 'me'.

The human intelligence is not a machine, whose parts are all discoverable and amenable to inventory and examination. The human brain cannot operate effectively without access to an external culture, which itself has roots in deep antiquity. And yet there is also something else at work, something intrinsic, something that might be called the human 'I', the indivisible and unique perspective of the individual human person who, while remaining mysterious even to himself, has access to a deeper intelligence that often defies his capacity for self-description and analysis.

Most of what mankind calls 'reason' is confabulation, a postrationalisation of emotional, intuitive or conditioned responses, using information assembled somewhat after the fact in order to 'explain' or justify a response or stated belief. The idea of pure reason, in the sense of a mechanical process of logic moving systematically through the facts and tying everything together, is confined to mathematics and related disciplines. Often what we regard as reason is merely the interaction of language and conscious thought, the *post facto* construction of decisions, viewpoints and descriptions, emphaticially delivered in a language that implies objectivity, creating the impression that what we say has happened is actually what has happened, and that the truth is a concept readily captured in words and arguments.

This becomes even less 'logical' at the collective level. Very often, in the throes of public discussion, it is possible to observe that, although those involved in the discussion insist that they are engaged in reasonable debate, their terms of reference are almost entirely emotional. Although such discussions can often manifest deep inconsistencies, there is no means of having these acknowledged or rectified, because illogic and unreason can always call in impressive resources of emotional rhetoric to drown out any insistence on reason.

Freud described the human brain as being divided into three elements: the ego, or conscious, logical element; the superego, a kind of societal or cultural policeman who sits on the shoulder insisting on compliance with the rules of society; and the id, which is the human desire for happiness and pleasure. We like to think that the ego is in control, and indeed the ego, because it has the final word on everything, because it has appropriated the levers of speech and language, manages to convince us that this is the case.

But neuro-science has established that this is an illusory impression of things, that very often what we 'decide' or 'know' or 'believe' is arrived at in the id, or dictated by the superego, with the ego coming in at the final moment to claim the outcome for its own efforts.

I remember once having a very clear insight into this process operating in myself. It was when my daughter was a baby and living with her mother in London, and I needed to buy a house there to be closer to her. I remortgaged my home in Dublin and had therefore a modest but hopeful budget with which to proceed. I began the search near where they lived, in Highgate, north London, and moved gradually outwards until I found a place that matched my means. Along the A1 in east Finchley, on the edge of Hampstead Garden Suburb, a beautiful sprawling estate of mix-and-match housing, I discovered some attractive-looking cottages spoiled only by the busy road, where the traffic droned and varooomed all day and all night. Because of this, there were quite a few houses for sale along Falloden Way, a stretch of the A1, all beautiful little semis with wooden floors and fairytale gardens.

After viewing a number of the properties on sale, I was torn between two, one on either side of the road. Having been twice to both, I couldn't make up my mind between them. I then decided to employ a strategy suggested to me for dealing with such issues by a friend of mine who considered himself of a highly logical disposition. This involved getting a large sheet of paper, dividing it with a line down the middle, and then setting out the pros and cons of whatever problem was proving difficult to resolve, and allocating points to each. The idea was that, by adding the points up at the end, you could 'logically' arrive at the best outcome.

I duly began to list the strong and weak points of each house, giving pluses for decoration, double-glazing and satellite TV, and minuses for dirty carpets and, for example, the fact that one of the houses had a pond in the back garden, which would have to be drained to render the place safe for a child. I remember giving the same number of points to each house under the heading 'Location', one because it backed onto a park with a children's playground, the other because it was on the same side of the road as the corner shop. I added up the scores and found them exactly equal. The 'logical' approach had confirmed my initial sense of things: that I was unable to decide between the two houses. Then I went back over the figures and started to review each one. But then something odd happened. I began to notice that I was tending to cheat, that I was trying to make one of the houses 'win' by tweaking the points in its direction. I stopped, stepped back and asked myself: do you really prefer this house? I did. Somewhere deep in myself I had already decided, but not on any 'logical' basis. As it happened, the house was the one without the garden pond, backing onto the park. It was more old-fashioned and less hi-tech than the other, and you had to cross the road to get to the shops. But somehow, at some level deeper than the 'rational', I had computed these elements in a way that my conscious mind did not seem capable of doing. Nor was it simply a question of personal preference. Surveying the outcome, I began to realise that I had not simply gone with the house that I liked best, but had somehow accounted for every conceivable consideration concerning the purpose of having the house in the first place, as a place to take my little girl. My desires, if you wish, had already factored in those elements that related to her, and were therefore not issuing demands purely on the basis of my own selfish needs. I bought the house and have never had any reason to regret the decision, which was therefore, in the purest sense, reasonable.

I have noticed a similar syndrome at play when occasionally I am asked to be a judge in, perhaps, a book competition or a students' award scheme. Because each of the entries is different from the others, it can be difficult to establish any kind of objective system of comparision. Usually what I do is read or otherwise absorb each entry and allow some sense of a preference to emerge within myself. Then, because the process of judging generally requires an explanation or a justification for a particular choice, I study each one again in search of evidence to substantiate my intuition. It can sometimes occur that, in this second assessment, a new contender begins to emerge, but this would be unusual. Usually I go with what might be called my initial 'gut' feeling, and usually, too, I provide reasons which make the decision sound like the most 'rational' thing in the world. And perhaps it is. But what this suggests is that what we call 'reason' is a much more complex process than we allow, that the conscious, logical dimension is often a *post hoc* communiqué formulated by the ego to 'explain' the outcome of a tug-of-war between the angel of desire in the heart and the moral policeman sitting on the shoulder.

Science tells us that the human brain is divided against itself – left against right, conscious versus unconscious, conditioning versus experience – and therefore delivers what are more like the decisions of a consensus of several entities, rather than the output of a single intelligence. The mind is such a complex phenomenon that it exceeds its own capacity to understand itself, and yet its conscious element feels obliged, at the completion of often involuted and deceptive assessments and calculations, to instruct the speaking apparatus known as the mouth to deliver a definitive judgement on what has occurred. This judgement is often wrong, or misleading, or subject to delusionary factors that render it much less 'rational' than the human mind in question is at that moment seeking to declare.

You get a sense of this sometimes, reading through a carefully constructed judgement of a court which moves majestically through the facts, arguing from point to point as a child skips across stepping stones. And yet, somewhere deep within your admiring response is a knot of doubt. Can things really be that simple? Can everything be established to such perfection? When you examine more closely, move to the foundations of the logic, you invariably find that the core of the judgement is based on certain preconceptions, prejudices and assumptions of the judge in question that he has internalised to such an extent that they are invisible to him. Seeking to build his structure of logic and arguments, he has dropped his assumptions like railway sleepers in the bog of doubt and confusion that is the human attempt at knowing, and, when a sufficiency of his preconceptions has created a kind of mutually sustaining solidity, has started to build.

Law is really man's attempt to create a bedrock in the nothingness of knowing in order to give his thought something to build on, the culture of the past preserved in the present. Thus, the law enables us to observe, in a relatively detached way, how fragile human thought can be, how prone it is to factors that, by definition, remain unacknowledged at the time. Often, laws enacted decades or centuries in the past can seem absurd, and yet they often exhibit clues as to why they made sense at the time. At any given time, what seems to be the 'logical' outcome of the thought process of society is governed not by objective laws in the manner of mathematics, but by the assumptions, desires, prejudices and objectives that dominate the culture at that moment.

We think of reason as a linear process: as we discover more about the world, our perspective changes, rendering obsolete the views we held on the basis of information now exposed as less reliable. But is this what happens in each and every human mind? Does each one of us come to each decision on the basis of considering all the facts as understood by humanity at that moment of advancement, and therefore in a manner more 'logical' or 'rational' than our predecessors? Hardly. In fact, our minds operate in much the same way as those of our distant ancestors: we process information coming in from outside, but usually this functions in our calculations as pre-cast blocks of assumptions to which we ascribe the status of established truth.

Most of the time, we do not understand the intricacies of the information, or the way it arrives at its final meaning. We take it as given. It is 'obvious'. Thus, what we think of as 'logical' processes are very often, in the individual mind, not that at all, but simply the cursory revisions of blocks of information which are never opened up to the scrutiny of the now. It is as though, having counted out an amount of money in notes and arranged it in bundles, we continue, even after apprehending that some miscalculation has taken place, to count and recount the bundles but without reviewing the accuracy of our conclusion as to how much each one contains. We are therefore doomed to make the same miscalculation over and over.

In any given period, the 'bundles' contain different things, different assumptions, different prejudices, different certainties. In what we term 'modern' society, there is an assumption that scientific progress has rendered mankind in general more 'intelligent' than his forebears because our bundles comprise tested scientific knowledge, whereas theirs contained assumptions now regarded as being superstitious or irrational. But no one of us can claim that we arrived by dint of our own intellectual resources at any more than a scintilla of the knowledge we claim.

At best we studied and absorbed it, checking it against our assumptions, floating its implications on the bog of our unknowing. Underneath the most advanced state of scientific knowledge that exists, there is nothing but mystery. We may have established some sense of solidity from which to build our logic, but our supposed 'rationality' is not, objectively speaking, any more advanced than the superstition of, for example, the rain-dancer who imagined that, by engaging in certain choreographed movements and prescribed noise-making, he could persuade the clouds to let loose raindrops.

In the popular mind, science tends to exist in bundled-up or pre-cast knowledge routinely assumed to be correct. In a 'rational' age, this can seem definitive, the policeman on the shoulder drowning out the angel of the heart. But this is only because the 'knowledge' available from the externally obtained bundles is more amenable to constructing what seems to be a coherent thread of logic. It is not that the individual in question 'knows', or 'understands', simply that, for reasons of cultural compliance, he chooses to accept. The very least one might say, therefore, is that our condescension towards those whose beliefs appear less 'modern' than the supposedly 'rational' beliefs of a technologised society is misplaced.

Science is the best understanding of things that mankind has arrived at up to the present moment. Logic is the process of working from what we know to what we can surmise about what is, in some sense, unknowable. Logic, therefore, requires a process of speculation, or surmise, in an attempt to establish something that is unclear or uncertain. In logic, there is, dare I say it, a leap of faith, which seeks to test something that is as yet only guessed at, and therefore unproven. By definition, therefore, the use of logic requires the departure from what, in political society, we consider the 'scientific mind-set'. The idea of God is simply the use of human logic pushed to its limits, in an attempt to arrive at a hypothesis capable of explaining everything. Far from modern science being in conflict with religious interpretations of reality, it is itself a creature of the Christian belief that the God-given powers of human reason were capable of divining the God-created workings of the world.

Whereas the assumptions, the 'conventional wisdoms' of our culture, can in many instances be regarded as reliable, they can never be taken for granted. Human knowledge advances apace. But, all the while, such shifting of understanding is underpinned by either a total, i.e. a religious, view, or by some perspective based on a combination of speculative openness and, implicitly, a repudiation of religious interpretations. In the heel of the hunt, if we apply what in our culture is regarded as 'rationality', we cannot definitely know. The core questions of belief or unbelief, therefore, really centre on the way we deal with this unknowingness.

What certainties we arrive at are sometimes reached on the basis of a kind of probability calculation governed by a number of factors not themselves all that reliable. One is pessimism, born of a natural fear which generally serves to protect us against danger. Our responses to danger, to threats, to attacks and to criticism tend to be faster and more refined than our responses to opportunities for pleasure and happiness. Mankind has an inbuilt negativity born of the need to detect danger in the environment, and, unless this bias is sufficiently modified in culture, this makes us lean towards the more negative interpretations of reality.

Another, related factor, is our desire for approval. We need this more than we are prepared to admit, perhaps more than we think. We want to be loved, admired, regarded as intelligent and good. This desire often contaminates our reason, leading us to short-circuit our deeper search for the truth of something. If those around us are seeking to convince us that something is true, or even more so if by their demeanour and language they suggest that no other perception is possible, we often arrive at the conclusion that will garner the most approval and then persuade ourselves that we got there all by ourselves.

While there is nowadays a developing trend towards 'logical' deconstructions of religion and faith, most people do not engage with this to any extent that would enable them to make up their minds one way or the other. Rather, what happens appears to be that, in the knowledge that such commentary exists, and vaguely aware of some of its content, people who have grown disenchanted with organised religion tend to become depressed about the possibility that religion can offer any answers to their problems. They then tend to rummage in their own experiences for negative evidence to bolster what is becoming their decision. In this, as in so many things, the public square, imagining itself defined by a profound attitude of rationality, is in fact governed by pessimism, by a dark vision of the world based on a petulant reaction against authority and a determination to believe only what is presented to its gaze. The first it calls 'freedom', the second 'reason'.

The human being whose very survival depends on accessing some channel to an understanding of his or her infinite relationship with reality, turns away from talk of 'religion', not in any sense of certitude but in a kind of wearied pessimism and a desire to be at one with the growing public sense of religion's impending obsolescence. Conflating the essential issues of existence with the concept of organised religion, some people lazily reject both at the same time. Perhaps weighed down by a sense that religion had been seeking to limit their freedom, they made a run for it. Their experiences of this 'freedom' did not satisfy them. And yet, nothing they remember of what they learned inside the edifice of religion seems to suggest any relevance to where they find themselves now. And anyway, conscious of the 'rational' nature of the culture they inhabit, and its insistence that faith is incompatible with reason, they could not, even if they could be bothered, find the language to get back in.

One of the remarkable things about our current scepticism is that it cannot see itself. It is hermetically sealed against the consciousness of its own despondency and bleakness. Proffering unbelief as evidence of our 'realism' or 'enlghtenment', we casually think of it – if 'think' is the right word at all – as the objective and naturalistic observation of reality. When the perspective of this pessimism is advanced in our culture, it is never advanced as a simple 'opinion'. Implicitly, it is more than that: a rational statement about observable reality.

When a religious-minded person implies that God exists, this is immediately signalled in the cultural codes as an 'opinion' – whether a naive opinion, an outmoded opinion, an irrational opinion, an inoffensive opinion or an unexceptionably well-founded opinion depends on the context. But, when someone speaks of what may be termed the opposing outlook in this context, the culture does not instantly apprehend such a statement as an opinion. The speaker is merely affirming what the culture, in its language, attitudes and assumptions, has already defined as reality. A priest talking about heaven is heard in modern society with a degree of cultural condescension, which simultaneously sanctions his intervention and dismisses it. On the other side of the argument, an atheist can come forward and, with a snort or a sneer, dismiss the very idea of a life after death and be regarded by our culture as having made a 'rational' observation. To be comprehended as reasonable, all one needs to do is quietly, almost in passing, refer to the nothingness that follows, the abyss that lies over the edge of reality, the extinction that awaits each and every human being. Even the religious-minded person, hearing this, has become so defeated by the culture that he is inclined to silently whisper something to himself along the lines of, 'Okay, so this is the rational position, but still, by virtue of my desire to escape the inexorable logic of this position, and retain a positive outlook, I am disposed to continue believing'. His belief is his alone, held against the will and grain of the culture, and, in terms of the language of everyday communication, impossible to justify in public.

Another strange thing we do is extend our claim on knowledge not just to what other people know but what might theoretically become knowable to other people at some time in the future. For all our progress, we know almost nothing, but still we know, we imagine, slightly more than we did. Therefore, our condescension towards our prior innocence leads us to assume that, more and more as we progress, our intuitive, non-'rational' sense of things will be debunked. Observing this process in what appears to be a beginning, we move immediately to the end of it, jumping to the conclusion that we imagine least likely to discredit or disappoint us. Impatient with our unknowingness, we clutch at the little knowledge that becomes available to take out a mortgage on all future knowledge, and then claim ownership of this as though we already knew all there is to be known.

It is not that the bundles of knowledge that we include in our calculations are sufficient to, for example, 'prove' to us that God does not exist. We do not now 'know' that there is no God, but having seen through certain of the formulations arrived at in what we decide was a less informed era, we jump to the conclusion most likely to enable us to avoid having to go through the same process again, and also, not accidentally, the conclusion most likely to gain us the approval of the prevailing culture. We know, if anything, only infinitesimally more than we did before, but having staked our claim on the totality of all potential future knowledge, assume that it will go on to reveal what our culture-assisted reasoning now tells us it is pointing towards, and settle on this as an understanding of reality. This makes us feel more sophisticated, less naive, more rational, less prone to disappointment and more likely to be loved. What it does not do is make us more intelligent or more knowing. We are neither. We are as subject to the mystery as our species always was. But, because this manoeuvre has also been completed by a majority in society, the train of our thought is rendered more plausible, and therefore more 'reasonable', than if we adopted a position based on the ineluctable fact that we simply cannot find words to say what our hopes tell us may be true.

The most fundamental hubris of which the human race has been guilty may be the belief that knowledge and competence are historically additive, whereas each new layer of knowledge supplants a previous one, pulling the ladder up on our awareness of how we got to that point. Our cleverness has enabled us to fashion technologies which liberate us from onerous physical tasks; but so successful have we become at transferring human activities to machines that we have diminished ourselves to the point where all but a tiny elite of our species may not much longer be capable of invention or creativity at all.

Among the many odd things this culture does is to colonise our own sense of the human enterprise, including our sense of ourselves as human beings. More and more it treats us as if we were, in fact, machines, reducing our human responses to technical, clinical and mechanistic functions that can be anticipated and remedied by the correct kind of technocratic intervention. There is, by this logic, an ideal form of humanity to which all of us aspire, and any failure to meet this is attributable to a pathology or 'machine failure'.

And this affects even the most 'perfect' of us. I remember a few years ago writing about the public admission by the footballer

David Beckham that he suffers from obsessive compulsive disorder (OCD). The principal symptoms of what is known as OCD include obsessions, such as unpleasant and intrusive fears about contamination, often resulting in frequent acts of handwashing, counting, repetition of certain words or mantras; and also obsessions with order, symmetry and neatness. In a television interview, Beckham spoke of his addiction to rearranging hotel rooms and lining up cans of soft drinks in the fridge to make things 'perfect'. He had tried many times to break his cycle of repetitive behaviour but could not stop.

'I've got this obsessive compulsive disorder where I have to have everything in a straight line or everything has to be in pairs', he said. 'I'll put my Pepsi cans in the fridge and if there's one too many then I'll put it in another cupboard somewhere. I'll go into a hotel room and, before I can relax, I have to move all the leaflets and all the books and put them in a drawer. Everything has to be perfect.'

What is called OCD is said to affect one in sixty people in Britain and Ireland, ranging from mild traits to debilitating dependencies on rituals of cleanliness, order or symmetry. The World Health Organisation lists OCD as among the ten most pervasive disabilities, yet many sufferers keep their condition hidden, perhaps because it is often the subject of scepticism and derision. It affects equally men and women and is said to run in families, suggesting a biological cause. Some research has shown that changes in brain activity and patterns, caused perhaps by a minor stroke, may also bring on the condition, which like some forms of depression and, in certain contexts, suicidal ideation, has also been linked to seratonin deficiency. OCD is frequently diagnosed in conjunction with depression and anxiety.

At the time I wrote that, as someone who had from time to time experienced symptoms not unlike those described by David Beckam, I repudiated the immediate pathologicalisation of the condition by professionals who insisted that it be treated with cognitive behavioural therapy and anti-depressants directed at seratonin deficiency.

While emphasising the importance of not trivialising such conditions or dismissing anything that might bring even minor relief to sufferers, I observed that there are ways of seeing such things other than in a clinical context. I suggested that what is called OCD, if it should appropriately be called a disease at all, is manifestly a disease of the spirit. Acknowledging that it can be perceived in a clinical context, I also argued that excessive emphasis on this aspect can obscure the fact that it is one of a host of increasingly visible symptoms of atheistic society, in which the contagion of disbelief is placing enormous and unacknowledged or misdiagnosed pressure on the individual to become the 'god' of his or her own life. Other such conditions include alcoholism, drug-addiction, gambling, overeating and excessive dieting.

I wrote in *Lapsed Agnostic* about my personal experiences with alcohol, and about how this undoubted symptom of spiritual disintegration can also be approached in a clinical context. But while such interventions can sometimes show superficial results, my own experience has told me that they can frequently result in the suppression of symptoms, leaving the underlying condition unresolved.

The desire to impose order on the universe and to become unsettled at our inevitable failure to do so may be ultimately a symptom of the expression in our collective mind-set of a compulsion to take over from a God we no longer acknowledge, or at least no longer fully trust to take care of such things on our behalf. In the modern world, saturated with unbelief, this can afflict both believer and unbeliever, humble citizen and godlike celebrity alike. Denied the certainties that informed the serenity of our ancestors, we feel increasingly pressured to occupy in our own lives the throne where once we would have acknowledged the presence of our creator.

Inevitably, as invariably occurs when you seek to approach such questions from a non-clinical perspective, the vested interests come teeming out of the trenches. One alternative practitioner wrote to the editor of the publication in which my article had been published to say that my views on OCD were 'breathtakingly arrogant and ignorant' and that I had 'recklessly suggested that there is but one solution to the problem'. This is typical of such interventions by people seeking to protect their turf from any attempt to present their specialisation in its broader human context. They never simply accuse those they disagree with of being wrong, but always of being 'dangerously' or 'recklessly' wrong, of endangering people's lives by seeking to delve into matter which, by implication, only the professionals are entitled to speak about.

The correspondent, objecting to my description of OCD as 'a disease of the spirit', seemed determined to close down an avenue of exploration that might not fill his own waiting room. Disingenuously, he asserted that I was diagnosing every individual incidence of OCD as rooted in a condition of agnosticism. In fact, what I was offering was an alternative analysis of the collective conditions in which disorders like OCD appear to flourish. I had not suggested that an individual absence of belief in God was necessarily the root cause of the condition, but that, in a society in which belief is on the wane, the condition known as OCD and other, yes, diseases of the spirit tend to grow exponentially.

Nor had I suggested that a personal belief in God was in itself sufficient armoury against the cultural onslaught of a disordered, atheistic society. Just as I'm sure it is possible for a devout believer to contract OCD, I am certain that there are a great many atheists who never encounter the problem, and many religious-minded people who battle it for years. But this does not mean that it is not a spiritual disease, the product of a general spiritual malaise manifesting itself in the souls of individuals.

A wise friend of mine, now dead, used to ask me in times of doubt or fear: 'Do you believe in God or do you not believe in God?' What he meant was: If I believe, why do I assume that God will not be interested in everything about me? The standard dismissiveness of the secular-rationalist treats as axiomatic the idea that some things can never be God's business. But how, if we believe in anything, can we dismiss the idea that unease within ourselves is symptomatic of a weakening of the current of faith? To deny this possibility is to conclude that spirituality is a discrete and containable element of the human make-up, having no relevance to anything for which a secular analysis is already on offer. This immediately strikes me as a prime symptom of the agnostic cultural context I was seeking to deconstruct.

In recent years, a new wave of allegedly rational thought has erupted to launch an onslaught on faith and the idea of a transcendent reality in a way that, because our culture is constructed around a reduced form of reason, seeks to use a form of semantic cleverality built on no foundations to contradict the human heart. When what is termed the New Atheism or 'neo-atheism' first reared its head above the cultural parapets, the response of people of faith, it seemed, went beyond mere irritation or dismay. These would have been natural responses, but there was, I believe, a deeper one: a sense that this represented something unprecedented, a feeling that we had reached a new staging-post on the road to silencing the human heart. This new wave of thought, and its zealous advocates like Richard Dawkins, Christopher Hitchens, Jonathan Miller and A. C. Grayling, seemed not merely to be claiming the right to speak for the modern moment, but to be speaking definitively about the nature of reality. And in the way they were received and feted by modern society, it appeared that they were being accepted at their self-declared face-value. They were to be heard all over the place, shouting down believers and sneering at their beliefs. Every time you entered a bookshop, you were confronted by their presence in the shedloads of their books occupying the bestseller racks. It seemed that, now this had started, not only would this never end, but it marked an end in itself, an end to the time when human beings might be able to speak of God and not be abused or jeered at. Believers might have been forgiven for despairing of the possibility of ever reclaiming the public square for the idea of mankind's relationship with infinite reality, and resigning themselves to fighting a losing battle for the hearts and minds of their own children.

But I'm not sure about that. The popularity of the neo-atheist books was due not to the lucidity of their arguments – which were largely attacks on the straw man of organised religion – but on the need of a particular generation to be reassured that its freedom-seeking repudiation of divine authority was still a legitimate position. In order to pursue the materialist and permissive ideas of freedom advanced centrally in Western cultures since the 1960s, the younger generations of that time and since have had a need to convince themselves that there is nothing beyond this world to inhibit their pursuit of desire in the most obvious and immediate ways. The problem now, and the opportunity grasped by Hitchens, Dawkins *et al.*, is that the pioneers of this freedom movement are no longer 21, but perhaps 61, or even 71, and that many of them no longer possess the certitude they had when their lives stretched ahead into quasi eternity. Hitchens and Dawkins are the scribes of this quest of reassurance, the success of their books a marketing phenomenon created by the desire of the freedom generations to hold on to their beliefs.

During the writing of this book, I attended the inaugural annual general meeting of a new organisation, Atheist Ireland, set up to campaign for a secular Constitution and 'an ethical Ireland free of superstition and supernaturalism'. Listening to their discussions, I was struck by several things. One was that their outlook and agenda appeared to be entirely constructed out of a reaction against a negative experience of Irish Catholicism. This was perhaps unexceptionable, but the most remarkable thing was that, although they did not seem to have thought beyond this initial difficulty, they appeared to feel entitled to feel superior to those who continued to believe. They talked a lot about 'reason', but seemed to imagine that reason involves only what can be measured, shown, described, computed or touched. I did not get any sense from anything said at the meeting that anyone present had contemplated reality in anything of the depth that any but the most superficial engagement with religion demands. And they all appeared to believe that this rendered them more intelligent than if they had.

These claims to ownership of reason are plausible only because religious people have come, at some deep level, to believe that such claims are legitimate. But when reason is extended to reintegrate heart and the spirit, and if the right words are found to give voice to the authentic claims of true and total reason, the spurious reasoning of the cynics and disbelievers becomes exposed for what it is: despair dressed as enlightenment.

And atheists are human too. They are no different to believers, except in the words they choose to describe their understanding of reality. In many cases, they are not even responding to reality as it is, but to some evil or wrong, real or imagined, in the past. They have the same longings and hopes as believers, and, deep down, many of them wish that their own pessimism could be debunked.

A couple of years ago, I was in University College Cork at the Philosophical Society, debating, with Professor Peter Atkins of Oxford University and the UK National Secular Society, the motion 'That This House Believes Religion Has No Place in the Modern World'. Professor Atkins was an exceptionally pleasant man, who, although rigorous and direct in the heat of battle, did not, in the manner of many of his fellow atheists, maintain the tone of the debate after it had ended. As we walked across the campus afterwards, I jokingly said to him that it was somewhat ironic, given his vehemence in the argument, that of the two of us, I alone had a chance of being vindicated. He asked me what I meant. I said, 'If you're right, neither of us will ever know, whereas if I'm right, we'll both know'. He laughed, fell silent for a moment and responded: 'It's much worse than that, I'm afraid, because if you're right, I'm going to be very happy!'

The fundamental needs of the human species for hope and a vision of some destination beyond the repetitions of earthly reality give rise to a deeper kind of reason, one that embraces everything, swamping the reductionist logic of the neo-atheists. Mankind will never be able to open the door in a demeanour of total knowledge, only in the fullness of human reason, which comprehends much more than we can prove, embracing heart and soul and imagination, as well as the mechanisms of the head. When we recognise this, faith becomes not merely reasonable, but an acknowledgment of what is – excepting nothing, postponing nothing, ascribing nothing to chance.

And this is to say nothing of what this simplistic reductionism has done to human hope. Our culture's prevailing reduction of reason leads us to deconstruct not just our beliefs but also our capacity to cast our hopes forward beyond the disappointing limits of the material world, and so our newfound 'rationality' bears down on us like a sagging ceiling.

— 9 —

The Poetics of Nothing

In April 2009, Ireland was pleased to honour, on the occasion of his 70th birthday, the Nobel prize-winning poet Seamus Heaney. On the national broadcasting station, RTE, there were many radio and television tributes to this distinguished Irish writer and his work. On the Marian Finucane Show, a year to the day after Marian had interviewed her dying friend Nuala O'Faolain, the poet was the subject of a lengthy interview, in which the conversation ranged over many subjects, including religion and the idea of an afterlife. I record the occasion for a number of reasons. One, that it is reasonably typical of the way such matters are dealt with in our culture today. Two, that it illustrates how existing ideas can be affirmed by an authoritative voice. Three, that is indicates how a particular definition of reason has been enabled to develop without ever coming under pressure to justify itself.

The poet said a number of things in the interview which were picked up by several newspapers and reported without significant comment or analysis. Because the author of these statements was not merely a poet, but a Nobel prize-winning poet, they acquired a significance far beyond their intrinsic content. In Ireland, poets are still seen as possessing some kind of 'other-worldly' insight, and the pronouncements of an internationally celebrated poet are therefore to be considered to have far more cultural power than those of almost any other category of public figure. In introducing the poet, Marian Finucane quoted the writer Joseph O'Connor as declaring in an article in one of the day's newspapers that Heaney was 'like an ancient bard, a druid who knows all the secret rhythms and rhymes of his time. He speaks for us all.' Allowing for a little rhetorical hyperbole, few would have demurred from the underlying idea that Heaney, by his work and stature in the wider world, had earned himself the role of a kind of Irish shaman of letters.

After some perfunctory questions about his winning of the Nobel prize, Marian Finucane asked Heaney about the fact that, some years previously, he had suffered a stroke which brought him into a close brush with death. Through her work on behalf of the hospice movement in Ireland, Finucane has been to the forefront of many campaigns and debates concerning death and dying, and how society should treat those who find themselves in the final stages of human life. It is likely, this being almost the anniversary of her interview with her close friend Nuala O'Faolain, that this issue was looming even larger than usual. Going through both his writings and interviews, she said, she was not quite sure that she knew where Heaney stood 'in terms of religiosity and death and faith'.

Heaney said he never thought of his illness as a brush with death. He had been paralysed down one side, but his speech and memory had been unaffected. 'I felt anxious but I never thought, "God, I'm going to go".' It was impossible, listening in, to avoid the idea that he was ducking the question.

Marian then asked him straightforwardly about his attitude to religious belief. He chuckled a bit and said that he was about to ask her the same question.

Pressed further, he began to explain that he had been reared in a traditional rural Catholic family. 'I think anyone born in our country, in our culture, certainly in my generation … the shape of the world, the religious eternal dimension was a given dimension in our world. And that sense of another dimension, the fundamental religious view, I think I will never lose that. Of course, the first part of my life the sense of religion was rewards and punishments, heaven and hell, judgement at the hour of death, and the fear and trembling of that. Now, over the years that has disappeared. Obviously.'

And Marian interjected: 'Has it?'

'Yes. I mean extinction. Yes.'

'You don't believe in extinction?'

'I do believe in extinction. That's what happens.'

So there it was. Nobel Prizewinner Says There Is No God.

It is an interesting word, 'extinction'. It has several meanings, all closely related, although in the way the poet used it, it had a clear and emphatic meaning. The *Oxford Dictionary of English* defines 'extinction' as 'the state or process of being or becoming extinct'. The word 'extinct' is itself defined in several ways, the relevant ones here being: '(of a species, family, or other larger group) having no living members'; and, 'no longer in existence'. The word has an etymological connection to 'extinguish', defined as 'cause (a fire or light) to cease to burn or shine'. It is striking that the poet did not intend a precise, literal equivalent to any of these meanings. He was talking about individual human beings, not of the species or any group within it. He clearly meant to convey something to the effect that when man dies he is 'no longer in existence'. This seems axiomatic: a dead man is clearly not 'in existence' in the way he was when alive – he has, in a precise sense, been 'extinguished', as a candle is extinguished when the flame is put out or dies.

Not even a poet can imagine what this might be like, or indeed if it is 'like' anything, since the process of comparison necessarily supposes a capacity to compare. If one has entered into nothingness by virtue of what Seamus Heaney would call 'extinction', it is doubtful if one would retain any capacity to apprehend what one enountered, since 'one' would not exist and therefore could not be said to encounter anything. Such an entry into a total absence of consciousness appears to be what Heaney had in mind for himself and everyone else. But in naming it – 'extinction' – he was relying on conventional assumptions that do not necessarily have the kind of reasonable basis that Heaney's rather telegrammatic disposal of the matter implied.

The very word 'extinction' in this context, as used by Seamus Heaney, is tautological. Anyone, regardless of belief, might loosely use such a word in observing that human life is extinguished by death. A religious person might loosely employ such a word to convey the process of the mortal body becoming subject to the inevitable, since an acceptance of mortality does not in any sense preclude the possibility of an afterlife. But Heaney used the word 'extinction' in a slightly different way. There was a hint of challenge both in his choice of word and in his delivery of it. In uttering it, he was confronting something, albeit something unstated. He was volunteering the weight of his poetic 'office' to make a reinforcing point on behalf of the prevailing culture. He was making a choice and doing so consciously. He was not making a neutral, passive statement, but denying something that for many people is of momentous importance: the idea of eternal life.

We throw the word 'nothing' around as though it were obvious what it means. But there is no such entity, knowable to the vast majority of humankind, as Nothing. A few mathematicians and philosophers may have some tenuous grasp on some abstract sense of what Nothing is, expressing it as zero or emptiness or vacuum, but for most of us this remains an abstraction. We cannot conceive of it. Nothing is beyond our grasp, like Infinity and Eternity and the Absolute. Nothing is an inverted reality, one that does not exist for us, even in its non-existence. We know nothing about Nothing. And yet, although we readily throw cold water all over the idea that a human being might live for ever; or that our humanity is an infinite phenomenon that, like matter or energy, cannot be destroyed; or that the reality we inhabit is part of an absolute reality that cannot be comprehended by our tiny minds; we speak of Nothing as though it was the most self-evident concept in existence, throwing the word around as though we had meditated upon the question at great depth and come up with words which by their very existences and in their essence contradict the concept we are seeking to communicate. Nothingness, extinction: names for things that cannot be seen or known. How, then, can they be named?

For a human being to think about nothing, not to mention think about Nothing, would require the thought and the human thinking it to disappear, and for the space from which both the human being and the thought had emanated to be absorbed into an absolute nothingness containing neither space nor matter, a non-entity that could not possibly exist and could neither observe nor be observed. No, it would require more: it would require this not to have happened, for time to reverse itself and erase even the possibility of such a human ever existing, never mind having such a thought, and for time then to curl itself up into a ball and evaporate itself into something that could not be air or space or anything at all, but would not be amenable to sense or description, even if these phenomena could exist without the intervention of humanity, which of course, because humanity had never existed or had become 'extinct', they could not. And by the evidence of anything you care to mention, even just the evidence of this sentence, this could never happen, or not happen, or not even be contemplated, which must surely mean, if it means anything, that Nothing does not exist. There is no Nothing. Nothing is not a thing we need to think about.

The nearest a human being can come to conceiving of Nothing is to wave his hand in the air, a ridiculous parody of an irrational idea. For what he engages with here is not Nothing. It is something: air. It bears no relationship to the concept of Nothing (if Nothing can even be a concept), may even be the opposite of Nothing (if Nothing could possibly have an opposite, which, being Nothing, it could not) because the concept of Nothing does not exist, or if it does we cannot imagine it, for in trying to imagine it we deny its existence and negate its very possibility. Or, perhaps that should be 'non-existence' and 'impossibility', for Nothing is a very confusing thing.

We use words in an attempt to convey Nothing, even though the words by their existence make this impossible, in the same way as it is impossible for a play or a book or a film – or even a poem – to convey boredom without itself being boring. We speak of Nothing as though it were an everyday thing, like water or chocolate, something that any ten-year-old could grasp and pack up into a little bundle of established and incontrovertible truth, and stash it away to be deployed in the course of thinking processes for the whole of a life surrounded by Somethings but no Nothings and handed on to children who must necessarily have emerged from this Nothing to do the same thing.

And we call this reason. It is not reason. It is laziness and unthinkingness and sheer intellectual sloppiness of a kind that would make Pooh Bear seem like Spinoza. The wonderful thing about rigour is rigour's a wonderful thing.

A belief in Nothing, or in 'extinction', may appear knowing in the culture we have created, but it is, so to speak, nothing but pessimism. It is despair dressed up as realism.

A key governing idea of present-day culture is that a perspective that looks into the eyes of the universe and concludes that there is Nothing rather than Something is the height of cleverness, that it is smarter than anything else, that it has been arrived at by a process of logical husbandry of the known facts. In contradistinction to the 'superstitious' and 'obscurantist' mind-set of religious believers, the culture insists, in both words and gritted silence, that this outlook is, self-evidently, more intelligent and reasonable. And yet it is difficult to avoid the suspicion that this viewpoint is held to, in the same way as religious belief and to perhaps an even greater extent, by the stupid as well as the brilliant, the slow and the razor-sharp.

It is easy to say that you believe in nothing, that there is no God, no heaven, no afterwards, no hope. The culture is currently well adapted to making such a statement seem intelligent, when actually it is as vacuous as the abyss it proposes is the destination of everyone. It is the laziest form of thinking masquerading as the most refined.

We have no way of knowing for certain that the life, like the body, does not simply change form. Reason has no means of, and no reason to, deny that, if the physical matter of the body simply undergoes a metamorphosis, then the same thing may happen to the life, that the relationship between the human body and the human soul is not analogous to the relationship between the candle and the flame. There is no definitive proof one way or the other. We just cannot say. Anyone is entitled to speculate, but nobody can say with any more 'reasonableness' than anyone else, or at least not in the language of what is conventionally called 'reason'. And a poet is no more entitled than a plumber to have his declarations on these subjects regarded as 'expert'.

Sitting in the studios of the national broadcaster, the most celebrated Irish poet since Yeats had declared that what we see is all there is. Speaking not just of himself, but of everyone who was listening and everyone who was not, and summoning up all his poetical authority, he declared human reality to be defined by an abyss of unconsciousness and death.

But soft. When asked if he believed in 'redemption', Seamus Heaney sought, as had Nuala O'Faolian a year earlier, to complicate things a little. It was, it has to be said, an odd question with which to follow up a declaration of nothingness as the aftermath of the human journey. Can the extinct be redeemed? Why bother? Redeemed from what? Why?

It is a symptom of what has gone awry with the Irish sense of the religious that this question would probably have made a kind of sense to most of those listening. Irish people expect discussions about faith to follow certain lines and employ certain buzzwords whose meaning is woolly but still approximately comprehensible. 'Redemption' is one of those neatly tied bundles of agreed meaning that seems to fit as a way of prolonging a discussion that is tacitly agreed within the culture to have no real basis in reality, but which nevertheless enables discussion to continue without ever becoming particular. In the Christian context in which it was here being used, the word 'redemption' signifies something about Christ having died to save mankind from the consequences of sin, or perhaps having risen to indicate the possibility of an eternal hope. Already, it was clear from Seamus Heaney's initial response that he attached no substance to either of these interpretations. This did not necessarily make Marian Finucane's question 'Do you believe in redemption?' a bad question, though it might reasonably be considered a *non sequitur* given what Seamus Heaney had already indicated about his beliefs.

'I believe in redemption', he replied. 'I believe in faith in this life. The Christian message is about faith in this life. It is about redeeming and being redeemed by ...' He paused. 'The message is one thing. The doctrine at this stage is not as practised, not as binding, on the general whole church itself. I mean apart from the Curia, I suppose, those entrusted with the Magisterium, the teaching of the Church, I think that clergymen, sisters, nuns, the official Church is much less dogma-bound than it was. And I think that the faithful, so to speak ... I mean my feeling is that the faithful are less, ah, less orthodox, certainly than they were.'

It is difficult to know where to start in attempting to parse this response. The stuff about the Curia and the Magisterium is the kind of thing people of a certain age engage in to convey that they are well versed in ecclesiastical terminologies, thereby signalling that anything they say has a greater value than might otherwise be apportioned it. 'Doctrine', 'Curia', 'Magisterium', 'dogma', 'faithful', 'orthodox': none of these words, in the contexts he employed them, would have meant anything much to most of those listening, other than to signify that the subject under discussion was Religion.

Does 'faith in this life' refer to the quantity, or quality, of faith exercised in this dimension or to the idea that this existence alone is worthy of faith? Based on Heaney's earlier answer, one presumes the latter. But how can you have faith in something that is self-evident? Or did he mean something else? If so, what? How about this: that he does not believe in faith in God, or in the idea of an afterlife, but he believes that the idea of faith is itself a good thing? In other words, that, even though God does not exist and there is nothing awaiting us but extinction, it is healthy to believe in *something*, even though this something may be invention or falsehood?

The idea that the 'Christian message is about faith in this life' might have seemed interesting if most of the possibilities it opened up had not already been dismissed in Heaney's initial verdict of 'extinction'. The idea that Christianity should be about living here and now in this dimension, rather than directed purely at some putative future existence, might have prompted an interesting philosophical discussion; but, given that Heaney had already emphatically ruled out the possibility of any future existence, it was difficult to avoid inferring him to mean that Christianity is actually a spurious programme of pseudo-spiritual engagement designed to make the earthly existence more palatable for everyone. It might well be argued that Christianity is 'about faith in this life' in the sense that it proposes the idea of faith as an answer to the fundamental questions of existence. It does not, however, propose that the meaning of life is centred on this existence. Theologically speaking, these are diametrically opposing positions: one, a widely held view among theologians, holding that Christianity invigorates this life with its promise of the next; the other, a decidedly untheological view, that the whole thing is a benign concoction to get people to behave in a civilised manner.

Of course, Heaney was not expressing any theological or philosophical position, he was simply blathering.

'And if anybody like myself goes through a literary education', he went on, 'everything in twentieth-century literature, everything really in nineteenth-century literature, or from the Enlightenment on, is a challenge to orthodoxy. So it's quite possible to live with a religious sense of the world, to live with complete faith in the Beatitudes, Christ's Sermon on the Mount, to know that this Christian ethic, ethos, is the one that you belong to and that it is, as far as I can find, the best method yet of proceeding.'

What does this mean? As a statement on what might be deemed one of the central questions of human existence, it seems evasive and confused. In name-checking the Beatitudes and the Sermon on the Mount, he was again signalling his familiarity with the chapter and verse of Christian culture. It would be surprising, indeed, if he was unfamiliar with these. But what is surprising is that he did not appear to have given any thought to the idea that, without the core meaning of the Christian proposal, the Sermon on the Mount would not long retain its cultural power.

And what could possibly be meant by the suggestion, coming from someone who believes in 'extinction', that the Christian message is about 'redeeming and being redeemed'. Yes, redemption has a precise meaning in the Christian context, but it seems that Seamus Heaney had something different in mind. If there is nothing afterwards but extinction, then the Christian idea of redemption is bunkum, and Christ was a lunatic with a God-complex and long hair. The poet seemed to have some other idea of redemption; perhaps the idea that suffuses the modern artistic sensibility, of a form of psychological cleansing brought on by cathartic events.

Marian Finucane, in her polite but firm manner, was indicating that she had picked up the vacuousness of what the poet was saying. She asked him: 'You say that it is on this earth that we find our happiness, or not at all, whereas you presumably were reared as I was, that it was in the next life that you find your happiness ...'

Heaney answered: 'Yes of course, but I'm saying that, ha aha ha, that disappeared, quite ... I mean who ... who on earth now, with a few orthodox exceptions I would say, believes that their reward is in eternity? I mean who among the Irish middle classes sits up at night and thinks that? Maybe I overestimate that, but it's a … it's a … it's a hazy area for those brought up with belief.'

There was that word 'orthodox' again, the suggestion being that a belief in something beyond the material world we know could only be a symptom of unquestioning adherence to an imposed world-view.

Who on earth believes that their reward is in eternity? Er, quite a number of people actually. Anyone who accepts the Christian proposal, for a start, which in Ireland would still account for a majority of the population. This is what religious belief involves.

Who among the Irish middle classes sits up at night and thinks that his or her reward is in eternity? All the poet has to do is walk to his nearest church on any given Sunday and ask people coming out. Where else might Christians think their 'reward' is to be found?

And what is meant by this: 'Maybe I overestimate that, but … it's a hazy area for those brought up with belief'? Has he in mind people like himself who have been brought up as believers but who no longer believe? Is he saying that he is unable to conceive of anyone having had such an upbringing and continuing to hold in adulthood to the belief in God or the hereafter? No other interpretation is possible, since, clearly, for people who have not been brought up as believers, the idea of eternity is not hazy at all. Either they believe it or they don't. For people brought up as believers, the situation is exactly the same: they believe or they do not.

Maybe he overestimates what? Maybe he overestimates the idea that eternity is still understood as the reward that follows earthly existence? Since Heaney clearly believes that nobody among the Irish middle classes believes in this, he is implicitly saying that this view is held, apart from by the orthodox few, by the poor and uneducated only, groups not embraced by his category 'the Irish middle classes'. Maybe what he means is that maybe he overestimates the importance of the belief in eternity as a constituent element of religious belief. But of what, other than a belief in eternity, does religious belief substantively consist? Of course it is much richer, much broader than that, but belief in eternity is necessarily at the core of it. There is no avoiding, no fudging it. There is nothing in the least hazy about it for those brought up with 'belief', which holds to the idea of eternal reward with the tenacity that a jockey holds on to a horse. Or at least it is not the experience of being brought up with belief which renders it hazy, but other things: extraneous elements, desires, agendas, intentions. If it is hazy, it is because the culture has rendered it so. It has nothing to do with the belief itself, which could hardly be clearer for those who hold to it. Believers may doubt sometimes, but there is no scope for haziness.

Then Marian Finucane asked Heaney about materialism – how money had become 'something of a religion' in the previous ten years or so. He eagerly picked up this ball and ran with it, observing that Ireland had been in danger of losing its 'religious unconscious and its Christian unconscious' during the years of the Celtic Tiger. The downturn, he declared, 'may have happened in time'.

> I thought the capacity for adaptability went far too far, adapting to capitalist, materialist, consumerist values. And the protection, the self-protection, of the culture we had, which was community-based, caring-based, charity-based, a kind of post-religious, if you like, sensibility. We had a religious unconscious, even though we mightn't have been so ... and we had a Christian unconscious, the idea that you could live on very little, that self-denial was a virtue, that there was a kind of virtue in helping others. That slipped, it seemed to me. And maybe what's happened happened just in time to rebrace the inner beings and the society generally.

This, together with his assertion that Christianity is 'the best method yet of proceeding', amounts to an odd position for someone who does not believe in the central idea of Christianity, which is that death shall have no dominion over mankind. Let us state it clearly: Seamus Heaney, for all his pessimism about the ultimate destination of humanity, thinks those who have been spinning untruths to the Irish people have been carrying out an important public service in laying down the 'Christian unconscious', presumably because this refers the human enterprise to a broader level of awareness than the purely material.

It is a position that seems to discount the centuries of Christian belief as empty superstition and yet to patronise this culture of belief as upholding something worthwhile for mankind.

From certain of his inflexions, one infers that the poet seems to regard any erosion of the 'Christian unconscious' as a bad thing – to hold that the collateral benefits of empty superstition are to be celebrated and valued. But the question then arises: how could such values be perpetuated for very long after the 'knowingness' of mankind, which he also appears to celebrate, had succeeded in debunking the underlying beliefs? Is Heaney's interest in this of a purely anthropological nature, or is there some element of moral judgement in his attitude? Certainly, from his apparently favourable references to the benefits of a 'Christian unconscious', it seems that his interest is at the level of social morality. And yet he not only appears to hold that it is acceptable that this morality be founded on a lie, but that it is also a positive development that the lie has been rumbled by all but the most orthodox and/or ignorant.

And there is a deeper problem in that Heaney's attitude appears to almost melt out of time, to remove itself from the immediate implications of his beliefs. By this I mean that the speaker appears to be indifferent to the question of how the moral cohesion that he extols, and which he traces to the influence of Christianity, might be perpetuated in the absence of the superstitions providing what might be termed its 'glue'. In this, the poet exhibited a strange quirk of the modern mind-set, which believes in the increasingly irreligious enlightenment of the species in relation to the ultimate meaning of reality (extinction and so on) and yet seems to agree with those of a religious disposition who argue that religion is essential to the moral cohesion of society.

This appears to suggest that, without religion, there is at least a risk that morality will be reduced. But what, as the exam questioner might have posed the question, is the poet's view of this? Does he think that something else will crop up to replace religion as the moral glue of society? Does he believe that the moral cohesion wrought by religion can continue even after its roots have been cut? Is he blind or devil-may-care concerning what happens next? How, in other words, does he tie the whole thing together in his mind? Or does he?

Of course it is possible to have no religious beliefs and still believe that religious beliefs are good for society. The believer may take the view that such a stance is somewhat hypocritical, since the unbeliever contributes nothing to what he says is in society's best interest. But the unbeliever cannot be blamed for this situation. He cannot help his unbelief. Faith is not something you can simply will into existence. At the very least, you might decide, the unbeliever who acknowledges the good that has flowed from religious influence must be given credit for magnanimity, for generously conceding the value of something he himself believes to be bogus. Many believers tend to take comfort from such contributions by those who say they do not believe in God or the hereafter, on the basis that at least they are not actively antagonistic to religion in the way many self-declared atheists tend to be. But there is, nonetheless, a semantic difficulty with this position. How, after all, if you do not believe in God or in the afterlife, can you reasonably suggest that a Christian consciousness is a positive phenomenon? You might observe that this has had a role in the civilising of mankind, but would also have to allow that, on your own declared terms, this civilisation has been based on falsehoods. What, then, do you propose will function in the place of these falsehoods when everyone becomes as enlightened as you are?

Seamus Heaney, it was clear, had already decided his position on these questions for himself, which is his absolute right. But here he was going further and asserting that the idea of eternity is so far-fetched that no thinking person, never mind a right-thinking person, could possibly hold to it. The entire drift of his thinking on this subject could be summarised as follows: we are now too clever to buy into the idea of God and the hereafter, but we still need the rules Christ gave us in order to live together in any kind of harmony. Implicit in his remarks is the idea that, paralleling mankind's growing belief in his own increasing cleverness is a process of undoing by which the rules we have come to live by are being undermined. This is the logic of what he was saying, and is perhaps a more interesting idea than anything he actually stated. Yet at no point in the interview did he seek to underline it, to claim it as his own. Instead, he remained content to state things that were no more than repetitions of the mantras of the secular culture he seemed to be conscious of addressing. He may well have been expressing a sincere personal perspective, but he was also saying something that he might readily have expected the listening culture to find unexceptionable.

At no point in the interview did Seamus Heaney elaborate on why he believes the idea of eternity is nonsense; he just appeared to assume that everyone listening to him would agree that it was, and that this was an opinion one did not need to have arguments for. Interestingly, his interviewer did not press him to move beyond his comfort zone. Neither was he required to produce arguments for the other semantic and logical flaws in his position.

A generation before, in a culture characterised by the most pious forms of Catholicism, such fuzzy philosophisings might have seemed to amount to a radical perspective and might well have involved the poet in a significant controversy. Now, however, his viewpoint was not unusual, even for a poet. Seamus Heaney was availing of a mechanism in the culture which, having already established absolute wisdom on these matters, requires only that the speaker nod in the direction of the prevailing assumptions in order to avail of the culture's consensual and intellectual protection. He was invoking on his side of the argument the culture of quasireason, which enabled him to make a point about a central question of existence without having to offer anything substantial in the way of evidence or argument.

It is, of course, possible to disbelieve in God, in creation and in the hereafter, and yet to believe in the idea that manufactured beliefs in these phenomena may have beneficial consequences for human society. But, if I believed this, I would, I hope, be at least the smallest bit interested in the idea that, now my own disbelief was being shared by growing numbers of my fellow citizens, we must be getting closer to a moment when the glue would begin to melt. I could not console myself with the idea that, whereas the superstitions I could so readily discredit and debunk were now being brought more generally into question, they had already fulfilled their useful function in creating the moral framework which enabled me and my fellow citizens to live together in a benign, 'post-religious' sensibility. If I believed these things, I would, I think, be all the time jumping ahead to ask what might happen when the superstitions eroded a little more. How would all this work in a hundred years? Can we be complacent about the chances of future generations being able to carry off the same pretence as ourselves?

If my position were anywhere close to Seamus Heaney's, I expect I might either construct a rationale based on the idea that man is capable of constructing a moral framework without reference to religion – which did not appear to be the poet's position – or I would be forced to imagine some apocalyptic scenario in which an increasingly clever population of middle-class sceptics started to boil each other's children with cabbage and potatoes.

But what Seamus Heaney appeared to be thinking was that the model he had grown up with would serve perfectly well for the moment, that, after a recent period of concern, he was now reassured that the civilisation of which he approved, built on the lies he had rumbled, was looking more safe. There had been a slight hiccup in the years of the Celtic Tiger, when people started to go a bit mad, but now things appeared to be getting back on track. Perhaps, one surmises, the shock of the downturn had sufficiently scared the population to return if not to the superstitions, then at least to the moral framework constructed upon them, clinging more tightly to the lies at the heart of their civilisation.

Interesting, too, beyond the content of Heaney's expressed opinion, was the way that, in the truncation of the discussion following his formal declaration of imminent extinction for everyone, a sense was conveyed that his verdict was, if not self-evidently conclusive, then certainly emphatic. The poet had issued his judgement and so the listening public was, depending on what each listener believed, either confirmed in a creeping suspicion about reality or challenged in a way that was impossible to answer. Heaney was working within a scheme of cultural logic that allowed his opinion to add itself lightly to the conventional assumptions he was feeding off and going along with. It was just a tiny incremental adding to the assumptions already 'established', but solid enough to add another microscopic atom of certainty to the prevailing cultural understanding of things. Either in the interview itself, or in its dispassionate treatment in the wider media, no resistance was offered to his views, which were accordingly conferred with an aura of conclusiveness.

What I found myself objecting to in the interview, then, was not Heaney's belief or disbelief. The point is not that I disagree with him, although I do, but that I am just a little shocked that someone of his intellectual stature should be so loose in his thinking concerning the core questions of existence. Even more shocking is that he was put under no pressure to account for his opinions.

What bothered me about the interview was that it was the statement of someone who has acquired the status of a cultural guru, and who, invited to say what he believed about the meaning of life and death, invoked the history and language of Christian civilisation to suggest that the central ideas that underpin this civilisation are pure unadulterated nonsense. He was able to do this in the nicest way imaginable, as though he were not really saying anything of significance at all. Who, after all, could possibly object to a gentle, seventy-year-old man sitting in a radio studio expounding his views of life and death? For one thing, it did not appear to occur either to Heaney himself or to his interviewer that he might well have been striking despair and distress into the hearts of some of his listeners.

There are questions which Seamus Heaney might have been asked which might have either led him to elaborate on his disbelief or else exposed his words as unthinking repetitions of conventional wisdoms. Why, for a start, does he believe that nothing, or Nothing, awaits him beyond this life? Does he have evidence of this? Is this belief grounded in his experience? If so, on what? Does he believe in anything he has not been able to prove? If so, has he found this a reliable basis for writing poetry? He might have been asked if he had never laid eyes on his own children, could he have believed it possible that such beings could exist. He might have been asked if, seeing a caterpillar for the first time, he could have had any intuition of its turning into a butterfly. He might, in other words, have been taken out of the safety of the culture to an intellectual space where his easy prejudices might have come under pressure. The reason he wasn't is not necessarily that his interviewer shared his views – perhaps she did, I don't know – but that the very exercise of delving into such an exploration would have issued a challenge not just to

Heaney but also to the dominant culture, and thereby would have run a greater risk than simply letting the matter lie.

The Nobel laureate had questioned the very basis of the belief-system that had sustained Irish society for more a millennium, and yet the public prosecutor sat down implying she had no more questions. And in the silence there was an acquiescence which, perhaps more literally than we know, reverberated in the heart of every listener to that interview. Each of us, in the intimacy of the human heart, was free to dissent from what the Nobel laureate had just said, but such resistance had become microscopically, but measurably, more difficult by virtue of his having said what he said and Marian Finucane having clearly received his declaration as a statement of the axiomatic. Those who shared the poet's view of the human destination were strengthened in their existing opinions by the fact that such a learned and celebrated man had endorsed their rational view of things. Those who had not shared this view, who held to a different sense of their humanity, were challenged by virtue of the same factors and, to a greater or lesser extent, were infiltrated by dismay.

And yet the exchange had brought no new insights to the matter. The discussion had simply added something tiny but tangible to the edifice that man had already constucted on the bedrock he had floated on the mystery. Those listening were either vindicated in their pessimism or shaken in their hopes.

Doesn't a poet have a duty to words and what they mean, and to ensuring that they make some kind of sense? Does a poet have any responsibility to the discipline of reason? Or can he just employ a colloquial form of expression to make observations that are, however loosely and lazily, in tune with the popular prejudices of the time? Is there any point, never mind any morality, in decrying the loss of a lie? Since this is unlikely to be Seamus Heaney's settled view of these matters, does he not have a poetic, human or civic responsibility to draw these apparent contradictions more fully into the light?

Heaney would be unlikely to deny that he is the inheritor of a particular tradition in Irish poetry that traces its line not so much through Yeats, the Irish poet whose names is on the lips of the world, but on Patrick Kavanagh, who, for all kinds of reasons having nothing to do with poetry, is not (yet) as celebrated as he might be.

'Is verse an entertainment only?', asked Kavanagh in his poem 'Auditors In', 'Or is it a profound and holy/Faith that cries the inner history/Of the failure of man's mission?'

Kavanagh was a poet of the people who wrote a gospel rooted in the countryside of Ireland, and for whom poetry was a moral and spiritual calling, a matter of theology rather than mere literature. His poems are rooted in the reality of nature and life's perpetual cycle. They seek with every word to capture the invisible reality behind the everyday and the ordinary. A staunch Catholic who wrote eloquently of the spiritual hunger created in Ireland by moralism and piety, he did not regard literature as a means of chronicling the human condition, but as a chink through which we might peer into the fourth dimension of life, that aspect of existence that remains invisible but is always present.

'The experience, as I see it, is really prayer', his 'sacred keeper' and brother Peter Kavanagh told me in a public interview in Dublin's Trinity College to mark the centenary of Patrick's birth in 2004. 'Patrick believed in the divinity, so what he hoped was to get a flash of that beatific vision, that supernatural place. Words are the least important part of it. In a poem, words burn up in a tremendous thread of something unusual. The important thing was what we called "The Flash", which was the Other World coming in to alert us to Its existence.'

Art and the artist stand in opposition to attempts by mankind to landscape the raw reality of his condition out of his vision. Social life, politics, commerce and entertainment try to convince us that our reality is knowable, controllable, manageable. Great art, like truthful religion (and they were once one) tells us that this is folly, that beyond our prefabricated, landscaped reality is an infinity of possibility, and that we did not, cannot and will not create one atom beyond what is already there.

In mankind, uniquely in the natural world, the mystery of existence becomes capable of expression. In our essence, we are the question which all art seeks to answer. The only requirement of the artist is an apprehension of the human situation, which is to say an awareness of the relationship between infinity and humanity. The true artist sees, hears or feels what is real, and reports faithfully the experience, in doing so reassuring us that, as Patrick Kavanagh put it, we are not alone in our loneliness.

Art has always had but one purpose: to kneel us before the mystery of our existence.

The essence of the mystery is within each of us, and the artist's task is to find a way of expressing it that will not short-circuit into a conventional wisdom. In approaching the mystery, the true artist understands that the object of inquiry will recede at a speed exponentially related to the effectiveness of the approach. Humility, the admission of defeat in the face of infinity, is behind all great works of art. It is what we see when we are moved by a poem, a painting, a song or a story. In the surprise of the revelation, we glimpse what is unknown, unknowable, but, instead of being downcast by this undeniable failure of capacity and will, are buoyed up. Our very smallness becomes reassuring.

This, essentially, is what happens when we read a book or a poem that moves us, or see a play that we find ourselves acknowledging as 'innovative' or 'interesting'. The epithets belong to the language of landscaping but the response belongs to our souls. The artist has taken us beyond the safe, landscaped area and enabled us to recognise ourselves. Each of us, in the intimacy of the heart, is touched, moved, changed, though outwardly we speak of intriguing plot devices, innovative chord structures and the subtle use of language. What touches us is something of the Source from which we come. There is a flash and we glance up, or prick up our ears. What was that? But 'the Flash' never affirms itself, is never more than a flash. It comes and is gone, leaving us bereft, confused but yet more certain of what we have witnessed. It strikes within us, resonating with the deepest desires of the heart, soothing our longing in the healing balm. It consoles, not because of some abstracted quality of beauty, but because it corresponds to the longing for perfection that resides at the centre of every human being. Without 'the Flash', a poem may still look like a poem. It may rhyme and scan and alliterate. It may even win the author a prize. But ultimately, without 'the Flash' it is mere imitation, a calculated copy of something that, resonating in his heart, was mistaken by the poet for an interesting novelty, influencing him to create his own interesting novelty, now masquerading as a poem, by which someone else will be sufficiently impressed to render his own reinterpretation.

Much of what we nowadays call art is hand-me-down craftwork, the mimicking of form and composition by people who, because they reside in a culture that seeks to deny the transcendent, wish to be artists without shouldering the artist's burden. Many paintings look like pieces of art but are actually mere compositions based on the idea of what art might be. The 'novel', seeming to pursue the most literal interpretation of its name, appears intent upon the discovery of variations arising from its own history, the novelist having forgotten that what affects us is not novelty but recognition of the truth when we encounter it.

Similarly with theatre. I go to the theatre to watch a play which, in the end, allows me to leave with a mere sense of being 'uplifted', of having witnessed some psychological 'catharsis', rather than having been touched by the common chord of humanity's longing for an external correspondence to its deepest desires.

Or I hear a song on the radio that causes me to pull over to the hard shoulder and sit wonderstruck for a suspended moment, but yet can continue about my businsss convinced that the reason I was momentarily slain in my seat has something to do with a clever interlinking of musical traditions. The glimpse is lost.

There is a sense nowadays that 'the arts' are something that people need, perhaps in much the same way as they need the odd glass of wine or a bar of chocolate, or perhaps as some kind of added extra to the enjoyment of a civilised lifestyle.

Once, there was the artist, such as Patrick Kavanagh, who looked at reality and perceived the essential nature of things. Now there is the draughtsman, the wordsmith, the versifier who, reducing the function down to a form defined by page or canvas, makes marks which appear to correspond to those once made by the enchanted, but without the enchantment. When, occasionally by the laws of probability, it still happens, we are dumbstruck. We stare at something and recognise ourselves, or our place in the true scheme of things, and wonder if it can be an accident. We look at the artist, who looks like all the others. Did he know what he was doing? Is this just another accident or the real thing?

And if you ask, the chances are that you will encounter a denial, not because you have been mistaken but because the language in which you must ask and in which the artist must answer does not have the capacity to bear what you have both borne witness to. The experience you have just had may be an intentional wink by someone who shares the culture with you but does not wish to acknowledge that his quest is as your deeper responses lead you to suspect. Or, it may be that he has simply randomly recreated some reference he learned at art school, either without conscious intention or as an ironic commentary on the form in which he has chosen to express himself. Either way, the society recognises it as 'art', and on balance will adjudge it better if it is devoid of the conscious intention to summon up intrinsic meaning. Because the criteria have been reinvented by people who would become alarmed if the Flash manifested itself in their presence, what is valued now is not the glimpse of the Beyond but the quality of the mimicry or the juxtaposing of incongruous elements. We live in a world in which the denial of the absolute realities of existence is so entrenched and determined that artists, too, have been recruited as landscapers to produce evidence of man's defiance of his apparent ultimate hopelessness. Artists are nominated as the consolers of a species that has decided, without much in the way of evidence, on its own intrinsic pointlessness.

I do not suggest that Seamus Heaney has not thought honestly and deeply about the great questions as his precursor Patrick Kavanagh. Anyone with even passing familiarity with his poetry knows this it not the case. 'What's the use of a held note or held line', he asks in 'Squarings', in his 1991 collection *Seeing Things*, 'That cannot be assailed for reassurance?' This is a far more succinct, if cryptic, way of saying what I have been trying to say about his interview. And perhaps it can also be said of the entirety of his poetry, which, though beautiful and proficient, is an example of something that, as he implied of Christianity, exists only as a residue of something that once extended something more than mere consolation. For without a faith in the held line, there is no reassurance, no consolation, and without faith the line cannot long hold. If the held line becomes a held lie, how long can the fiction be maintained?

Nobody, then, could casually accuse Seamus Heaney of unthinkingness. And yet, in a single, short episode of public reflection, he contributed significantly to the unthinkingness of the public realm. Although his poems indicate that he reflects on the deepest matters at least as much as anyone else, and delivers the fruits of this imaginative voyaging in a language that opens up himself and his readers to the totality of possibility, he confined himself, when asked a straight, literal question in the context of a prime-time radio interview, to the declaration that all his reflection, all his introspection, all his imaginative adventuring have led him to nothing except the conclusion that the material realm, the one we know, is all there is, with the implicit rider that the best we can hope for, from art or poetry or anything, is perhaps some kind of imaginative refuge from this reality, to be maintained and curated by people like himself.

— 10 —

The Anatomy of
De-absolutisation

In the middle of 2008, as the world economy started to go into freefall, an odd proposition started to float around Ireland's public conversation. Mixed in with the shock occasioned by the sudden departure of the Celtic Tiger was this strange undercurrent of sentiment suggesting that now, at least, we could turn our attention to less material concerns, that a return to poverty would at least render us more 'spiritual'. As the global economic crisis deepened and Ireland's recent bout of prosperity began to dissolve before our eyes, the President of Ireland, Mary McAleese, during a visit to Phoenix, Arizona, remarked that Irish people were paying a big price for a radical shift in values. 'I think that every one of us would have to say with our hands on our hearts that we were all consumed by that same element of consumerism', she said.

> Somewhere along the line, we began to think that we weren't happy with deferred gratification. We had to have it now and in this moment, and I think that we have paid a very, very big price for that very radical shift. And now the balance presumably is going to swing back the other way and it will be no harm. We clearly have come from quite unbalanced times and they have not been able to secure for us the kind of peace of mind, peace of heart, contentment that we would have wished for. Now we're trying to find our way back to a more rooted and possibly more modest time.

There was some truth in this, but also a little humbug. Yes, there had been a shift in values. Yes, most of us had been swept up in the swell of these unbalanced times. Yes, there was going to have to be a period of readjustment. But the idea that this 'will be no harm' was a more complex and potentially controversial suggestion. The humbug element related to the President's chiming in with a some-what platitudinous view emanating mainly from religious sources in Ireland that a little bit of recession might restore some of the 'values' we had lost in the Tiger years. The idea that people, having allegedly turned their backs on God in the years of prosperity, might now find cause to rediscover Him seems to me to suggest that God can legitimately be seen as a fallback position for those whom earthly life has disappointed. This odd idea seems also to have emerged from a concept of faith as consolation, one of the less helpful strands in Irish Catholic tradition, implying that God is something we rely on when times get bad. It does not appear to occur to those who give voice to this idea that among the things they imply is that God is a contrivance designed to make poverty more palatable.

This idea in turn offers an insight into one of the ways Irish Catholicism came to be formed in its historical context, without any real sense of being grounded in the essential human personality. It grew mainly as a system of social organisation, supplying the society with a moral framework, as well as a long-term reassurance about the transitory and dispensable nature of this existence, but never really engaging people about the precise details of their relationships with reality. There was something innocent about the kind of piety that suffused Irish Catholic religiosity in the past – as well as an inescapable sense that, rather than a renouncement of materialism and libertinism, Irish asceticism was predominantly a sour grapes response to the non-availability of other options.

The Irish model of Christianity, which in Ireland seemed to be the only possible kind, tended to emphasise a moral distinction between wealth and poverty, in much the same ways as it empha-sised sexual continence over the sensual. Because Irish Catholicism developed through centuries of poverty, and offered Christ as a comfort to those who had little else in their lives, the link in the Irish imagination between faith and consolation became almost absolute. Although nobody had actually expressed it like this, it naturally followed that, when we became more prosperous, Christ could be allowed some time off.

In the years of the Celtic Tiger, the population had become divided, essentially, into three: those who set out to 'find' themselves by improving their lot materially; those who lacked the opportunity to do this in a serious way and who availed of the surviving undercurrent of moralism to continue transforming their failures into moral capital; and the genuinely poor, who just wanted to join the ranks of the rich. The first group, picking up from the deeper culture that their aspirations were incompatible with Christianity, decided to be hanged for sheep rather than lambs, giving the second group an irresistible opportunity to feel morally superior by virtue of their involuntary asceticism. The third group was relentlessly patronised by the second, which never really explained why, since it took such a dim view of prosperity, it wanted to remove the poor from poverty and thus condemn them to the same eternal flames as the rich.

I recall a headline from some time in the early days of the third millennium: 'The Economy is Awash with Money.' Although we may now blush at the memory, many of us would spend our leisure time in those now dim and inscrutable days sitting around counting how much the value of our houses had gone up, our reveries punctuated only by intoxicating visits to financial advisers who showed us how to renegotiate our mortgages to conjure up new kitchens or automobiles. Not everyone participated in this altered culture of Irish life, but its dubious benefits certainly touched many people who might now wish to downplay the extent to which they did so.

It seems impossible in the present changed climate to believe that, at the height of the boom, in the late 1990s, the Irish magazine market was briefly graced by a publication called *Spend* (subtitled 'How to & Where') containing lifestyle splurges, intense celebration of materialism and articles about the consuming habits of middle-range celebrities. *Spend*, as its title made clear, was a magazine about spending money. In the first, perhaps the only, issue, a successful Irish pop singer, asked to name the most 'unusual' thing he had ever bought, revealed that he had purchased 'a really expensive Gucci dog-bed for his wife's dog'. He also shared with readers details of his 'last impulse buy': a WG HSE Range Rover.

'It was very impulsive', he said, 'because I already had a 4 x 4, so I guess I didn't even need it. But I just had to have one.' The main driving force behind *Spend* has been, since the onset of recession, one of the most strident voices in demanding salutary treatment of all those who 'lost the run of themselves'.

After the collapse came in mid-2008, we seemed to speak about nothing for months on end but the appalling thing that had happened to our dreams of wealth and freedom. One of the great themes of these discussions, interestingly, had to do with the allegedly unhealthy obsession with money we developed in the Tiger years, when we allegedly 'lost the run of ourselves'. But anyone listening would have been in no doubt that we were even more obsessed with money now that it had disappeared than we had been when we imagined our society to be awash with it.

Day after day, we talked of little else. Blaming and scapegoating had become national pastimes. The private sector blamed the public sector, the public sector blamed the politicians, and everyone blamed the bankers.

Anyone listening to our public conversations might easily think we had forgotten about the stars and the moon, about birth and death, about love and passion. It is as though our entire collective life had been reduced to a balance sheet, and the mystery of our human journey expressed in marginal rates and pension levies, with all the great questions of human existence treated as bad debts that have been written off and out of our collective consciousness.

The idea that this moment would throw us back on 'more funda-mental values' was proving to have been better left as an untested theory. For one thing, nobody seemed all that clear what these 'fundamental values' might be, and for another nobody seemed to be able to remember all that clearly how they tied in with religious faith. We were hearing an echo of a refrain from the not-too-distant past, which told us that we had a duty to be good and a related duty to embrace 'spiritual' values, but without anyone spelling out why we had these duties or what their observance might achieve.

When we thought at all about the decline of religious belief during the Tiger years, we tended to speak about the incidentals –

either bemoaning the loss of moral values, or welcoming the 'opening up' of society on the grounds that we were now freer than before – free to, among other things, accumulate money and do what we liked with it. By the turn of the millennium, this had indeed resulted in a new value-system, which was what President McAleese alluded to in Arizona.

For centuries, we Irish, or most of us, had nothing. Wealth and prosperity were mysteries. We imagined that such blessings were destined always for others. Our national defeatism, induced by centuries of interference and abuse from external sources, led us to disbelieve in the possibility of entitlement. Then, before our eyes in the 1990s, things began to change. We didn't fully understand what was happening, but were not about to look a train of gift horses in the mouths. For us, the windfall prosperity of the Tiger years seemed to have the same sources as the centuries of misfortune. Suddenly, we began to become convinced that, at last, good fortune was our due. History had ceased to frown on us. Why shouldn't we be rich like others? Perhaps understandably, we did not question our change of luck, but embraced it to the full.

Into the mists of history, the measure of worth in Irish society had been a moral one. Where you ranked depended not on what you possessed but on your rating in the society's understanding of 'goodness', which was largely dependent in turn on the standing of your parents and grandparents before you. But, although this way of seeing things was inspired by religion, the outcome was not overtly recognisable as a religious phenomenon. The Catholic dimension flowed into a cultural stream in which religious faith was just one of the subheadings, and by no means the most important.

There was a list of unwritten criteria, which everyone understood. Hard work was perhaps the most indispensable element. To be deemed a 'great worker' was in the past to be accorded one of the highest compliments in Irish culture. It was not a question of what you did, but how you did it, your attitude to the doing of it and what this said about your character. Also valued were thrift, honesty, decency, composure, quietude and the ability to keep oneself to oneself. The roots of this culture lay in the devastation of the Great Hunger, the famine that had obliterated so much of Irish life, culture and society in the middle of the nineteenth century. Its echoes can still be detected in the obituary notices in provincial newspapers, where a deceased person may be described as 'quiet and inoffensive' or 'hard-working and unassuming'.

It is impossible to convey a precise sense of the criteria, because these were, to a high degree, personalised to the circumstances of the individual. Someone could be sweeping the roads and living in a local authority estate, but might gain extra points for courtesy, cancelling out the disadvantages of occupation and address. On the other hand, a man might be a chemist or a bank official and destroy the benefits of these advantages by keeping bad company.

A few people in any community might try to break away from this evaluation system, seeking by their lifestyles or possessions to place themselves ahead of their stations, but this tendency was always regarded with a vicious and strategic irony. There was no expressly stated view concerning how wealth and good fortune were to be worn, but generally you found that those who maintained their status over the long haul were people who played down their affluence and blended in.

The traditional method of social evaluation began to change in the Ireland of the 1990s, when social worth came more and more to be predicated on what you possessed. For all kinds of reasons the older hiearchy based on character was no longer sustainable. The nature of work had changed, for one thing. In the old culture, what you did, as a rule, was visible from your person. You wore working clothes, or office clothes, or you wore the uniform of priest or police officer. In the second half of the twentieth century, work became largely a sedentary activity, so that it was no longer possible simply to look at someone and see what they did and determine whether or not they were industrious about it. It became more and more the case that, in order to assert your character and identity, you needed to accumulate things, to possess things, to display the signs of yourself externally.

Having just written this down, I am unable to escape the idea that it reads as a judgement. It implies that the old way was better, and that the 'descent' into materialism represents a decline from some more elevated form of morality. In as far as I can tear myself away from the culture of which I am part, I sincerely believe that either way of judging people is no better and no worse than the alternative. But the language does not allow me to say this. It grabs me into a clammy, tendentious embrace, forcing me to agree with the culture that certain things are self-evidently good and certain things self-evidently bad.

And yet, although most people would quietly and sanctimoniously nod at the idea that material wealth should not be the barometer of social worth, most people have also, over the past couple of decades in Irish life, determinedly set about trying to become wealthier as a way of declaring themselves to the new dispensation.

In an individualist society, he who tries to buck the trend discovers a devastating form of loneliness. It is not open to any one of us to effectively challenge the means by which our society values its members, and most of us are therefore imprisoned within a cultural paradigm that, for all it may oppress us, we must continue to observe and respect. Alain de Botton describes, defines and names this modern condition of material enslavement in his 2004 book, *Status Anxiety*. What we seek when we pursue the material, he explained, is not something trivial or superficial, but the very essence of what our human natures demand. 'It is the legacy of those who have felt pressured by the disdain of others', he writes, 'to add an extraordinary amount to their bare selves in order that they too may lay a claim to love.'

We seek love in the things we have, the places we live, the people we call our equals. Is there something morally wrong in this? Perhaps there is. But, long before we come to this point in the argument, we recognise that it is not good for us, that we need to help each other to unravel the culture that subjects us to this ultimately unhealthy anxiety.

In this light it becomes clearer that there is little to be gained from hectoring people about their fascination with the baubles of the marketplace, or with simply demanding that they give their money to the poor and creep back to the churches. A responsibility falls on religious leaderships to go beyond sermons about the evils of consumerism: to develop and articulate a radical theology of materialism. There is also a responsibility on the voices of the public square to begin describing the situation for what it is. From these starting points, we need to begin the discussion that might allow us all, together, to redefine the project of mutual valuation in human society.

One of the remarkable things about the post-meltdown squabbling was that it demonstrated the extent to which the old way of seeing things had somehow survived underneath the culture, in some cases in a slightly altered form, in others pretty much intact. It was interesting, for example, to note how some of the ascetic fundamentalism, which had earlier characterised elements of the Catholic clergy, was now manifesting itself in certain commentators who decried our obsession with money and property. Generally speaking, these tended to be individuals who repudiated every other aspect of what was thought of as Christian teaching.

Religion, too, became less a barometer of adherence to a common code of behaviour and more a badge of identity for the dwindling numbers who remained interested. The general sense was of escaping from the old way of being, shaking off authority and conformism, finding freedom. People had begun to reject, in their daily lives, the writ of Rome in relation to sexuality. This was made easier by the succession of sexual scandals which beset the Irish Catholic Church from the early 1990s. The overall sense was of an outmoded form of authoritarianism being cast aside, personal freedom being embraced. Irish society began, from the 1960s onwards, to get a smell of the incoming breeze of cultural liberalisation. This suggested a choice between Christianity and freedom and, quietly but determinedly, people surveyed the options and whispered, 'Freedom!' They had no way of knowing that, in making this choice, they were making another one as well: the choice between two forms of hope, one of which was eternal, and therefore the only form of hope that can be so called; the other seductive in the short term but ultimately empty.

It gradually emerged that the years of prosperity had been a mirage. There was no element of the indigenous economy that had suddenly blossomed to an extent justifying the scale of our fancied success. Our apparent overnight prosperity was down to a range of factors owing much more to global conditions – and even in this regard to an illusion created with smoke and mirrors – than to anything we had suddenly started doing right. Ireland, offering bargain rates of corporation tax, had become more attractive to transnational industry at a time when demography and a competitive cost of living index made it seem an attractive place to operate. Later, our adoption of the euro currency and lowering interest rates meant that there was plenty of cash with which to grease the wheels of this newly sprung economy. Infrastructure was rapidly and radically upgraded. Property became the mechanism by which the new-found largesse was released and pumped around.

Really, what happened in the Tiger years is that we allowed our desires to overrule our reason. It was obvious, if we had stopped to think about it, that the kind of prosperity we were enjoying was unsustainable. Indeed, a few people did point this out to us, but we chose not to listen to them. Like children dressing up and playing 'house', we had got caught up in the fantasy of the game. When the game was over, we faced the fundamentally unchanged facts of our existence. The core problems of the Irish economy over many decades persisted. Despite the conjuring trick of the previous decade, we still had an undeveloped economy that continued to exist at the whim of external agents and factors.

As time passed and things got worse rather than better, we began to perceive that words like 'downturn' and 'recession' were inadequate to convey what was happening. One morning I heard an unusually sensible-sounding eonomist on the radio listing the problems standing in the way of a world recovery. He seemed to take it for granted that the economy was an expression of human values, and could therefore be understood only by reference to human behaviour. Nobody had any remaining confidence in the capitalist system, he explained, and without confidence, the system could not be made to operate again. We had exhausted the illusion of endless credit, having borrowed for 25 years on the basis of a postponement of consequences. There was nobody left to buy anything, because everyone had borrowed and bought until they were waist-deep in things they now realised they did not want.

This seemed plausible. What was emerging seemed not so much a periodic dip in economic fortunes as a self-inflicted wound arising from the fear and insecurity of human beings. Because we could not trust the future, we had destroyed even the present. This crisis, it became clearer, had flowed directly from a collapse in our understanding of our own natures, and was at its root a human crisis rather than a merely economic one. A recession is, of course, an economic phenomenon. But more fundamentally it tracks something deeper in the human pattern of interaction, an inevitable failure of the human capacity to replace providence and create cast-iron guarantees against uncertainty and want. And what we call the economy is really just a mask, a projected explanation for the interaction of human efforts which, in many ways, defy description, quantification or logical analysis.

What had happened was a crisis in the relationship between human beings and the systems they created to serve their wants. Human desire had burst at supersonic speed through the fragile edifice of the money system, leaving nothing in its wake but shattered illusions and unsatisfied appetites. The problem lay not with the system, but with the fact that human longing, being infinite, remained incapable of earthly satisfaction.

In the early years of my life, just into the second half of the last century, our public square held to an explicit connection between the affairs of state, economy and government, and the absolute, eternal dimension of man's relationship with reality. Of course, this understanding was crude, simple-minded and dogged by agendas concerning power and wealth; but it was, nevertheless, a context in which the ordinary citizen was able to function with a general sense that events, either in the economy or in his personal day-to-day circumstances, were not the last word on everything. There was something more enduring and important beyond – something, moreover, that could either positively or negatively influence the day-to-day realities.

There was, in other words, hope that, beyond the problems of the public or private sphere, a more enduring process was at work that mattered far, far more, and that this process was fundamentally linked to the human structure – to the body, mind and spirit of each citizen. This enabled previous generations to maintain a somewhat wry attitude to times that were, by any objective criteria, much worse than anything facing us in our time. They believed in providence, in the idea that underneath everything is a divine plan that may be lamented or complained about, but ultimately, in its ineluctability, offers the only hope there is.

Nowadays, however, day follows day, week follows week, year follows year, without this sense of things being invoked at all. It is not that the sense no longer exists, but that it is not allowed to surface as part of the public logic. It has been privatised, compartmentalised, cordoned off, separated from three-dimensional reality and accorded a place in the spiritual, imaginative and mystical dimensions only. It has been reduced to a kind of play, in the childish and theatrical senses: recreation and ritual to make us feel better, a sacramental icing on reality which makes it taste a little more exotic but doesn't suit the flavour of the cake.

We value the tradition of historical faith as a kind of scaffolding which we hope will sustain the ethical edifices we depend on. We dabble in faith, when we do at all, so as to reassure ourselves, console ourselves, elevate ourselves. But we do not take it seriously as an element of everyday reality.

And yet, it should be obvious that, if faith is not connected to everyday reality, it has no meaning. Either God exists or He does not. If yes, then nothing that happens can be taken literally, or as definitive, or irrevocable, or can legitimately lead to despair, or be devoid of hope, or be thought incapable of instantaneous change. If there is no God, then, yes, there is no hope except what mankind can conjure out of the illusion of temporality that is earthly existence.

My reckoning was that we needed another year, perhaps two, of good times, before there could have begun a gradual and general move to formulate some deeper understanding of things. We knew the good times weren't going to last for ever, and may even have been quietly preparing for some tentative attempt at a better balance, but the collapse happened a little too suddenly and unexpectedly for us to take anything positive from it. We had begun to be a little jaded by the endless party patter about house prices, but we didn't want it to end like this. We needed more time to think it through, to prepare for the quieter life ahead. Prosperity having lost its novelty, we might in time have come to understand the meaning of the word 'enough' – enough of partying and enough of insatiability.

We might have begun imagining into place a ceiling on our wants. But any hope of this was scuppered by an unscheduled meltdown of the materialist dream.

Our culture takes hope for granted. Since so much of what happens in the public domain seems concerned with satisfying human desires for pleasure and happiness, this insight seems far-fetched. But it is nevertheless observable that our culture increasingly seems to regard such satisfactions as add-on benefits to human existence, which is assumed to be automatic and self-firing. We do not think very much about what sustains us, only about how we might survive, prosper and enjoy a life that is assumed to be self-evidently liveable. Of course, we recognise exceptions to this: those who, because of personality or psychiatric difficulties peculiar to themselves, are incapable of seeing things in this way. When an episode occurs which makes the existence of such exceptions impossible to avoid, we scramble around for an explanation that will not require us to look at the bigger picture. A man we know who appeared to 'have everything' suddenly kills himself, and we respond with a strange admixture of ostensibly contradictory thoughts. On the one hand, we are shocked at this deviation from what we think of as normal behaviour; on the other, we readily settle for a proffered explanation: he was depressed, he lost everything, his wife left him. And yet we know others who have lost everything and who have gone on living.

Embedded in our collective conversation is the delusional notion that human life continues in the manner of the machine, requiring only the correct physical conditions for maximum efficiency and the fuel to drive it. But human beings are delicate entities, depending for their survival and propulsion on the survival of a deep sense of meaning, like a flame burning at the core of being. The great artists once understood this, but nowadays great art has been compartmentalised in our cultures, housed in an annex that is removed from the main thoroughfares and accessible only to an elite who insist on interpreting it as the creation of elevated human sophistication. And in the end, what? Extinction?

Human life needs more to sustain it than mankind is capable of imagining, proposing or generating. Ultimately, all we can create for ourselves are false hopes, which sustain us for an instant and then dissolve, leaving us grasping for the next. What gets us out of bed on any given morning may be identifiable as the promise of progress, the lure of money, the call of duty, the prospect of love, the imminence of spring, the sight of a new sunrise, the thought of a fix. But ultimately all these will lose their power. If our hope for the future remains exclusively rooted in such phenomena, the process of anticipation followed by disappointment, occurring again and again, will lead to a dwindling enthusiasm, which our society will insist on explaining as depression.

Because we have dismantled the heavens and replaced them with a low-slung ceiling of our own construction, this disillusion is inevitable and, with a savage irony, progressive.

In a crude sense, the crisis arises from the loss of what used to be conveyed, even if often clumsily and ineffectively, by religion. Because of the corruption of our public thought, the loss of religion is regarded in our cultures as, at worst, a neutral phenomenon. By the same token, injunctions that we re-embrace faith and God, because the material world has started to go awry, convey a rushing to a spurious form of consolation because of what is implicitly regarded as a temporary glitch. But this is not temporary: this is the way of the material world. What is collapsing is not reality, but the flimsy construct that man engineered out of his own desire to replace God on the throne. What we need, then, apart from fixing the broken systems, is to become conscious again of the essential nature of the human entity: mortal, dependent and primed with desires that nothing on earth can satisfy.

Hope is the core of the Christian message, but the power of this concept has been dulled in our time by virtue of the success of mankind in creating systems that appear to answer human needs in ways that spuriously suggest a potential for limitlessness. The economic implosion tells us, surely, about the folly of this. Hope lies not here, but in the very facts of the universe, in our human capacities and in our various relationships to the mystery from which the human species emerged.

But, short of a cultural revolution, there seems no way of circumventing the stratagems and constructs of a culture that has rendered all but impossible a demeanour of openness to the eternal dimension, without seeming, even to oneself, to have merely capitulated to sentiment and fear. Somewhere along the line, we have lost the essential meaning not just of religion but, since religion implies everything that relates to the human mechanism, of ourselves. Instead of perceiving God as the eternal reflection of our own infinite natures, we have allowed to have invoked on our behalf a kind of cosmic policeman, watching our every move and writing down everything. This perversion of the essence of human and transcendent reality is at the heart of our recent slide away from what we call religion. The most harmful aspect of this is that it has led us to understand religion as something external, imposed on us from outside as a means of controlling our freedom, and this in the name of this God who, for reasons to do with His age and temperament, disapproves of everything we most enjoy.

This is religion turned inside out, the cart put before the horse, the moral universe that is insinuated by a religious view of human nature and reality emphasised in a way that reduces the Truth to a set of rules. The questions that every living human person represents are treated as secondary or even irrelevant. Why am I here? Do I matter? Why do I get up in the morning? How do I divine the meaning of reality? Indeed, does reality have any meaning? In our culture, you might be forgiven for imagining that the fundamental religious questions have to do with abortion, divorce, contraception and homosexuality, and this reductionism has spawned a tremendous backlash, enabling to triumph an unthinking pseudo-rationalism that now suffocates the spirit of the young and the old.

Why has the language of the most fundamental element of mankind become so antiquated and irrelevant? Why does religion, which should really embrace the entirety of universal possibility, seem content to wallow about in a mess of petty issues relating to perceived ethical dimensions of reality? Why, for example, do we not expect to find in our religious publications articles about (to outline a short list for the sake of example) poetry, motor cars, Mozart, football, beauty, ice-skating, mathematics, Plato, black holes, the molecular structure of water? It is conceivable that each of these subjects might come up for mention in a religious publication, but inevitably this would be in a narrow context: the 'religious' or 'obscene' content of poetry, the materialism associated nowadays with motor cars, the religious beliefs of Mozart, and so forth. You might, occasionally, encounter a subject that surprised – a discussion about Harry Potter – almost certainly critical on the basis of implications of 'occultism', or an analysis of a topical political issue in the context of its alleged ethical implications for Christians. Invariably, though, such subjects are dealt with in a particular fashion, with particular emphases.

Is it not odd that, if religion is supposed to encompass everything, it is so easy to predict what will preoccupy religious-minded people?

The obvious and conventional explanation for all this is that religion has in our time been consigned to a ghetto by the encroachment on the public square of what are regarded by religious people as secular ideologies. Not only have these thought-systems succeeded in seizing control of the public thought process, they have altered the public language to normalise their narrow forms of perception. But something even more remarkable has happened here also: the partial explanations for reality have increasingly succeeded in suggesting themselves as total explanations, whereas religion has been consigned to a compartment of reality, where it is treated with growing public disdain. Thus 'religion' has been turned into, at best, just another ideology, battling for public space in increasingly hostile conditions.

What is most ominous about this, however, is not that it has been imposed on religion, religions and the self-declared religious, but that religious-minded people have acquiesced in the idea that religion is simply another partial world-view competing for attention in the clamour of the public square. For if, in discussing what we call religion, we are so tediously predictable in our concerns, do we not implicitly concede that our perspective is indeed just one more partial conception of reality? Indeed, does not much of the content of religious discussion conform to the so-called secular prejudice that religion is no more than a series of objections to the drift of the modern world, admonishing the tide of progress as it sweeps all before it?

We lazily use the term 'secular' to describe our society, and are at best ambivalent as to whether this amounts to a good or a bad thing. But really the word 'secularisation' is useless in communicating to modern societies what has happened to them. It suggests a retreat from the sacred, yes, but also a rejection of organised religion. It is used, too, to describe the process of separating church and state. It tends to be used to refer to a political process that seeks to diminish the role of faith and religion in society. Yet, strangely, the same word is used both by those who approve of and drive this process and by those who resist it. Not only that, but the word appears to embrace something of the zeal of the anti-religious mission and the dismay of the religious-minded who resist it. This is unusual and should alert those who are dismayed by the process to the fact that the word 'secularisation' is inadequate to describe, from the religious point of view anyway, the precise nature of what is happening.

For what is happening is not simply that the religious world is being divided from the material/political world, but also, and far more crucially, that our societies are being reconstructed to obscure from sight any possibility of a consciousness of an infinite, eternal or absolute dimension. The idea of mystery is being abolished in the construction of a new ceiling calculated to create the illusion that human beings can function within a self-defined, even a self-created, space.

The concept of secularisation does nothing to alert us to the enormity of this change in our culture, merely signifying a liberation from the shackles of religious authority that is, at most, ambiguous. To describe what is happening underneath this process, we need another word. The one I have come up with is 'de-absolutisation', which describes an existential process as much as a political one. It is, I know, a clumsy word, but I have not been able to find another term that comes close to describing the real problem.

In Christian societies, de-absolutisation means the occlusion of Christ in culture. But, as with so many aspects of the fundamental cultural changes taking place now, we speak evasively of this phenomenon. Christian leaders warn of its consequences all the time, but somehow they seem to be speaking of something that is merely dismaying from an institutional or organisational point of view. Christ is invoked in the context of the authority of the Church, or at least this is what it tends to sound like. The consequences of losing Christ, by this hearing, seem to have to do with the loss of moral values, and perhaps also the loss of the possibility of consolation in the midst of life's trials and tribulations. And given the shallow nature of the Christian education experienced by most of our societies, this sounds like the loss of something optional, rather than of something central, to existence.

The important issue is not the decline of power of churches, nor even the decline of ritual and practice in society and culture, but something that happens to every one of us, regardless of beliefs: that the nutrients we need as the very basis of survival have been removed from the culture, so that the question that was raised by Christ Himself, 'Who do you say that I am?' is almost impossible to respond to except in the deepest, most hidden parts of ourselves.

Before I come to Christ's question, there is another question I must answer: 'Who do I say that I am?' How can I describe myself in this society, how can I express the deepest yearnings of my heart in a culture that is hostile to certain forms of thinking in ways that I do not understand? These are fundamental realities, as real as timber or concrete, which affect us moment to moment, which we take for granted, which we do not name, but which bear down profoundly on us.

Because Catholic teaching has emphasised morality above other aspects of the Christian proposal, all references to Christ tend to read in our cultures as warnings about the loss of His love owing to a slide into sin. The idea that, in losing contact with Christ, we are losing something far more fundamental to our human natures simply does not translate. This may well be included in the intention of the messenger, but it does not communicate itself through the fog of the culture. Our cultural understanding simply does not comprehend what is meant by the love of Christ, other than as something sentimental and optional, an accessory-of-choice that can be abandoned without immediate consequences. The idea that the Person, Presence, of Christ embodies something vital, something indispensable to human nature, something non-negotiable within the human condition, is so strange an idea in our Christian cultures that many people who have no difficulty calling themselves Christians, stumbling across it somewhere, would be shocked at its implications. Could we possibly have heard about Christ all their lives and missed this? Surely not. Why did nobody put it like this before?

And this implies that the process of de-absolutisation was happening long before the process of what we now call secularisation. Secularisation arrived to a ploughed field and was able to sow its seeds without much effort. What this suggests is that the Christian message itself, as relayed in many of our Christian societies, has been deficient; that it emphasises many of the secondary elements of Christianity and talks about the essence of the proposal in a certain way, but does not succeed in conveying to the culture that the essential meaning of Christianity is that Christ can rescue us from the limitations of our humanity. The very words in which such an idea is conventionally expressed do not have the capacity to convey the core of the idea, because they have been overused, reduced, sentimentalised. The full weight of statements about Christ does not carry in our culture, other than to the already convinced, and it is impossible to detect from their responses what precisely such people hear. Judging from the words they utter in response to some cultural trigger, it might be that they have heard merely the sentimental idea, or the authoritarian idea, or the moral idea, or one of the other partial understandings that have attached themselves in our cultures to the name of Christ. Or it could be that they are briefly directed towards the most sensational idea that anyone ever spoke but, because this is so rarely alluded to in terms appearing to do it justice, they think that nobody else seems to have observed this, and that therefore they may have misunderstood.

—11—

The Gulag of Unhope

In recent years, the already disastrous relationship between Irish Catholicism and the wider culture was further crossed by a series of revelations about abuses of authority by priests, brothers and nuns who were discovered to have taken advantage of their positions of power to physically or sexually abuse children in their care. For many people such revelations have provided the impetus, or the pretext, for a formal abandonment of Catholicism and for the justification of an intense rage expressed in its direction.

In the summer of 2009, after nearly a decade of investigation, a tribunal appointed by a previous Irish government to investigate allegations of abuse in over sixty Church-run institutions finally filed its report. The five-volume *Report of the Commission to Inquire into Child Abuse*, popularly known as the Ryan Report, is a vast document that threads together various strands of testimony about a selection of industrial schools where abuse was a way of life, including Artane, Beechpark, Cabra, Cappoquin, Carriglea, Clifden, Daingean, Dundalk, Ferryhouse, Glin, Goldenbridge, Kilkenny, Letterfrack, Lota, Marlborough House, Newtownforbes, Salthill, Tralee and Upton.

It is said that the Ireland of these horrors was a theocracy. In so far as the word has any meaning, this is probably correct. It is difficult to outline now the fabric of a culture in which the Catholic Church was the effective moral government of Irish society, deferred to by State institutions and personnel.

What the Ryan Report described was a wholesale State-driven system of child abuse. The Catholic Church was centrally implicated, but with the collusion of the Department of Education, the Garda Síochána and the courts. Usually, when this is said, it is interpreted as an attempt to in some complex way 'excuse' the Church, to spread the blame. But in Ireland now the opposite is more common: an avoidance of State responsibility so as to emphasise the Church's wrongdoing. Without seeking to diminish the evil that was done by people who claimed to walk in the way of Christ, it needs to be recorded that not a single Irish child could have been taken into one of these institutions without the approval of the State. None of it could have happened had the State not colluded, had the police and the courts and even the (alleged) national child-protecton agency not arranged for a steady flow of victims to be provided to the Church-run institutions of torture and degradation. The report describes a wholesale State-sponsored system of child abuse and mentions in particular the 'deferential and submissive attitude' of the Department of Education towards the religious congregations on whose watch the abuses occurred. It is clear that State-run systems of the time operated to a reflex impulse of denial, at the heart of which lay a knot of ideological rationalisation, called upon by each component to justify its own role. The dominant ideological proposition was that troublesome children were a threat to public order, rendering justifiable almost any means deemed necessary for their subjugation. A child sucked into this system was rendered beyond the embrace of public compassion.

It is important to stress that much of what is recorded in the Ryan Report was already known about. The report is, of course, the first substantial official examination of this dark history and contains shades of detail that add something to the texture of popular understanding. But, substantively speaking, there was nothing particularly new, nothing in the general picture which had not been widely known and understood for many years.

Yet the filigreed letter of these horrors was met in the summer of 2009 by ritualistic expression of shock, horror and disapproval across Irish society, as though nobody had been prepared for what the report contained. In a strange reversal of earlier cultural responses, the details were greeted with ostentatious shows of outrage. Now that these events were safely in the past, Irish society and its political establishment could become enthusiastic in their condemnation.

Most Irish people over thirty-five recall being beaten in school, corporal punishment in the education system having been abolished only in the early 1980s. In my childhood, forty years ago, the threat of being sent to the reformatory at Letterfrack, in beautiful Connemara, was one of the most effective instruments with which to subdue an unruly child's spirit. In other words, the wider society, including its official elements, knew at the time that decency had been abandoned, but the corruption of State power and the felt impotence of individual citizens unleashed a deadly cultural concoction of fear, powerlessness and contrived scepticism, as well as impatience with those few who insisted that something evil was happening. It takes courage to challenge people with powers to incarcerate children in State gulags, and so the popular perspective on these obscenities was expressed in nods and winks and nervous jokes whispered behind hands.

Oddly, when RTE, the national broadcaster, transmitted its purportedly groundbreaking television documentary series on the matter a decade before the Ryan Report, the public response comprised the same mixture of horror and surprise as would later greet the 'official' chronicle of these horrors. *States of Fear* was a well-made series, outlining its case with sincerity and precision, but its essential content was not new. For twenty years, there has been a parade through the various communications media of former inmates of the Irish industrial school system, all seeking to draw attention to their experiences. There had already been a number of books, in which the facts were outlined in a manner at least as compelling as in *States of Fear* and the Ryan report. The dismaying truth is that, even in adulthood, those whose childhoods had been stolen were still far from cherished.

The intelligence of a society is a strange phenomenon. Especially in what is termed a 'modern' society, you would think that, given the speed of communications, what is known to one is known to all. But it doesn't work like that. Tempered by fear, prejudice, deference and collusion among the powerful, the mind of society at any given moment 'knows', or admits to knowing, only what the powerful are content to have acknowledged. There are occasional exceptions, but generally the rule holds. Power is never accountable until it is on the wane.

And yet, underneath the official, formal intelligence is another form of knowledge, existing at the level of rumour, humour and gossip, in which everything, or almost everything, is understood. Here, nothing is really surprising.

Perhaps the most important and useful study to be undertaken of these matters relates to what it tells about a society's capacity to turn away from things that are known. Instead of smugly condemning the past, perhaps it is telling us that we need to look closely at what this sickening saga says about the toxic dynamics of an ideological apprehension of reality, in which prejudices and fears are given the run of a society to an extent that empowers authorities to abuse those from whom the affection of society has been tacitly withdrawn.

Whistle-blowing, from a safe remove, supports our present-centred sense of moral superiority and the prevailing imperative to turn away from different kinds of inconvenient truths. We have unlimited appetites for hearing about obscenities that require us to do nothing about the now. The present is less expendable than the past, but is bound by the same kinds of compromises, vested interests and loyalties that once held together a different combination of hurts and brutalisms. To enquire too closely into what goes on now would not be containable in the manner of even the most rigorous examination of yesteryear.

It is, of course, true that nothing, or very little, was suspected about the sexual abuse that was occurring in Church-run institutions for orphans and 'wayward' children. But the State not merely turned a blind eye to the industrial-level corporal punishment being administered in these institutions; it also, for many years, refused to change its policy on corporal punishment, then in widespread use throughout the Irish education system.

One of the most interesting aspects of the discussion in the wake of the publication of the Ryan report was the apparent desire of many of those leading the attacks on the Church to avoid the question of corporal punishment policy, which was maintained by all governments, including 'liberal' governments, right up to 1981. The most courageous and consistently raised voice against this culture was neither a journalist nor a politician, but a medical doctor,

Cyril Daly, who in his early thirties in the 1960s, began speaking out against the axis-of-evil comprising Irish State and Catholic Church. Dr Daly was, and remains, a committed Catholic who opposed violence against children from – odd as this may have been made to seem – a Christian perspective. When Dr Daly denounced the Irish education system on American television in 1971, he was declared 'anti-clerical' and accused of letting down Ireland in the eyes of the world.

The Ryan report, then, provided an opportunity, in a single snapshot, to survey the extent of the damage to Irish Christianity, and not just the damage to the institutional Irish Church or to those it directly damaged, but the damage, deeper down, to the relationship with the fundamental elements that religion provides and which human beings depend on.

This damage includes direct and close to unimaginable destruction to the lives of many Irish citizens. The fact that it involves also untold damage to the Church itself might well be regarded as a deserved judgement. In the immediate aftermath, many people were unwilling to venture beyond this point. But, while the discomfiture of the Church may have been welcomed by a minority who mindlessly wished to remove all traces of religion from public culture, and while this purpose might be passively acquiesced in by many more who could not see past their anger and confusion, the outcome of such a purging would be, by any objective assessment, disastrous for the future of Irish society and its members.

I do not mean that there is a danger that Ireland may lose its religion. In fact, I am moved to wonder yet again if Ireland ever had any real religion to lose. Nor have I any desire to defend the Church. In many ways, the Church is beyond defending. I wish, yet again, to try to bring this discussion back to basics. What is religion? Who is Christ? Where might Christ be found?

To suggest that what happened was a betrayal of Christ is to insult Christ with the idea that somewhere about these activities was something of His imprimatur, but that this went slightly out of control. There was no Christ. There was only the Devil. And the Devil's work here embraced not only the torture, violation and destruction of innocents, but also the silence, denial and cover-ups, which continued in the case of some of those implicated until in some instances several weeks after the publication of the Ryan Report.

It returned to me, listening to the frenzy of debate about the Ryan Report, that, many times in my childhood I had gazed fearfully upon some trembling wreck of a cane-wielding nun or brother and wondered if, since these people wore the effigy of the crucified Christ and claimed to be acting in His name, this meant that, if Christ were physically present at that moment, He would be deploying the cane with similar vigour?

No, something had happened long before to remove Christ from the picture. For reasons suggesting a degree of historical mitigation too distant in time to be of any relevance, Irish Catholicism jettisoned Christ, was overcome by a love for power and so unleashed a warped and corrupted culture of religiosity in Irish society. In a sense, the Church made children of us all, destroying any true sense of God and Christ and nurturing only fear and guilt. This mutant version of Catholicism usurped the Church's teaching on human sexuality and then deployed it as an instrument of control and subjugation, vacating this teaching of any sense that it is a body of knowledge about man's structure, finally reducing Christianity to one puerile idea: that sex is bad. One of the most shocking elements of the Ryan report is the descriptions of episodes in which children were first buggered and then flogged because, having been sexually defiled, they needed to have the 'badness knocked out of them'. This is a parable of Irish Catholicism in the twentieth century.

Deep in our psyche is a sense, placed there by those who stole Christ from us, that if He comes, He will come to condemn. The greatest abuse perpetrated by the Irish Church – and it was perpetrated by the Church as a whole, rather than by a minority of abusers – was the promulgation of the idea that religion comes from outside, that it is primarily an imposed system of control designed to police the instinctive desires of human beings. For 150 years, since the Great Famine of the 1840s, this moralism was a form of idolatry in Irish society, which is to say that the Irish Church a long time ago broke the first commandment. How, then, could it be expected to explain any of the others? Even worse, of course, is that some of those in authority in the Church were secretly intent upon exploiting that which they condemned, implying that even the moralism was invented, was not believed in by many of those seeking to enforce it.

At the centre of the problem was a denial of human desire, an intuition that desire was dangerous. There was, then, to begin with, a misunderstanding of the human structure and its relationship to Christianity. The resulting suppression of natural desires led to their eruption in a dissociated manner, burdened also by the guilt imposed in order to police them in the first place, and this led to unforseeable psychotic reactions as the desires emerged in mutant forms that were inevitably destructive. To speak here of 'celibacy' is misleading, because, among other things, it implies that what occurred was confined to celibate clergy. Rather, there was a society-wide suppression, and this led the natural desires to force themselves upwards and outwards like a nuclear reaction.

Because there had been no proper sense of the Church's teaching on human sexuality as comprising values that serve man in his deepest needs (how could there be, given that the corruption of the teaching had demonised the very desire that perpetuates mankind?), the 'freedom project' of the 1960s was defined as the purging of the Church's teaching on sexuality. The emerging evidence of historical abuses provided many people with the impetus and alibi to choose 'freedom' rather than God. In spite of generalised education and increasing openness to external influences, the Church remained reluctant to shift its ground or to explain its teaching more fully. Thus, a new generation was deposited into a vacuum between the reductionism of the Church's seemingly baleful view of human sexuality and the promise of total satisfaction through sexual expression. Irish society became trapped between two ideologies: the ideology of moralistic Christianity and the ideology of absolute freedom. There we remain.

The prevailing wisdom of the now dominant culture of 'freedom' continues to hold that sexual liberation is the answer, though there is also a sense that the reason this may not be delivering total satisfaction is because we are still constrained by the memory of historical repressions. Once we shake off these, we are led to understand, we will be truly free.

The Church's voice has been silenced, even on those things it comprehends better than anyone else, precisely because of the perversion of its teaching to begin with. Each new round of revelations tends to consolidate this situation. The human being, therefore, remains lost betwen the old, twisted understanding that human sexuality is problematic because it is sinful, and the new understanding that human sexuality holds out the key to perfect happiness. Neither representing the full truth, the unhappiness that is inevitably unleashed has no possibility of coherent explanation – other than the idea that, if the Church had left us alone in the first place, we would have been fine. This suggests a rather deeper inventory than is currently mooted. The damage did not start with institutional abuse: it started with the mangling of Christ's message in the name of power, in the sabotaging of Irish sexuality and in the infantilisation of the population.

Everyone says now that the Irish have 'grown up', but it is hard to see how we could have done so. When did this growing up begin? What was the moment of epiphany when we understood what had happened and moved to put things right? Yes, we reacted against the corrupted notion of Christianity, but we never at any point moved to recondition our sense of religion. There was nobody around to give us any reference point from which we might begin such an initiative. There was nobody to tell us that religion begins in the human heart. There was a lot of platitudinous guff about Christ's love, but Christ was by then long gone below ground. Nobody invited Him back because nobody acknowledged that He was no longer there.

We may not be children any more, but we are not grown up either. We are stuck in an adolescent rebelliousness towards a false idea of religion, and it is difficult in this condition to say whether the rebelliousness or the warped sense of religion it repudiates has been doing us the greater damage.

From a certain perspective, it is understandable that we shrink away from the institution and the moralisms that led to these abuses. If it were a matter of adherence to the institution alone, then that might well be unproblematic. But this would also miss the point of why the institution exists in the first place: to serve our need for the infinite relationship which remains indispensable regardless of how well or how badly the institution has carried out that duty. It exists to carry the proposal of Jesus Christ to the people as the only conceivable answer to their infinite desire. It can truly be said that the institution of the Irish Church has in many ways failed its people, but it should seem obvious that the people do not stand to gain from simply walking away from the institution and all it represents, for then they risk losing the truth to which the institution, for all its human flaws, bears witness. It is not, in other words, a matter purely of the future of the Church, but of the future relationship between the Church, as curator of the Christian proposal, and the people in their infinite need.

It is insufficient, then, to simply observe that the failures and weakness of the Church in Ireland have rendered it unsuited to the needs of the people. This would be to add to the damage already inflicted by personnel attached to that Church the further damage of removing from the reach of the people the only possibility of hope into the infinite future. Indeed, when we look at it like this, we perceive that the initial wrongs, on account of which the people are rightly angry, would emerge as just the beginning of a greater and indeed final wrong, to be inflicted out of the facts of the first. This surely cannot be right. It cannot be, other than out of a superficial petulance, what we desire. What we desire, instead, is surely that the first wrongs be healed by a greater adherence to the proposal that became so monstrously mangled in our time.

— 12 —

Only Wonder Knows

As I child I had what I thought was this normal idea: I was unique. I used to marvel at the idea that, out of all the aeons of time, I happened to be here now, inside the structure of my body, looking out. I wondered if other people had the same wonder, but, even when I imagined I had successfully explained the idea to them, they tended to look at me blankly, as if they had never thought of themselves as different to other people in that they were first persons, whereas everyone else was, or appeared to be, third persons, walking around the face of the planet as human beings had done for a few million years.

Still, I couldn't get over the fact that I was 'in here', as opposed to just another of those 'out there'. I used to wonder if something had happened to the brains of other people to stop them wondering about this, or even being aware of it. All the time, from as far back as I can remember, I had a sense that I had been created by someone or something, and nothing I have heard or read since, of biology, evolutionary theory or history, has convinced me that this perception was not, in its fundamental sense of things, correct.

My father was born beside the sea in Sligo, but still I did not see the sea until I was nearly twenty. Now I see the sea continuously from my back window and could not be without it. From my living room, perched high on Dalkey Hill, I look over Dun Laoghaire Harbour and across to Howth. On a clear day, I can see the Mountains of Mourne, heads raised ghostily over Sutton.

At my front door I look onto Dalkey Quarry. Sometimes, especially on Tuesday nights in summertime, I stand at my front door listening to the voices of the rock-climbers in the quarry, invisibly calling to each other across the rock, and once again I cannot believe my luck in being here now, at this moment, of all the moments of time, those that have appeared to pass and those I have been led to believe are yet to come.

Sometimes, as we come to the end of a rough winter, when the winds have pummelled us from the north and the east, and we have stayed indoors more than is natural in such a place, I find myself walking again across Dalkey Hill as though for the first time. It is not a place you can take for granted. Walking off Torca Road, where George Bernard Shaw once lived, and along a path that weaves its way around the side of the hill, you suddenly emerge onto a vista that some people claim to be more beautiful than the Bay of Naples. Whether it is or not does not matter: this is beauty you cannot ignore.

Every time I come across it, even after a few days' break, I think, 'How could I have forgotten this? Why have I been neglecting to come out and look at such an extraordinary place?' Walking home each time, I am visited by the same thoughts, as I try to retrace the steps that brought me here from the flatlands of County Roscommon and enabled me to call this my home. The beauty of this place seems to challenge something in me that seeks to normalise everything, to pretend that experience can be taken for granted as the natural order of things. Each time, something in the encounter seems to draw me back to a faint awareness of some prior consciousness, reminding me that I have a broader existence in both time and space.

Strangely, too, a collateral benefit of these rather enhanced experiences of beauty seems to be the opening up of my eyes to the beauty of Roscommon as well, so nowadays I am far more inclined than previously to be struck by the raw beauty of parts of my native county, pausing by the roadside at its north-easternmost corner to gaze across a misty Lough Arrow, or just standing on the back road behind the house where I grew up, in Castlerea, in not-quite-the-West-but-not-the-midlands-either, to gaze in awe at the landscape I played in as a child, its long wild, communal gardens converging into the Suck River Valley stretching to the Dublin-Westport railway line beyond.

When I say 'beauty' I mean something deeper than I am capable of conveying in words. It is a kind of recognition, a sense of some broader and more tranquil existence, a sense of being perfectly at home.

Dalkey represents for me much more than aesthetic beauty. It is a place where I can encounter the wilderness, albeit in a distilled form, and yet live near to the street. Both aspects are, I think, vital to me. People who think they know where I come from always seem to regard me in a certain way because I come from what they call 'The Country'. But I come from no such place. When I was a child growing up in Castlerea, I lived on Main Street, which, when I think about it now, had about it the qualities of a short stretch of city. It had a roadway with near constant traffic which I could listen to as I fell asleep. It had those incessant sounds that make the city live in the imagination as much as in space, the sound of Guinness barrels being unloaded at dawn and the drone of a train in the distance. It had the regular lines of the streetscape, the calculated bends and ordered corners, the footpaths and road markings, the signposts that tell you where to go, which create a kind of box for your humanity that both contains and seems to explain it. It had the Fair Green, two churches, a couple of small cafés, where the people congregated in various manifestations of themselves. It had shops – where you could get food, ice cream, things to read or wear, and where you could get your shoes repaired or your radio fine-tuned and where the tradesmen, without yet having a name for it, multi-tasked as they talked to their customers about the life they shared, without questioning it much.

When I walked out my back door, I was in the wilderness. The gardens behind our houses had long since run into one wide continuity, bordered at the end by the river, which had an island in the middle which you could access by means of a tree felled on the town side. It only now occurs to me that, as a child, this wild place existing so close to the beat of the street was fundamental to my formation in accordance with my nature and structure as a human being. The street sought to seduce me to a new reality, but the condensed wilderness of those gardens kept me in touch with what is infinite within myself. I used to walk around with my life's companion, Fumble, a skinny, ugly, but intensely loyal animal, a dog trapped in the body of a cat. Usually I carried an iron staff, a spear, and we would go hunting together, as though we had walked straight from the pages of *Huckleberry Finn* or *Just William*. And in an eternity of a summer's afternoon, I would lie in the hollow of the island with Fumble purring at my head, utterly alone in the human universe, connected to the sky and the core of the earth, part of the continuity of time and yet momentarily resting on some cosmic journey. Then I would return to the street and be seduced once more.

There is something about a town, especially a town of a certain size, that touches me as nothing else does. There are few things I enjoy more than going to a new town, or better still an old town I haven't seen for a while, for any old excuse, staying overnight and just walking about looking at how the town fits together. Cities do something to me also, but the draw of cities is, I suspect, more superficial, seeming to be fundamentally about sex, whereas the excitement of what we call towns is about a more subtle form of attraction. It has to do with the history and taste of a community, of the interaction of the lives of people largely unrelated but con-nected by space and story. To look at any town, even one without a formally recorded history, is to know that it has seen both great sorrow and great happiness. A town has a visible DNA which bears the record of its backstory, expressed in incongruous ways: the juxtapositioning of bingo hall and funeral home, the bright colours of the jolly-mixture town houses like face-painted children on the verge of laughter or tears, the church at the centre, the graves ranged behind, perpetual reminders of the open wound that marks the fate of mankind.

There is a particular time when the town comes into its own: on a fine summer's evening in the hour or two before nightfall. This is when the magic is most potent, when the inhabitants come out devoid of their business senses and move in that golden light in a way that hints at something deeper in their togetherness. I like to watch them call to each other across the street and guess at their relationships. I am enchanted by the sense of their collective ownership of their surroundings, which varies greatly from town to town. The city does not have this, except in a more localised neighbourhood sense that you occasionally stumble into, and the countryside is too sparsely peopled for such intimacy. The town, therefore, is the repository of community in its purest essence, a physical representation of the togetherness wrought by people who live, by a combination of accident and design, side by side.

Sometimes I go into the centre of Dublin, where I once lived too, and walk from my former home on Grattan Street, which I shared with a friend from home for a while in my thirties, to Baggot Street Bridge. I sit on the bench beside the bronze statue of Patrick Kavanagh and watch the moving water of the canal and think of time passing and growing old and getting what is called sense and finally learning, after Kavanagh, not to care about anything, except whatever place I may have in the greater scheme of things.

I look at the lunchtime hordes streaming through the ancient streets of the city and reflect that these streets, which were here before us, will be here long after we go wherever it is we are going. They are older than the oldest of us and younger than the youngest. They have their own mortality, but it is not ours. And that thought always momentarily fills me with a kind of grief, because I cannot be a building or a tree. But this thought is wiped away by another: that I have a kind of dominion here. I see the potential for hubris with which the city is immanent at all times: the ancient city, even while telling me of my transience, also tells me that reality is defined by man's achievements.

I remember the first day I came to Dalkey, in 1990, when I began house-hunting after getting my first real job, with the *Irish Times*. My initial encounter was with Castle Street, with its castellated walls and its mid-morning hum of life. There was a tiny café then just opposite the Ulster Bank, and I went in and had a cup of tea and a bun. I had come purely out of curiosity, my house-buying budget seemingly dictating that I live somewhere else. But those twenty minutes looking out on the life of that Dalkey street was enough to convince me that this is where I should stay. I had no idea how I was going to do it, but I knew I was going to live here.

Eventually, putting my shirt on the line, I bought the cottage on Ardbrugh Road where I imagine I will stay for as long as this cosmic pause endures. The street is a little more distant from me than was that of my childhood, but, although I cannot hear the Guinness barrels clatter onto the concrete, I can see the distant and reassuring movements of Castle Street from my attic window.

In the night, I hear occasional cars passing by my bedroom, enough to half-wake me occasionally to the sense that I have regressed forty years. And then, the car having disappeared into the infinity of sound, my ear shifts to the wilderness just across the road, to the pre-dawn chorus and the hum of the other reality. I stand at the door on a summer's evening listening to the rock-climbers and sometimes fancy I hear the purr of a cat who thinks he's a dog, and have to pinch myself awake. If I half-close my eyes, I might be under Ben Bulben.

My father was born at the foot of Ben Bulben, the mountain made famous by William Butler Yeats, who is buried at its foot in Drumcliff. Every day of his childhood, when he walked out of his front door, my father would have been as aware as Yeats ever was of the presence, to the east, of this most majestic and mysterious of mountains.

I never thought of my father as connected with the sea. He had about him a sense that he came from an exotic place. But he never talked about the sea, or implied any special knowledge of it. He did, however, talk about the mountain. I remember the words 'Ben Bulben' being uttered by him with both a deep pride and a tinge of regret.

When I set eyes on Ben Bulben, I felt instantly its uniqueness and its mystery. It's as though something had been practising to create the perfect mountain – and here, just once, has almost succeeded. This feeling is beyond mere 'love of nature', an attraction so deep it feels like deeper kinds of love. It provokes in me a Yes – but one that is at first ambiguous. Could it be mere sentimentality, provoked by discovering this lost garden of my father – or, something else?

When I watch the mountain from Lislary in the west, I see it like an animal in the middle distance, crouching, about to pounce. But, nearer, on the road to Grange, it rises above me, stately and proud, like something with a mind of its own. And not just a mind but an entire emotional apparatus that seems, strangely, quite like mine. More than any other mountain, I like to believe, Ben Bulben shares my humanity. In the veils of clouds that hang around his brow; in the light that plays tricks with time in the folds of his back – he mirrors my temperament and shares my joy or sadness. On a clear day, approaching from the east, to catch a glimpse on the horizon of that unique and noble profile – you can glimpse it to the right just after Boyle – is to be transported as by the face of a true love.

The geological explanations for Ben Bulben's existence – its shape, its geometric integrity – interest me a little, but not much, for such are merely superficial explanations born of the limited human intelligence. I need to know merely that Ben Bulben has come before me out of the cosmic order, to bear witness to the facts of existence, to assure me that there is an order and that it is not what I, left to my own devices, would have made or shaped. Ben Bulben is for me a sign, a nodding brow towards something infinitely great, an intelligence the human mind is too earthed to contemplate.

For Beauty is not a matter of aesthetic appreciation of shapes and colours, but the reawakening to the original Beauty whence we come. We rummage through the world for traces of it. Sometimes we catch a glimpse that keeps us going. Sometimes, because it is too much or too little, we turn away, or accept some plausible explanation rooted in aesthetics, or geology, or civilisation, or what is called science. But knowing is more than gathering information. Knowing is standing in awe before something that defies expectations – because it strikes a chord in harmony with something deeper. The evidence we need is before our eyes, accessible not through comprehension, but through the sheer power of wordless wonder provoked in us by what is there. Only in wonder do we really see, because only wonder knows what we are looking for.

But strangely, it is in the street rather than the wild that the pure condition of man can sometimes become most strikingly visible. It is there, in moments of repose, caught in the contradiction between his place in nature and his place in his own schemes, between his createdness and his own striving to control, that man occasionally emerges from the murk of civilisation to become visible in his pure state.

One Friday afternoon in the autumn of 2008, when my daughter was twelve years old, we were driving through Dublin city on the way to the airport, when a strange experience occurred, implicating us both. The traffic was heavy and we were making slow progress, but we had plenty of time before our flight and so were enjoying the trip, talking intermittently as we do and otherwise listening to Johnny Cash on the CD player. In one of the silences while Roisin was changing the CD, I became aware, at a bus stop just ahead of us on the right, of a scene that struck me in some exceptional but not immediately identifiable way. Paused in the line of cars, I idly directed my attention at the tableau. There were perhaps a dozen people, mainly adults but also a couple of schoolchildren in uniform, all waiting for the next bus. What was remarkable was that, at that moment, all of them were looking in our direction, though not exactly. Their gazes were directed upwards, just above our heads, or the tops of the line of cars – perhaps craning to read the numbers on one of the buses coming towards them. But in this brief instant it occurred to me that I was looking at one of those occasional moments when life betrays its inner meaning and briefly lapses into the demeanour of art. If I had been a photographer, I would have grabbed my camera, jumped out and captured this instant. A painter would have soaked the scene into his memory and gone away to recreate it almost exactly as it was.

What I was seeing, I realised, could be described in two ways, and it was this dualism that made it striking. On the one hand, one could easily come up with a prosaic description of the scene: a dozen or so harried commuters waiting for a bus. This would be the everyday interpretation of the signs contained in the scene, the significance our culture leads us to draw from scenes as we go around our cities in the citizen's general condition of metaphysical numbness, reading the signs and the lines and the lights so as to find the quickest way to where we want to go. But what made the scene exceptional was that it also contained a different pattern: something deeper and more resonant.

Drinking it in, I became conscious that I was momentarily observing a number of human beings in something like their pure existential state, stripped of the meanings which become attached to us in consumer/commercial/political society. They were waiting for a bus, yes, but also no. They were waiting. They were gazing upwards in anticipation of something. And looking at this dozen or so people looking upwards, I became aware that it was possible to see them, almost simultaneously, in these two different ways – that it was actually possible to 'flip' backwards and forwards between the two interpretations, now seeing them as commuters waiting for public transport, now seeing them as human beings caught in a moment of repose in the midst of existences mysterious and brief and shockingly beautiful.

I sat almost hypnotised by the scene, overcome by its beauty and significance. And then, beside me, my daughter spoke: 'Dad', she said, 'why do people in the city look so different from people in the country?'

Already moved by what I was seeing, I now almost burst into tears. It was all I could do to ask her what she meant, though I sensed immediately what she was asking. We had never spoken of these matters in such terms before, but, in the course of a brief exchange, which scratched around the surface of the moment, I established that she had seen the same thing I had, in much the same way, and had been struck by it also.

— 13 —

The Tapestry of Hope

In that last interview they did together, Marian Finucane asked Nuala O'Faolain about how, when she got the news concerning her terminal condition, she had gone at once in search of the things which had given life meaning. 'You decided that in the time you have that you would see or examine what it is that gives life quality or what is it that gives life meaning or significance for you. Tell me the kinds of things you might do and what you have done.'

It was strange to hear Nuala describe what she had done, a litany of the kinds of things we do every day without thinking too much about them. Now, however, they possessed the added significance of being done in the prospect of imminent death.

For the first few weeks she had been able to do nothing, because of undergoing brain radiation treatment. Then they told her that there would be a gap of three weeks before the chemotherapy started, and it was then she decided that she would not have the chemotherapy. The only point of it, she decided, would be to win time, and this was not something she could see the purpose of. 'What do I want to win time for?', she wondered. 'What is the quality left in life?'

She then described going to Paris on her own, booking into 'the best hotel' to see if she could revisit some sense of the joy of living. 'In the morning', she remembered, laughing, 'in a ridiculous piece of economy, I didn't have their €40 breakfast and I wandered out and I sat in a café and I had a tartine – you know – and a milky coffee and I just thought, "Well this is it. I love this".'

'I loved being in a café with my *International Herald Tribune* and my big crusty piece of bread and my coffee that I'd forgotten the smell of. And it worked great for half an hour. But then I walked too far and fell down and stuff and that didn't work out too well.'

Nuala mentioned again her room in New York, which she would never see again. There was in her words a sense of a childlike attachment to a safe place, a place that might be called home. She began to describe through the detail of things her sense of losing everything.

'I had to say goodbye to my room. It simply absolutely broke my heart. Because if you look around any room of your own, you remember buying those good pillowcases, and you remember buying that series of books, and my logs were there. I'd a fireplace, you know. And I had beautiful yellow silk curtains that I'd spent a thousand dollars on, you know. I remember thinking, "Look at all the stuff that I've acquired, just to leave it". And you think that about your inner life too, because … I know so much. It's not that it's important information, but things that, you know, when I was at St Louis, Monaghan, in the Fifties there was a whole sub-culture of romantic love, very very innocent and it had a vocabulary, like you were such and such a person's "daft" and if you gave them a present and they thanked you it was a "soiree". Now all that doesn't matter, except it was a vocabulary, and I knew it, and nobody else as far as I know is bothered collecting stuff like that. And I know loads of songs, and what's the point? And what's the point? What's the point of all I know? I worked in Iran, before and after the Shah. I've been a lot of places. I've loved a lot of people, usually unwisely. So much has happened and it seems such a waste of creation that with each death all that knowledge dies.'

'I never did think, nobody does think, what is the point of today's behaviour? But, on the other hand, now that I have to … go … like, I take so much with me that nobody knows about.'

Later on, Marian Finucane said: 'You said it wasn't so much you leaving the world as the world leaving you …'

'That's right. Like, I thought there would be me and the world, but the world turned its back on me, the world said to me, "Well, that's enough of you now and what's more we're not going to give you any little treats at the end".'

'Like …?'

'Well like, let's say, adoring nature. Let's say.'

'Is that gone?'

'Yeah.'

'Music?'

'Well, music is not quite gone, but I'm afraid it will go if I overdo it. So I'm trying to listen to as little as possible. But one of the reasons I went to New York was to hear live music, which I did the night before last – a wonderful string quartet, and thanks be to God my heart responded because if I had had to sit there listening to Schubert's quartet 'Death and the Maiden' meaning nothing to me, I really think I would have thought I am going to throw myself under the subway train. But it wasn't. I came out elated. So there's things left.'

'Reading?'

'Not much. No. I'm reduced to reading old copies of *Vanity Fair*.'

'But I still occasionally like food and above all I like sleep and what I'm hoping for, and I don't think this is going to happen, but if I could have this ... I kinda hoped there was some kind of way of fading away; that's to say you lay on your bed and you were really a nice person and everyone came and said goodbye and wept and you wept and you meant it and that you weren't in any pain or discomfort, that you didn't choke and didn't die in a mess of diarrhoea, that you just got weaker and then in the end they say that the cancer migrates into some other organ. Mine is already in my liver and I don't know what that means, but if that means that sometime in the middle of the night on your own as you must be, you know that you are just about to go into the dark ... that's what I want.' Here, she broke down, weeping.

In 2007, in the second encyclical of his papacy *Spe Salvi*, Pope Benedict XVI talked about hope in this way: 'Day by day, man experiences greater or lesser hopes, different in kind according to the different periods of his life. Sometimes one of these hopes may appear to be totally satisfying without any need for other hopes. Young people can have the hope of a great and fully satisfying love; the hope of a certain position in their profession; or of some success that will prove decisive for the rest of their lives. When these hopes are fulfilled, however, it becomes clear that they were not, in reality, the whole. It becomes evident that man has need of a hope that goes further. It becomes clear that only something infinite will suffice for him, something that will always be more than he can ever attain. In this regard, our contemporary age has developed the hope of creating a perfect world that, thanks to scientific knowledge and to scientifically based politics, seemed to be achievable.... In the course of time, however, it has become apparent that this may be a hope for a future generation, but not for me.'

There is something in Nuala O'Faolain's almost forensic reconstruction of the little things that held her life together that is ineffably resonant because most of us can identify with the idea of attaching meaning to little pleasures, and with the idea of these little pleasures, all strung together, seeming to add up to a kind of meaning in a world where the question of meaning is either taken for granted or avoided. If we zoom in close and take a look at the fabric of our lives, we probably find that these lives owe much of their sense of worth to such pleasures: bananas for breakfast, a clean shirt, walking in the sunshine to the train, coffee at eleven, a phone call from a beloved other. In our societies anyway, the human existence, from dawn to dusk, is a series of strategically placed motivational baits, treats, which, set out before us like stepping stones, take us through the day. Moment to moment we negotiate these steps unthinkingly, rarely if ever stopping to imagine our lives if they were not there. Most of us in our modern societies rely on this tapestry of tiny hopes for the pattern of meaning that takes each of its citizens through the most tedious or difficult of days. Much of the commercial activity of our societies relates not to the purveyance of necessities but of these alleged luxuries, without which we might have to stop and ask ourselves, 'What is life actually about?'

— 14 —

We Shall Have Stars at Elbow and Foot

I had an epiphany not long ago in a Texaco station on the N4 near Lucan, on the road westwards out of Dublin. I had fallen into the habit of stopping there whenever I drove west, for a fill-up and a takeaway coffee, finding few things in Irish life as exhilarating as driving west out of the dawn, with no company but Bob Dylan and a hot skinny latte. Then, one Sunday morning, I encountered an 'Out of order' notice on the coffee machine and a truckdriver manfully making himself a cuppa from a jar of Nescafé Gold. I was devastated. I don't mean I was a little annoyed: I was beside myself with disbelief and disappointment.

By the time I hit Newtownforbes, about halfway to my destination, it had begun to occur to me that this was a disproportionate response to the temporary unavailability of coffee-coloured milk. That's when I decided I should see how life felt without it. It was, you might say, a modest sacrifice arising out of a minor hedonism, but dimly perceiving that this seemed to be about something fundamental, I decided to give up coffee for Lent.

I hadn't 'done' Lent since my childhood. As a child, Lent had been emblematic of an experience of Christianity seemingly fixated on pointless self-denial, as though the very pleasures of life were themselves suspect, as though we had been let loose in a garden booby-trapped with temptations designed to test our capacities for some ethic of restraint whose objective claim to virtue was never satisfactorily explained. Reacting against a childhood tendency to go unthinkingly along with this, I later on began to see Lent as a time to indulge myself in doing and consuming things I wouldn't normally be bothered with, by way of elaborately repudiating the tyranny of imposed self-denial. I would eat fish any day except

Friday and give up blueberry muffins as soon as Easter was over. Childish, I know, but there it is.

Alcohol had been for me an adventure embraced largely because it seemed to be disapproved of. The results were both disastrous and eye-opening as to the validity of at least some of the cautionary messages, in the form of preachings and prohibitions, directed at my growing-up self. But this did not, of course, mean that my experience educated me in the underlying context of these patterns, nor did the salutary lesson concerning alcohol translate into a general theory of freedom in reality.

At the level of collective culture, our societies misunderstand addiction, thinking usually of chemical dependency and outright junkie disintegration. But addiction is a much more subtle and ubiquitous phenomenon, having as its principal symptom the evasion of reality. It's not just the chemicals: sometimes it's the distraction, the comfort, the habit or the sweetness, and always the blocking out of the real. Things we tend to think of as making us free are often the sources of our enslavement.

Sometimes it is good to contemplate that letting go of things we think essential may not cause as much pain as we imagine. Self-denial is not always a penance: sometimes it can become an exercise in self-liberation.

My coffee experiment was an instructive experience. Over the next couple of weeks, although I encountered no obvious symptoms of withdrawal that might readily be attributable to my 'penance', I began to note something deeper in myself that I had no doubt was connected to my abstinence. I don't actually like coffee that much, my addiction in this instance being more in the nature of circumstantial ritual: buying the beverage in the crowded filling station, putting on one of my favourite CDs and sipping it as the countryside of the midlands opens up before me. In these moments, it is as if Freud's policeman takes a break from sitting on my shoulder and insteads sits in the seat beside me and starts telling me that he, too, enjoys a little Bob Dylan, that that song on the CD player, 'Mama, You Been On My Mind', makes him think that Dylan seemed to have the capacity to watch his own intelligence at work from a distance, observe the calculated duplicity of his own thought and get it all down in a couple of lines. *Maybe it's the colour of the sun cut flat/And coverin' the crossroads I'm standin' at/Or maybe it's the weather or somethin' like that/But Mama, you been on my mind.*

On a surface level, being off coffee didn't affect me. There's almost no coffee in a latte anyway. When I made a journey as before and had a cup of tea instead of a latte, it didn't seem to make much difference. But, then, one morning when I woke up, I noticed that I had just the tiniest bit less than usual of an urge to get out of bed. I got up, I watched myself and waited. The next day, I felt the same thing. After a few days, I realised that what I was experiencing was that my sense of the balance of meaning in reality had been ever-so-slightly affected by my removal of this single, tiny pleasure from my life. I had lost a little of the moment-to-moment hope that suggested life as being worth living.

Have you ever stopped what you are doing to enter fully into the present moment, to look at it and compare it with other reference points you might be dimly relating to, in the past or the future? Have you ever stopped and asked: what is the nature of my reality, what defines it, how might I describe it? When I do this, from time to time, I become conscious of a strange and unsettling fact of my ordinary existence: that it is, as Pope Benedict has intimated, fundamentally disappointing. When I look, briefly, over my shoulder, I become conscious of some forces that drove me to this point, and that seemed, while doing so, to be whispering to me that I was going somewhere special. And yet, when I gather myself up in the present, I invariably find that where I thought I was going, in as far as it was a thought at all, is not where I am now. I have not yet arrived at the promised place.

And then, entering further into myself, I become aware that the desires are still there, driving me forward, promising me something, cajoling me to go on. If I were to become strictly logical, I might decide that it is all a sham, knowing that, when next I pause in this manner to reflect, I will find myself in the same place, still looking over my shoulder at the desires that drive me ever onwards, still aware of something propelling me forward, but still, too, in the same condition I find myself enveloped in here, now.

There is, I recognise, a hope inside me that is bigger than I am, that overwhelms me with confidence and optimism and that rests too in the light that it has placed just beyond my sight, a light that I see only in a reflection on the telegraph wires overhead, a faint shimmer of something engaging, promising, comforting or seductive. My desire still tells me that something is coming, something is happening, something is waiting for me just as I am waiting for it. But nothing on earth has come near to satisfying this desire.

With pleasure, beauty and happiness there always comes regret, because of the sense that what is being experienced is really just a sign for something behind it, something unreachable. I find myself in a moment of tranquillity, perhaps on a Sunday morning in April walking by the forest beside Annamakerrig lake in the grounds of the Tyrone Guthrie Writers and Artists Centre in County Monaghan, where I am writing parts of this book, first hearing voices and then catching a glimpse of a father and his two little daughters among the trees. I have been happily strolling along, enjoying the sunshine and the racket of the hedgerows, when suddenly something happens to discommode me. I am overcome by a lurching sadness, which I find impossible to pick up and look at.

It may, I think, have to do with the years of my own daughter's childhood, in which we had mornings like this, perhaps in Hyde Park in London or on the beach at Lislary in Sligo. Partly, I guess, what I feel is regret that these moments are past, these particular moments, I mean, since it is still possible for me to take my now teenage daughter to all these places and others as well. Perhaps there is a streak of envy because this man has his children with him now, whereas I am preoccupied with the business of making black marks on white pieces of paper. But there is something else as well, a feeling that the beauty I crave within me is not entirely here, even in this near blissful moment, a feeling that we are all scratching at the face of beauty, seeking to enter, all trapped outside something we can sometimes glimpse or smell or hear, but cannot enter in the way the urging inside us tells us should be possible. This beauty that we sense will move on, or wither or dissolve or leave without us reaching it.

Sometimes, sitting working inside my attic window in Dalkey, I glance upwards and am swept away by something that has manifested itself for what I am certain will be a brief and once-only performance. I look east and see that, in the murk of the low-slung cloud, an oasis of sunlight has appeared, trapped in a clearly defined area between the Great South Wall and the coastline beyond, which is probably Clontarf (although my grasp of the geography of north-side Dublin is still, after twenty-five years in the capital, a little ropey). There is an intensity of brightness to the sunlight that seems impossible, perhaps the contrast with the gloom over the rest of Dublin Bay. It is as if it has erupted spontaneously in the space allotted to it, like a visitation of light from another place, with no visible evidence of source. I stare at it in wonder, delighting in the idea that I could be blessed to witness it, a little dismayed that there is nobody in the house right now with whom to share it, and at the same moment consumed by a sudden tremor of sadness. I have taught myself to remain in such moments and look at the sadness.

What is it? It has a little to do with the pre-programme that sends out signals every moment of my waking life, sending me hither and thither in search of perfection. The sudden rush of beauty makes me regret that my perfect life has not yet come together. I stay with it and look hard into the feeling. I see, or hear, something else: this beauty that will pass. This beauty that will be here when I am not. This moment that may well recur, perhaps a billion times, but I will not be here to see it.

Deep inside I feel something else, like a ball of frustration that has nothing to do with sadness as I normally understand it. It is like I can't quite get to something. Do I want to reach out and touch this moment, to snatch it to myself and store it away? There is a little of this. I look again at the shining wash of light on the fortunate bay and think I feel something greater than possessiveness: perhaps a yearning for something that it not quite there, a barely awake sense that this sight before me is something I almost know, only not quite anything I know and not quite the whole of what I feel.

Then it strikes me: I have been expecting this. I have known about this, or something like it, and now its picture has materialised before me, I am on the hazard for something else to happen. Except that it doesn't happen. I have seen something a little like this before, but something far more beautiful, something perfect or at least more perfect than this, and the recalled sense of this something, or Something, seems to be accompanied by an understanding, or an event, or a state of consciousness that is absent from the present picture. But the strangest thing, then, is to hold that feeling and look at it, as into the eyes of a beloved, and realise that it contains all these things: the regret of not being able to share this moment with some-one who will affirm it and spread the risk of it being lost forever; the fear that this will be the only and final occasion on which I will witness this precise manifestation of beauty; and the deeper sense that even this intensity is just an echo of something, that it is really no more than a crude representation of something already seen, or known, or distilled and implanted in my heart as pure and limitless desire.

To comprehend the experience in this multiple way is to achieve something not unlike the process of learning to swim or ride a bicycle. When you have done something like this a couple of times, it ceases to frighten and starts to exhilarate. You become proficient in the process of entering into the totality of what is in front of you. The epiphany of beauty followed by the sudden lurch of sadness ceases to be the conclusion. I refuse to scrunch myself up in fear of what I might discover. If I stay with it a little longer, it turns again, and becomes a sweetness, a peaceful but ineffable understanding that, yes, this beauty is not the end of itself, but merely a hint of something beyond or behind – something I have been awaiting in some way for some time – and that my witnessing it now is not a meaningless happenstance but more in the way of momentarily catching sight of a slipped mask on the world behind. It seems obvious that such moments are striking because they are exceptional. They don't happen often but often enough to keep at bay the idea that beauty is either something accidental or something perverse and teasing. Conventional wisdom and everyday experience dictate that, though beauty exists, it is not available in this dimension all the time. But these moments tell me something else: that beauty is the norm, that the pain and sadness or sometime ugliness of this dimension are nothing like the truth of reality. Somewhere out there is the true echo of the desire I feel.

As you grow older, life sends little messages, sometimes with the most unlikely messengers, to tell you that you've been getting it all wrong. Such moments occur to tell me that, although the sense of perfection that governs me is not realisable in this dimension, this does not mean it is not real. Perfection exists, even if it can't be found right now. The rain falling on my face tells me it's okay. Breathe and be. Even after the loss of love, love remains. Nothing can be lost because nothing is quite here yet, just the shadows of things and the echo of the future sneaking in.

Father Luigi Giussani, in a talk entitled 'The Risen Christ, the Defeat of Nothingness', said: 'All things have a vanishing point toward the infinite, the eternal, and that is what attracts us, because it is according to the measure of the heart.' This 'vanishing point' is the aperture opening into the mystery. This, in the shape of a mountain or the face of a beautiful woman, or indeed man, is what attracts the eye. It is possible, of course, to look upon such things without knowing this, and still be moved, carried away. But to look upon things all the time without understanding this is to move, slowly but inexorably, towards disappointment. One day, even in the midst of beauty that once transported me, I will, without this insight, be struck down by loneliness and tedium and a desire to be someplace else. I will be forced to conclude that either life has no point or I am missing it. These moments do occur, and in doing so present a challenge and a choice: either I succumb to their implicit despair or I move through them, focusing on the hard facts of reality, first gazing, then moving through what is there to what is beyond. In a step or two I have shaken the weight of unhope from my shoulders and moved towards the future.

After years of observation of myself and others, it occurs to me that there is something counter-intuitive about the human engagement with reality. Much of the modern self-help philosophy urges man to 'live in the moment', but in truth this is impossible. The moment does not stand still for me to live in it. It passes and another arrives, but this too is gone before I can engage it. In his sublime essay 'The Dimension of the Present Moment', the scientist, philosopher and poet Miroslav Holub observes that comprehending eternity is easier than comprehending the present moment, which is 'a dimension without a dimension'. But Holub insists that what he calls 'the subjective present' can, in fact, be defined. Describing various experiments concerning the human capacity to recall, exactly or otherwise, the content of very short sounds, he concludes that the present moment, perhaps of slightly different duration for everyone, lasts approximately three seconds, just enough time for a 'tick' and a 'tock', denoting the unit, perhaps the temporal quark, of human perception. Even this quasisatirical exercise in empiricism merely serves to accentuate the transient nature of the human gaze, the difficulty in being able to look at reality for long enough to say what the real is like as it happens.

What requires to be entered, then, is not the present moment, but something beyond it, not in the future or the sky, but a point related to the present moment by a measurement that is not of this dimension. A crude metaphor is provided by the golfer's method of addressing the ball. There is the matter of the proper stance, or demeanour, but also there is the question of how the ball is addressed. When the club strikes the ball, the golfer is not focused on the point of contact, but on a point through and beyond the ball, where the head of his club should rightly end up. The club strikes the ball, which is despatched into its trajectory; but the club follows through to the position the golfer was seeking to achieve in his stroke. The optimum result is achieved by focusing not on the present moment but ever so slightly into the future.

The point is to hit the ball correctly, but the point can also be defined as the necessity of ending up in the correct posture, which seems to have nothing at all to do with the ball, long gone when the end position is achieved. Mankind's sense of meaning resides at least marginally ahead of him, and ideally an absolute distance in front of him. The meaning of what he does here, now, is enhanced by adopting a posture predicated on that other point, rendering him in harmony with the earthly and transcendent realities at once.

The genius of Luigi Giussani relates not so much to his startling re-presentation of the Christian proposal as to his understanding of what had been happening at the heart of the culture of modern society. He seemed, a half century ago now, to see things that were only just beginning to show their earliest signs. Giussani stared at what was happening until it began to yield up its patterns. He observed that human curiosity seemed to have lost its intrinsic capacity for positive affirmation, its sympathy with being. Man's curiosity had become detached from the fundamental longing that underpins the human appetites, so that he no longer felt pushed towards a universal comparison between himself and what he encountered beyond himself. Instead, he was focused on his desires in something approximating to the present, in the banality of the here-and-now. Giussani recognised this condition as fatal to man. And, having observed, he prepared an antidote comprising both his re-presentation of the Christian proposal and a new way of explaining modern man to himself. Eliding the traps of language, he created a new description of man's condition and his alienation from his true nature.

The antidote was Christ, yes, but in a particular way, a way that opens up again the circuitry of man's total relationship with reality.

In the past few years, as a result of stumbling over the work and story of Father Giussani, I have been thrown in the path of many people I would not otherwise have met. It is hard to say what these people are like. It is easier to get across what they possess to render them different by noting how other people seem to lack this essence. There is no sense of evangelical zeal, but rather an intensity of ease that seems to seek nothing but the happiness of the other. They look at me in a different way, as though they can see me always in my timeless, spaceless dimension. There is a sense that the people I have met in Communion and Liberation (the movement established by Giussani to pursue his intuition about Christianity in modern culture) have integrated themselves into reality in a different way, having stretched themselves again between the stars and the earth's core, floating in an infinity of time. Each new moment arrives to them not as an ephemeron but as a revelation, an event relating to the total potential meaning of their existence. They have no need to capture or measure it, their gazes always directed slightly beyond it to what is not quite here yet. Every little thing gives them a greater sense of who they are and why they are here. They are filled with a wonder that is infectious. I have encountered nothing like it any-where else.

In my experience of living in the culture I have inhabited for over fifty years, there is a moment somewhere not far beyond the middle of life when something fundamental changes about your understanding of life and its meaning. I don't mean a rational apprehension, a penny dropping, a new level of understanding suddenly arriving. In fact, this moment does not announce itself at the time, but only in retrospect, gradually revealing itself as having begun to occur at some critical moment beyond the halfway of life's expectancy, perhaps a fortieth or fiftieth birthday, the death of a parent, or the birth of a child. This moment is not a revelation, but more like a chill that creeps into your bones, an understanding that everything you have been working with as a map of reality has been bogus. I sometimes think this may be what the medical profession has come to call 'depression', though I have no wish to prove this theory even to myself.

It has, I think, something to do with repetition, with the idea of doing the same thing over and over while each time expecting something new or unexpected to occur. This impulse drives us through much difficulty in life, the insistence of the culture that there is something meaningful in the next experience, that a purer form of happiness is just around the corner. At a certain moment in your life, you rumble this idea and, drawing in the totality of your experience, begin to comprehend that, if you continue to see things in the same old way, what will happen in the future is pretty much, in essence, what has happened in the past, and this will no longer contain the illusory promise it has held before. The specifics of your experiences may change, but the outcome, measured in happiness and satisfaction, will become reduced.

Another thing I notice as I grow older is that something odd is happening to my sense of time. Once, time seemed to open up before and behind me in a linear fashion, measurable by some approximate process of comparision. When I reflect back on a particular past moment, some intense three seconds of joy or peace, I am surprised by how recent it seems. Once, time seemed to open up before and behind me in a linear fashion, reliably measurable by some approximate process of comparision; now, it seems to have become more fluid.

Gradually I began to perceive that my vantage-point was no longer on an axis extending backwards and forwards, but at the centre of a not-quite completed circle. One consequence of this was that I was no longer able to measure reliably the emotional distance to some future moment by comparing it with distance into past time. Whenever I tried to do this, my sense of time seemed to become mangled and confused. Time seemed to have changed form and begun to surround me, rather than extend itself before and behind. An event that had occurred six months before might seem like either three days or thirty years in the past. When I found myself in a place I had been in some time ago, the sense of that past time would overcome me as though it were only moments, rather than thirty or thirty-five years, before. I would be in Galway, in Eyre Square, where I worked in 1978, and, though the place had changed a little, feel a kind of continuity with the person I had been back then, even though the intervening period had spanned many years when I had barely thought of that experience. My childhood and adult selves are blurring into one, my whole life converging into a single moment. It is as though my life has risen up before and behind me, like the Milky Way. Already, as Dylan Thomas promised, I have stars at elbow and foot.

When I turned fifty, I now realise, something began to happen to me that, though unrelated to any physical change, was having a palpable effect on my sense of myself. I was breathing in from the surrounding culture a new message about my evolving description. Birthdays affect everybody differently and you can almost never tell someone's attitude to his age by simply asking him about it. It is possible that he has convinced himself of what he tells you, that it doesn't matter, that he hardly ever thinks about it, that we're counting from the wrong end, ahaha, ahahahaha.

It is not that, when I passed my fiftieth birthday, I suddenly noticed a change. But, although the implications of what was happening did not sink in for a long time afterwards, I can trace a fundamental shift in my relationship with my life to this exact moment.

Deeper down there was a process, of which I was only vaguely aware in my emotions and not at all in my head, of a kind of disquietude developing within me. I found myself, listening to radio adverts directed at the over-fifties, wanting to hide away. Although I am generally open about my age, there is, I recognise, a certain implicit and paradoxical reluctance in my too-emphatic declaration of my truthful age. I blurt it out almost by way of implying that it doesn't matter, or that it isn't what it seems to be, or that I am above all that nonsense. And yet, if you were to ask me, having just heard an advert for vitamins for the over-fifties, I would probably deny my age until the cock crowed. For someone of my generation to be fifty seems beyond impossible, because we have been trapped in a bubble of cultural certainty that reassured us we would always be young. There is therefore for us a certain dreamlike quality to the process of ageing. Whether we try to deny the truth or admit to it, either way we do not quite believe it. We are always on the verge of asking for a recount.

In our societies, age, after sex and colour, is perhaps the most fundamental element of human identity. Each of us, consciously or not, factors in, as part of his apprehension of his fellows, an instant computation of chronological age. And yet, each of us also, within him- or herself, does constant battle with his own indicator. We lie about it to the world and fudge it to ourselves.

There is a melancholia, too, that seeks to descend on me as I grow older. It is a strange mixture of an attraction to the beauty of the world, growing in inverse proportion to my sense of the putative time that remains to me, and a consequent fear of losing this forever. There is a kind of weight that descends, like a rain-bearing cloud. It seems to consist mainly of fear, but not of fear of death, or at least not obviously so. It is, instead, a fear of smaller things, a fear that very often cannot be traced to anything in particular.

If I stand back from it and try to document what it comprises, I find myself zeroing in on the oddest of phenomena: the pile of undealt-with correspondence on the top of my microwave oven, unpaid bills and unsorted documents, most of which I could simply throw away; the ironing board buried in crumpled garments that accuses me every time I enter the room; the telltale streaks of dust along my skirting boards; the weeds sneaking their heads up between the atoms of gravel in the yard; the skipload of Johnny Cash CDs my daughter has abandoned on the floor of the back of our car, in the wrong cases and exposed to the traffic of shoes and the detritus of a driving life cast unthinkingly behind as though there were no tomorrow. Such a forensics of fear is an interesting exercise because it enables you, by sorting out the components of these dull but gnawing feelings, to understand the irrationality of such phenomena and therefore the possibility of dispersing them.

Sometimes, too, I experience a fear of death, or rather a fear of being in the situation where death is, if not imminent, certainly more real than it was before. You could call it a fear of old age. Sometimes, walking through the house I have lived in for nearly twenty years, I am struck by a sense of passing time that momentarily becomes visible in the way my life is reflected in my surroundings and causes me to shiver. It reminds me momentarily of the house of an old lady I used to do messages for as a child. My father called her 'Mrs Wower', though not for any reason I recall ever being aware of.

She lived directly across the street, a small, stern woman, who seemed to take it for granted that childen existed to do her messages. She kept to herself, having just a couple of friends who called to her for chats. She was by then well into her eighties and did not waste her wind on small talk. She had two sons, one of whom had several children whom we used to watch rather enviously from our bedroom window when they would come on their summer holidays in a caravan which they would park in the lane behind the house. Her other son had moved up North and was reputed to have become a protestant, a source of no little disgrace which she carried without outward sign of perturbation.

She would be out polishing the door knocker and would call my mother across on the way from the shops and instruct her to send myself or one of my sisters over. Usually, when I arrived, she would have made a list of all the things she needed, and counted to a few pence the cost of her purchases. But sometimes she would still be in the throes of her inventory or calculations, and I would have to wait while she counted out her money and wrapped it in a small, carefully cut piece of brown paper. When she was doing this, I would look around her mausoleum, a place from a different age. There was always a smell of furniture polish, for she spent most of her time polishing things. Everything seemed dark and burnished. But for all the cleanliness, there was something about it that smacked of age and decay and a sense of the pointlessness of such order and cleanliness in a place where nothing beckons but the end.

There was an old man who lived across the road from us whom I used to visit also, mainly because he seemed to have been a close friend of my father's many years before, though they maintained a respectful distance in later life. My father called him 'The Gentleman', because he never seemed to do any work. In his old age he used to invite me in for chats, which generally meant him talking and me listening. He would want to talk about everything he had heard since he had seen me last. He would have a bunch of cue cards on which he would have written notes about things he had heard on the radio and he worked through his agenda systematically while I listened. His home was a good deal messier than Mrs Wower's, and gradually he moved himself into the back of the house, setting up his bed in a small room off the kitchen. These two rooms became his world.

I think of these people often now, coming to realise how misplaced was the sense I once had that I was not like them. The culture persuaded me to see them differently to myself, to avail of the freedom that youth offered without thought of my fundamental structure, spanning the days of my life, from birth to death. This sense of things was persuasive for a while, but gradually I began to comprehend that nothing the culture offered seemed to take account of my fragility, my mortality, or the exile from the source of my life.

At the heart of the cultural obsession with youth is a fear of death, itself a symptom of loss of faith. Because our generations lack a convinced belief in a Hereafter, all our hopes hinge on the realisation of our appetites in the only existence we know about. The idea that our lives might pass and leave us still full of longing is one that terrifies us to where we seem to remember our souls used to be. Our societies tell us that our chances of happiness depend on the number (denoting chronological age) we carry around in our heads, a description existing just behind our faces, keeping us ever more awake as fear of the ultimate sleep encroaches. All the time we seek an unattainable perfection, waiting to freeze-frame ourselves in that optimal moment, except that this moment never quite seems to arrive.

Sometimes nowadays I have a momentary sense of my life as becoming more like either Mr Wower's or The Gentleman's. I walk though my own house and see it as though in the moments or days after my death, full of things which mean nothing to anyone but me. In terms of orderliness, it is closer to The Gentleman's, but sometimes the light of a particular afternoon will bring back those childhood moments waiting for Mrs Wower to parcel up her coppers and finish off her shopping list. Again I have this sense of timelessness, but something else as well: the feeling that my sudden identification with Mrs Wower's reality and my childhood innocence as I gazed around at her surroundings are somehow forged, parcelled together in a ball of longing hurtling through space and time.

Pope Benedict wrote in *Spe Salvi*:

Obviously there is a contradiction in our attitude, which points to an inner contradiction in our very existence. On the one hand, we do not want to die; above all, those who love us do not want us to die. Yet, on the other hand, neither do we want to continue living indefinitely, nor was the earth created with that in view. So what do we really want? Our paradoxical attitude gives rise to a deeper question: what in fact is 'life'? And what does 'eternity' really mean? There are moments when it suddenly seems clear to us: yes, this is what true 'life' is – this is what it should be like. Besides, what we call 'life' in our everyday language is not real 'life' at all. Saint Augustine, in the extended letter on prayer which he addressed to Proba, a wealthy Roman widow and mother of three consuls, once wrote this: ultimately we want only one thing—'the blessed life', the life which is simply life, simply 'happiness'. In the final analysis, there is nothing else that we ask for in prayer. Our journey has no other goal – it is about this alone. But then Augustine also says: looking more closely, we have no idea what we ultimately desire, what we would really like. We do not know this reality at all; even in those moments when we think we can reach out and touch it, it eludes us. 'We do not know what we should pray for as we ought', he says, quoting Saint Paul (Romans 8:26). All we know is that it is not this. Yet in not knowing, we know that this reality must exist. 'There is therefore in us a certain learned ignorance (*docta ignorantia*), so to speak', he writes. We do not know what we would really like; we do not know this 'true life'; and yet we know that there must be something we do not know towards which we feel driven.

I think that in this very precise and permanently valid way, Augustine is describing man's essential situation, the situation that gives rise to all his contradictions and hopes. In some way we want life itself, true life, untouched even by death; yet at the same time we do not know the thing towards which we feel driven. We cannot stop reaching out for it, and yet we know that all we can experience or accomplish is not what we yearn for. This unknown 'thing' is the true 'hope' which drives us, and at the same time the fact that it is unknown is the cause of all forms of despair and also of all efforts, whether positive or destructive, directed towards worldly authenticity and human authenticity. The term 'eternal life' is intended to give a name to this known 'unknown'. Inevitably it is an inadequate term that creates confusion.

Each of us in his own heart must occasionally sit or lie alone, all distraction momentarily quietened, and face the fact that, without an eternal dimension, life is going nowhere rather than the Somewhere our sense of purpose and intensity seem constantly to insinuate. In such moments, reason may take a different view of everything, as we are returned to the original state of consciousness defined by wonder and surprise. In such moments, the truly reasonable position is one that, wondering at what is, can see no point in being amazed by anything. Everything is possible. There is no reason to be pessimistic. But then we must get up and go out into a world that, in its every inflexion and nuance, rejects this perspective as unreasonable, and which tells us that such interventions are unhelpful to the project of human happiness, that all these questions have already been settled, if only by avoidance. Again and again, we are forced to vacate that state of original wonder and embrace what is called 'realism'. And the 'real' is this connection is the urgency of coming to terms with a world that does not embrace or even contemplate our human hopes and longings except for the purposes of selling us things.

Our conventional culture still treats it as axiomatic that time is a consistent entity, a measurable quantity that ticks its way through our lives and onwards into the future. This idea forms an integral element of our thinking about lots of other things, like age and death and the order of the universe. But there is ample evidence that, at the very least, it is nowhere like as simple as this. Most people are aware of Einstein's theory of relativity, and even though this is in an academic sense old hat, it remains in our mainstream culture implausible that time might actually pass faster or slower depending on whether you are sitting on a red-hot stove or a lap-dancer's knee. To conventional culture this seems like a joke, both counter-intuitive and scientifically unreasonable. If we think about it at all, we understand this perspective as existing somewhere between a metaphor and a gag.

But Einstein was deadly serious. He wasn't speaking in metaphor and he wasn't making a joke. At the very least he was alerting us to the idea that things we take for granted are sometimes not what they seem. Because time is connected to the earth's gravitational pull, time passes faster where gravity is weaker. It seems ludicrous, given our sense of the nature of time, to think that someone who lives at the top of a skyscraper ages slightly faster than someone who lives at ground level, but this is implicit in what Einstein asserted in his Theory of General Relativity.

And this is just one of an array of theories about time that, regardless of which ones you believe or which ones you regard as implausible, at the very least demonstrate that we cannot safely create any logical equation with time in it without running the risk of arriving at conclusions that are entirely false. Physicists differ with physicists about what time is; philosophers cannot agree among themselves; but the man in the street thinks he can tell the time by looking at a small mechanical device on his wrist. Our culture is all like that, and many of the ideas we take for granted are arrived at in much the same way.

Some physicists argue that there is no absolute concept of time, that it is purely a human construct and meaningless outside a narrow usage within human civilisations. Others argue that we construct both time and space from our sense of the relationships between things within the physical universe, and this changes under different conditions. Even within our internalised, circumstantial concept of time, our sense of a constant force derives entirely from the approximate conditions of the world we know, which is just one of billions, in each of which the natural laws may be utterly different. Other scientists claim a degree of success in proving that time does not necessarily always move forwards, that it can, in certain situations, travel backwards from the future. We call this 'science fiction', underlining just one of many examples of how the condescension of conventional wisdom creates fallacies that remain in the popular consciousness regardless of what science suggests.

There is an odd resonance between this thinking and what the Pope Benedict XVI says about eternity. In *Spe Salvi*, he wrote:

> 'Eternal', in fact, suggests to us the idea of something interminable, and this frightens us; 'life' makes us think of the life that we know and love and do not want to lose, even though very often it brings more toil than satisfaction, so that while on the one hand we desire it, on the other hand we do not want it. To imagine ourselves outside the temporality that imprisons us and in some way to sense that eternity is not an unending succession of days in the calendar, but something more like the supreme moment of satisfaction, in which totality embraces us and we embrace totality – this we can only attempt. It would be like plunging into the ocean of infinite love, a moment in which time – the before and after – no longer exists. We can only attempt to grasp the idea that such a moment is life in the full sense, a plunging ever anew into the vastness of being, in which we are simply overwhelmed with joy. This is how Jesus expresses it in Saint John's Gospel: 'I will see you again and your hearts shall rejoice, and no one will take your joy from you' (16:22). We must think along these lines if we want to understand the object of Christian hope, to understand what it is that our faith, our being with Christ, leads us to expect.

Conventional culture, in other words, forces us into a way of thinking that identifies a line, a kind of border, between this life and the next, when really Earth and Heaven exist in a continuum, approximately corresponding to what physicists call space-time. There is a line, but it exists neither in time nor in space, but rather as the horizon between the three-dimensional reality we see around us and the absolute dimension to which we also, simultaneously, belong. This means that every action, thought and word of ours occurs in both dimensions at once, resonating through space and time as well as falling like a raindrop in the three-second here and now. There is therefore no choice between doing things now or postponing them to the next life. Now is all there is, in this life or the next, though not in the three-second sense, but in an eternal sense of 'now' going on for ever. There is no future and no past. Everything we do we do for all time, for eternity, in the infinity of space to which we belong.

And this is what I already sense happening within myself. Perhaps it has always been happening, but now I have reason to be more aware of it, having less reason to be seduced by the culture of the street. I am drawn to the beauty of the world far more than I was when I had, in theory at least, decades to look at it. But I am filled, too, with a sense that it is only a shadow of the beauty that exists, that beyond this, somewhere, somehow, is the Beauty I have been searching for since the first time I opened my eyes.

— 15 —

Courtesy towards Christ

To introduce the name of Jesus Christ into a discussion, in the cultural conditions I have been describing as existing in today's Ireland, is to risk bringing all conversation to a sudden stop. It is not that the name itself is resented, but that it immediately sets off a short-circuit. Something has happened to the way that we speak about Christ that we cannot explain. It is as if the mention of Christ is an invitation to agree to something you cannot quite sign up to.

We know too much and not enough. We understand, or imagine we understand, ourselves too well. Our cultures create hermetically sealed logics which seduce us by their symmetry. Our self-defined understandings of our own natures seem increasingly plausible. Having detached ourselves from an absolute consciousnes of reality, it is difficult to go back to seeing ourselves in the old way, even if we have any sense of what the old way was like, and especially because there is no immediate reason to, and since by doing so we might have to surrender certain ideas about freedom. In the culture I speak of, the very name of Jesus has become contaminated by prejudices and fears that render it all but impossible to utter it without setting off the alarm bells that the culture has installed within our heads.

Language, again, lets us down here, because words in this context have become sclerotic and no longer enable us to get beyond the fossilised notions which, while seeming to contain what there is of the religious, the transcendent and the sacred, actually reject all our attempts to relate what is around us to something fundamental in ourselves. I believe that everyone is 'religious', whether aware of it or not, or like it or not, because religion is no more and no less than the total relationship with reality. I contrast this with the ideological view of reality, by which I mean a partial understanding, one that arrives at concepts of reality that appear coherent, and which allow the believer to move about within that reality in a fairly easy and familiar way, but which are nevertheless partial in that they deliberately exclude the full truth about human being across the spans of their lives, as well as excluding certain possibilities about what might be 'out there', even in the absence of certainty as to what, beyond what we 'know', is actually true.

'Religion', on the other hand, requires me to invite everything in, to open up to the whole of reality, a large element of which is mysterious and unknowable. We live in a culture that insists that reason involves only what is knowable, excluding the idea that, moment to moment, I must deal with things, like death and time, of which I have only the most partial understandings. Instead of trying to redefine these concepts to fit an ideological concept of reality, I must live with them as they are, hoping to understand more but accepting that they may well remain unknowable. For reasons that remain unclear, modern societies have jumped to the conclusion that advancing human knowledge, because it seems to undermine certain past formulations of the human attempt at self-description, is *ipso facto* opposed to the religious way of seeing things. Some religious people, reacting to this simplification, have developed a suspicion of science. But science itself is neutral, being no more than the pursuit of a natural curiosity about reality.

Some of the greatest scientists I know or know of have been or are deeply 'religious' in the purest sense. Their religious beliefs have provided no impediment to their searching for knowledge. Nobody ever suggested it should, except for a few frightened souls who think of Adam and Eve as literal history.

Science is simply the pursuit of knowledge, and this is self-evidently a good thing. What people often appear to be reacting against is an obscurantism associated with some religions, which encourage people to blinker themselves against knowledge for fear that it will unseat their present understandings. I do not believe this is religion at all, but merely a form of refuge for those who are so frightened by reality that they need to pin it down and put it in a box, another excellent working definition of ideology. An ideological understanding allows the human being to achieve coherence of a sort, but it closes down the relationship with infinite, absolute reality. The relationship with the infinite embraces a near infinite degree of unknowingness, which needs to be accompanied by humility, and this seems a difficult position for ideologues to adopt. There is a difference between the hunger for knowledge about what is not known or knowable and the idea of accepting that the unknowability of infinite reality implies a dependence, a weakness, a lack. To live in the consciousness of the Mystery is not a matter of simply being randomly or even systematically curious about it for the purposes of conquering it, but of accepting it while remaining open both to the possibility of more knowledge and also the inevitability that this knowledge will remain partial.

There is, so, nothing wrong with a thirst for knowledge. But there is, however, an important question in relation to demeanour: how do I accommodate what I learn within a schema that allows for my potential? Do I fight my unknowingness out of a misplaced sense of myself, or do I persist in my searching with a sense that I am defined by the Mystery and not by my potential to unscramble it? How, in other words, do I live with the knowledge that I am defined by these three characteristics: I am created; I am dependent; I am mortal?

No amount of knowledge of the external world is of any use if I do not achieve a similar level of understanding of myself, of my essential structure, of how I relate to reality, of what patterns emerge from this relationship and what these tell me about what I call my freedom. It is here that organised religion has focused its main attentions, sometimes clumsily but usually with the proper intention of offering to man the means to avoid the grief that comes from abusing his own freedom, which he is instinctually inclined to do. Thus, my relationship with reality is defined not merely by the vast expanse of the Mystery, but also by the internal dynamics that define my humanity, which is also mysterious. The details of our personalities and our functionality may change through time and culture, but we continue to be driven by a desire for something that does not appear to exist, or does not exist in what we can discover, but seems to draw us over the horizon towards what we cannot see. The idea, then, of 'living a good life' becomes not an obvious pursuit of freedom but a far more complicated engagement with the totality of the facts, external and internal.

All this is mere words, and God is beyond words, which renders the entire exercise as pointless as it is essential. This is the kind of paradox that the Mystery throws at us. Reality is reality. God is just another word, a tool for getting to grips with this. But it is a word that, used in a careful way, can be made to open up things rather than close them down.

Christ, the incarnation of God in our culture, is nowadays peripheralised in that culture, as much in language as in reality, indeed perhaps in reality because first of all in language. Except that He is not outrightly rejected, but placed in a cultural Limbo, a figure with whom we associate love and consolation and mercy, but not anything concrete to do with the present, with our natures as they are in this fleeting moment. The harangues of the disgruntled priests and religous-minded, far from driving us back to any sense of the absolute connection which Christ represents, merely confirm for us the correctness of our decision. For surely if Christ was as He seemed to be, then he would not associate Himself with such simplistic moral blackmail?

Reviewing in 1984 the volume *Letter to Olga*, the then recently published letters written to his wife from prison by Václav Havel, the German writer Heinrich Böll observed that Havel's book appeared to be the manifestation of a new form of religious expression, 'which out of courtesy no longer addresses God with the name which has been trampled underfoot by politicians'. Böll noted that Havel used careful constructions, such as 'absolute horizon' and 'spiritual order', rather than applying the name that is in general use, such as, he implied, 'God' or 'Christ'.

Havel had indeed wrestled with the subject in many of the letters. 'I have the feeling that something more than intellectualistic subterfuge is preventing me from admitting my belief in a personal God', he wrote to his wife. 'Something deeper is concealed behind these subterfuges: what I am lacking is that extremely important "last drop" in the form of the mystical experience of the enigmatic address and revelation. There is no doubt that I could substitute the word "God" for my "something" or for the "absolute horizon", and yet this does not seem to be a very serious approach.' He acknowledged his closeness to Christian feelings, and was pleased when others recognised this, but still he felt that one must choose one's words well. He baulked at the articulation of words that, though they might literally convey the reality of his belief, could also place him in a camp that would make him uncomfortable.

But although Havel avoided the intentional use of the word 'God', Böll concluded: 'I dare say that Christ is speaking in these letters, albeit a Christ who does not describe himself by that name and yet is still a Christ, and yet I must quickly erase this description again before those ever ready Christian drummer boys, representing their explosive version of Christianity, lay their hands on it.'

This is a perceptive description of the modern, or perhaps the postmodern dilemma in respect of accessing the absolute dimension. These phenomena of semantic confusion and evasion are replicated thoughout our culture: in the language we use, in the convolutions we engage in, in the irony we employ to deflect the gaze of the domineering culture that scruntinises our every gesture. It is even possible that this domineering culture is by now unmanned, in the sense that it is theoretically possible that each and every one of us is quietly looking out in search of the something else that defines us, while at the same time imagining ourselves to be alone in this forbidden search and more conscious, from the semantic definitions with which we grew up, of what we are not looking for than what we are. 'Our' cultures, in other words, may be on automatic pilot, dictating, imposing, oppressing, but ungoverned by actual living human beings. Human beings operate the culture and police its logic, but nobody any longer remains in control. The problem is a tangle of semantics rather than a hierarchy of authority. Each us has had his stock of hope diminished or defused, but each of us also contributes to the sabotage of the hope of others, because we refuse to bear witness to our own unique humanity.

Good Friday is the darkest day in the Irish Roman Catholic calender, the day that is all night. It is a remarkable commentary on the power of a Catholic childhood that, despite the moveability of the feast and the social changes that have in recent years rendered Good Friday largely indistinguishable from other days, at 3pm every Good Friday, no matter where I find myself, it grows dark all around my head. In ways beyond metaphor, the clouds gather and the sun shrivels away. Even if I should find myself sitting in Starbucks in the Dundrum Town Centre, the biggest shopping mall in Dublin, I will shiver a little and feel bereft. The death of the Saviour will assert itself as the remembrance of a real event and I will experience the horror all over again. This is the power of culture.

Remarkably, for much of my life, Easter Sunday has not for me had an equivalent religious power. Somehow, the meaning of Easter, as I apprehended it as a child and younger adult, seemed to derive more from myth than history. My impression, born of the culture, is that Easter represents a lifting of the shadow of the Crucifixion, but only in the sense that I feel permitted to cast off the sackcloth and embrace the spring, to live again in the world with a sense of undeserved reprieve. It is my favourite time, but mainly because it brings this sense of release and relief. I may have caused Christ to be crucified, but somehow He has gotten me off the hook. Whereas Good Friday is unambiguously religious, Easter Sunday in our culture feels more like a secular feast, a celebration of the fact that we have shaken off the guilt and gloom of religion. The chocolate eggs accentuate this feeling: a corrupted symbol of rebirth which diverts rather than deepens meaning. Good Friday reminds me of my mortal structure; Easter Sunday gives me permission to re-enter the constructs that man has built to deny his own nature.

A couple of years ago, talking to a Puerto Rican monsignor with an acute gift for simplicity, I found myself embarrassedly asking if he could explain to me the core meaning of Christianity. He urged me not to feel bad, since about 95 per cent of Christians do not understand Christianity either. He said that, a short time before, while lecturing in a Catholic seminary in the US, he had been approached by a young man, about to be ordained, who asked him a related but more specific question. He wanted to know the meaning of the Resurrection. The monsignor took him to a graveyard and picked a grave at random. The headstone indicated that a man, let us call him 'Daniel', was buried there. What, the monsignor asked the young seminarian, do we know of Daniel? The young man shrugged. 'We know', said the monsignor, 'that Daniel is dead; that his body is inert, his mind a void; that, even if we were to bring twenty dancing girls and have them cavort around his grave, Daniel would continue to display a radical disinterest in reality.'

On the evening of that first Good Friday, he went on, this is how it was with Jesus. But then, forty hours later, something happened that would change everything. Jesus came back to life. Let us be clear, he emphasised, Jesus began to breathe again, grew warm, started to move, re-engaged with reality, became interested in things around Him. Having been as dead as Daniel, He became, once again, as alive as we are. This too is history.

This, the monsignor told me, is both the meaning of the Resurrection and the central idea of Christianity: that death has no dominion, that beyond the end there is a new beginning. Christianity, he said, is the announcement to the world of the death of death.

In fifty years of immersion in a Catholic culture, I never heard it put like that. Although none of the story was new, I had never before quite grasped its meaning. In a life spent in Catholic churches and schools, reading Catholic periodicals, nobody had ever succeeded in communicating to me that the central message of Christianity is about hope beyond human imagining. If you had put me on the spot to explain the core of Christian belief, I would have mumbled something about Jesus dying for our sins. Why? Not sure, I would mumble and possibly flinch in anticipation of a clout on the ear for the outrage of being ignorant about the reasons Christ died for me. He had died for me and I could not even trouble myself to understand why!

This was my sense of Easter. Being responsible for the death of Jesus, I was relieved that He had managed to get out of the pickle I had got Him into.

I don't think I'm alone in this warped thinking. Something in the kind of Christianity we have inherited suggests that the point is to feel bad mostly, but occasionally to celebrate because, though we are unworthy, God is merciful and good. In its constant reiteration of rules, the Catholic Church in Ireland has seemed to forget that there is a need to tell people why, rather than out of blind obedience and some weird desire to be told how to live their lives, they might want to listen to its message. Very often those who are the voices of the Church fail to emphasise the most important part: that, once in history, 2,000 years ago, God came to earth as a man to demonstrate that death is a myth born of the limited human imagination.

Conscious that I am at least as badly damaged by the culture as anyone else, I have in recent times started to think differently about Christ. I cannot simply utter words that seem to invoke Him. I cannot imagine Him into being. How, then, can I acknowledge His existence? It is a paradox, but no worse than many I have to deal with every day. I wait for Him, but do not quite know what I am waiting for. I am waiting for whatever it is that my humanity asks for, and I see no particular reason not to call this Christ. I find it helpful, in the first instance, to think of Christ as an essence, a presence in reality, which defines what is there, not in the way we see it, but in terms of what lies behind – the Beauty for which the mountains and the beautiful women are but signs. This enables me to use the name of Christ in the way it is generally used, as an agreed cultural indicator of a transcendent being, without necessarily signing up to everything each of those who claim to follow Christ would seek to have me believe He stands for.

Recently I have found myself experiencing a strange and new perspective. I have taught myself to place myself in the situation of the Apostles Andrew and John, that first time they met Jesus, and then to think of this moment as if it were happening to me. I might be sitting having coffee with a friend and then find myself looking towards the spare chair at our table. I begin to think: 'What if somebody was to come now and sit here before us?' What matter of exceptionality would it take me to begin to understand that this was the Christ? What would He look like, in this moment now? Would he surprise me? In what way would he surprise me? Would he be dressed casually or would he wear a suit? Would he have a beard and would it be trimmed? Would his hair be long or short? – and so on. I try to enter into the feeling of Andrew and John and all those others who encountered Jesus Christ. What would it take in another human being to strike me sufficiently to convey the true drama I was witnessing? And of course this is beyond my imagination. I cannot imagine somebody who is both a man and a God; I cannot think of how this might manifest itself.

I realise this is a fairly improbable scenario. I do not rule it out, but it seems unlikely. For me, however, there is a necessity for another kind of encounter, if not with the person of Jesus then certainly with what I undertand Jesus to represent, the Presence of the Mystery in three-dimensional reality, an encounter with Christ in the culture of the moment.

In spite of my best efforts and what I think of as my infinite openness, Christ remains for me an idea. Although I have, after many years of searching, the desire to meet Him, I have not yet actually done so. I have met many people who have met Him, or who have told me they have met Him, but I am reasonably certain that, for me, He remains an abstraction. Listening to many of those people who told me of their encounter with Jesus, I remained unconvinced by the literal content of their descriptions, and yet conscious from their demeanour that they had indeed encountered something exceptional. I believe this had more to do with language than anything intrinsic to the experience they were seeking to relate. I did not doubt that they had come to know Christ, but was unable to glean from their talking about this anything that would take me to the place where they had met Him. It was as though the words fell apart as soon as they parted the lips of the speaker, and could not be reintegrated as they reached my ears. Even worse, I noticed in myself a tendency to pretend that I understood when I did not, to imply in my demeanour and body language a sharing of the experience, which in fact remained mysterious to me.

As a child I had been given what I had imagined to be a profound relationship with Christ. Growing up in the Ireland of the 1960s, I was a devout and pious boy. I loved Jesus, or so I resolved. How could I not? It would have been impossible not to love this perfect Being, this Beautiful Jesus who had died to save me. And yet, on the threshold of adulthood, seduced by the freedoms of the world, I had turned my back on this Jesus. This turning away was accompanied by considerable emotion on my part, mostly anger at the abuses I perceived in the administration of Christianity in my own culture, though there were other emotions as well: relief, guilt, excitement, trembling.

It strikes me now that I never once attached any of the anger I felt to the person of Jesus, never once had a negative thought about

Him, never once felt that I should blame Him for anything. This is interesting, because I don't think I am alone in this. Strangely, although our modern, once Christian cultures have turned their backs on Jesus, they have never actually rejected Him. Despite the many harsh things said against faith, religion, Church and Bible, there is almost no suggestion in our cultures that Jesus was anything other than an exceptional Being.

We cannot look at Him, but still we do not condemn or castigate Him. None but the most insistent, and often the most demonstrably damaged secularising voices in our cultures do not, as a rule, attack the person of Christ, or suggest that He was not who He claimed to be. Usually, they attack the authority or record of those who through history have claimed to speak for Christ. Despite everything, the icon that is Christ remains intact in our culture – venerated by some, but quietly respected even by those who deny belief in or adherence to the Christian proposal. This is strange and interesting.

It is as though the impulse towards freedom has required us to turn away from Him, but that we have done so with a degree of reluctance, of regret. In fact, if you were to try to identify the central emotion that governs our present rejection of Christ, you would possibly fix not on something like anger or contempt, but rather on something close to shame. We are ashamed of our rejection of Jesus, but our desire for freedom seems to give us no alternative, because He had become so inextricably linked to the former culture of oppression and denial. What resentment we have towards Him is like the resentment of a child towards a mother who does not instantly embrace him, even though, in his fear of something, he is trying to kick her shins. Perhaps she is waiting for him to calm down a little, but this pause seems to exacerbate the tantrum and so extend the moment. Only when the boy tires does an embrace become possible.

This suggests that the processes of secularisation and what I call 'de-absolutisation' are in certain senses quite disconnected. On the secularising surface, there is this repugnance of the record of Christian stewardship in the world. In many respects this is easily recognisable as an alibi for the pursuit of forms of freedom which have been identified as contrary to the Christian statute (it would be foolish to deny that the accusations levelled at institutional Christianity have, here and there at least, considerable merit). But underneath this desire for an alibi is a continuing affection for the person of Jesus, an admiration for his life and his teachings, a desire for whatever it is that, in Christian thought and culture, Christ equates to in the life of mortal beings.

But there are difficulties. One is that, as I have observed, this affection is unconnected in our conventional cultures to any sense of an absolute significance to be associated with the person of Christ. The other is that, even when the process of exploration begins tentatively to assert itself, as it has in me, the possibility of meeting Christ in modern culture seems remote. Deep in ourselves, we know that, in our burst for freedom, we have left something vital behind. But now we are as refugees from our own misconception of what it means to be free. We look around wistfully at the figure of Christ, still there in our imaginations, but cannot find a way of reintroducing ourselves. We have not walked away, at least not entirely, and yet we cannot bring ourselves to simply engage in what, to the profound blindness that feels like omniscience, seems the charade of embracing the figure from whom we are voluntarily estranged. And even if we could find the willingness, the humility, to do this, we cannot find the words.

The Beautiful Christ still haunts us, but the culture we have created so as to pursue our own sense of freedom has sabotaged the channels by which we might hope, in harmony with the deep longing within ourselves, to recommence this most fundamental friendship of all.

— 16 —
A Language to Hope In

Nuala O'Faolain had spoken many times for a particular generation of Irish women, and in the end she spoke for several generations of Irish people, men and women, who have imagined for themselves an abyss in consequence of pursuing the failed hypothesis that humankind can live without God. The despair she expressed is the despair of a generation which imagined it could establish a utopia of reason free from the encumbrances of tradition and the dread of the absolute. What she described so perfectly in this moment when she had nothing to lose is the abyss that our culture has created for us, the abyss that we have conjured up out of some fatalistic, pessimistic, joyless perception of ourselves. We look in the mirror and we see hopelessness. A society speaking of progress and happiness for its people through time can imagine nothing but oblivion for the individual human being.

Most of the time, people who know they are close to death are either too distracted by illness, too medicated or too engrossed in prayer to come out and put words on the moment. Nuala applied to the process of dying the same talkativeness she had applied to so many things in her public life, but afterwards we insisted on patronising her to, as it were, death. People talked afterwards of her 'honesty' and 'courage', but what moved me was not so much her honesty as her articulateness about despair. What she did really was make visible the feelings that lie in wait for any of us in the culture we have helped to create. This culture is functional in many ways to do with what we think of as living, but is a bad culture to be dying in.

We call it reason, but it is not that at all. What, remotely, might be the reasonable basis for the idea that the answer to the question that is humanity might be a void, an abyss? How reasonable is it to believe that, after chasing illusions all our lives, we face the dark alone? How, driven by the deepest desires of the human heart, can we reject such a miraculous incidence of correspondence between the question of the human heart and the answers contained in the stories and traditions we have inherited? What, other than a life-denying pessimism, could have convinced us that the accounts handed to us through history, verified along the way by countless human beings much like ourselves, is not the most persuasive evidence concerning the meaning of human existence? How can we gaze on the beauty of the world and imagine that this is all there is, that this is possible because it is, but nothing else is possible because we cannot see how? Perhaps we can arrive at such a conclusion, but it is not reasonable. It is pessimism, pure and simple. It is despair.

And it is not what our hearts tell us. Beating within us, our hearts bear witness, second by second, to the idea that there is hope beyond the hope we can rummage through, the flimsy hopes of the marketplace that draw us to themselves and then dissolve in our hands, before our eyes. If this is all there is, why do we continue?

The wonder in our hearts knows that there is more than what we see and hear and touch and taste. For such deep-set hopes to be merely imagined, conjured up, an invention of a self-deluding human intelligence, is not merely unthinkable, but actually unreasonable. For the human heart to nourish the hopes it does and for these to be baseless, delusional, would be a betrayal of nature of unparalleled proportions. Nowhere in nature do we encounter such a betrayal.

Reason belongs not just to the head, to logic and proof, but to the heart also, to the fruits of experience, to feeling, intuition, instinct. When we recognise this, faith becomes not merely reasonable, but an acknowledgment of what is – excepting nothing, postponing nothing, ascribing nothing to chance. Our culture's prevailing reduction of reason leads us to deconstruct not just our beliefs but also our capacity to trust and hope.

Almost everything we do involves faith. Faith, therefore, is the greater part of reason, because to reason is to live in the light of infinity, totally connected with reality, accepting what exists and seeking to live in accordance with everything we truly know, which is so much more than we think.

A cosmic detective might say that mankind had a strong motive for inventing God, whether God existed or did not. In a way, it doesn't matter. These arguments do not reach conclusions that serve any purpose for man in his need. If my reason tells me I have a need for something greater, I do not solve my dilemma by deciding that this something does not exist. By doing so, I resolve, ever so quietly and deep within myself, to wind up my existence, and to convey to my descendants that they should not bother with these questions.

In the main, atheistic objections to the God hypothesis seem to centre on cultural notions of probability – is it likely that God would behave as religious culture would have us believe? It is possible for even deeply religious people to have sympathy with elements of this outlook, but generally they allow themselves to perceive the content of religion as the material that has emerged in human cultures to enable the limited human imagination to know what is essential.

Of the two possibilities – God or no God – only one serves my need. I have therefore two good reasons for adhering to its logic: it is useful and it does nothing to contradict my sense of my humanity. Already the cosmic detective may be coming to the conclusion that, since there is no smoking gun, this case will be decided on the circumstantial evidence. But he must examine all the evidence and test each hypothesis in the light of man's reason, and not just the parts that render themselves easy to measure and count.

Let us postulate that the idea of God is simply an imaginative mechanism of mankind to simplify the great questions of human existence, the mysterious and unknowable aspects of reality that define us and yet cannot be seen or understood. Let us put aside, for the moment, the idea of Christ, leaving the issue of its validity or meaning for another time. It is possible, then, to see that, quite apart from what anyone thinks of religion in general or any specific religion in particular, there is an imaginative problem in a society which seeks to remove religion from public sight and public discussion. What happens to such a society is not that it finds some new kind of language to embrace the great questions in its new-found 'rational' belief system, but that the mysterious and unknowable elements of reality disappear from the conversations by which the society and its members seek to understand their human journeys.

The 'truth' of 'God' is beyond description. But if, in an attempt to combat the rational-atheistic logic, which inevitably closes down not merely the issue of God but also the semantic path to the absolute dimension, you suggest that religion is simply a metaphorical way of summoning up the unknowable, you are in difficulty with religious people who insist that their beliefs are literal and anyone who claims to believe in God but seeks to fudge the specifics is actually worse than those who lay claim to no beliefs at all. There is something in this viewpoint, but not enough to overcome the urgency that the preent moment presents for those who seek above all to restore our culture's capacity for openness in the interests of their children. Specificity is essential to even limited comprehension of what matters, but the problem with specificity is that it provides also the straw men for the pseudo-rationalists to knock down. The knocking down, then, becomes the total event in the eyes of a culture with little capacity for poetry or mystery.

I have never had a supernatural experience. I do not really understand what mysticism is. I know almost nothing of theology, and to be honest most of it bores me stiff. I am not good at praying. My back goes up at the slightest sign of piety. Many religious people annoy me tremendously with their pat assumptions about what the idea of my believing implies. I resist with every fibre of my being the clubbability of what is called faith, and the sense believers often give off that all this is obvious. To me it is not obvious. To me, in the culture I must live in, the idea that there is no God is more 'obvious' than the idea that there is. But this is my problem: this answer does not satisfy me, at any level of my humanity. My attention is therefore directed to the question of how our cultures decide what is obvious and what is not.

Because, of course, I am part of this culture, or perhaps I should say that it is part of me – I too am infected by the national pessimism. How could it be otherwise?

Sometimes, as I have explained, I feel great sorrow at the prospect of the loss of the beauty of this world, however qualified this may have been or may yet become by virtue of the pain inflicted on me by reality and the absence of a consistent and central sense of meaning. I have in recent years felt such an acute increase in my sense of this pain of impending loss that I wonder if I will be able to bear it all if it increases to any significant extent. My intellectual and sometimes emotional acceptance of the reasonable probability that there is more to existence than I encounter in this reality can sometimes be eroded by a sudden incursion of despair, or a sense of pointlessness, or even occasionally a sense that, no matter what happens in the next life, it cannot be better than this one is, right here, right now.

When I think about it in such moments, I too am unpersuaded by the versions of the afterlife on offer, not necessarily by their probability, possibility or even plausibility, but by the detail of them, the sense of – to take the most crude and banal example – walking around on clouds for ever, being nice to everyone in a rather bland and, frankly, sickening way. I can imagine worse things, but still none of the standard tableaux seem to me to be worth the trouble of achieving them.

I wonder if, in heaven, I will be able to tell someone to fuck off if they are annoying me, or if I will be past annoyance and will be able to tolerate the kind of people I am now moved to cross the road from when I see them drawing near. Or, I think about Saint Peter manning the gate and imagine him like one of those guards you see at Dublin airport who stop people with black skin but give me a wink because they recognise me from the telly and nod me on without even glancing at my passport.

All this, of course, is nonsensical. I know that, whatever comes after, it will be nothing like what I know now, and nothing like the mind I have now is capable of contemplating, and nothing like any of the things the words I am capable of using are capable of evoking for myself or anyone else. I sense that my present thoughts are like the caterpillar in comparison to the butterfly. If there is a language in heaven, it will not square up to or bite into reality in the way our languages do in this dimension.

But, trapped in my earthly logic, I have enough sense by now to know that if I allow these undoubted facts to govern my relationship with my ultimate destiny and its meaning, I will come to conclusions that fall far short of what my humanity at play in reality tells me is possible without showing me how.

So, all these words are pointless? Perhaps; perhaps not. At the very least you have to admit that words are all we have. We cannot know God, if He exists, if He is the right word. Our attempts to invoke or describe this reality must necessarily be worse than pathetic, but we have nothing else to work with. Words are pretty much all we have to think, to imagine with.

I do not think the words exist to say the things my mind is incapable of formulating about God and the meaning of human existence. I am caught with my desire on the one hand and on the other the sense that in order to create a harmonious connection between this desire and all earthly reality, I need to construct something that might be termed a set of beliefs. I cannot even think about my own total reality because most of the language I can locate to do it in has already been colonised and/or discredited.

I need a language to hope in. I need words to express my infinite longing that do not make me sound mad, superstitious, reactionary or stupid. It's not that I care what people think of me. I really don't, or at least not as much as I did once. When I was younger (there I go again!) I used to care what my peers thought of me, mainly writers, artists, left-wingers – all people who had the best of reasons for taking up certain stances against the way things used to be. There was a time when for me the scorn of such people would have been among the worst things imaginable. But now I care less and less, because the questions concerning my place in reality and what my ultimate destination might be are much bigger than any consideration of fashionability or acceptability.

I ask these questions not because I have suddenly capitulated to conservatism in middle age (perhaps I have, but, if so, it is an unrelated phenomenon) or because I am terrified of the Last Judgement or preparing for the next life. No, I ask them because I have to, because the need to understand myself to the fullest extent that I can before it is too late exceeds any other consideration, even the friendship of those whose love I still crave. I wish it were otherwise, but that's the way I find myself.

This is as frightening as anything about death. It seems I am destined to step out of the culture, or, even worse, to remain in it while seeing through its insubstantiality, but still unable to make out what lies beyond.

I don't 'believe'. I can't. If believing is just gritting my teeth and adhering to some proffered concept of what is and might be, I cannot do it. If a 'faith' is merely a collection of people, a club, in which everybody affirms everybody else, and together they affirm a set of dogmas that have been agreed long before by others, then count me out. Unless my 'faith' accords with the knowledge derived through my own existence, it is not faith at all, but blind acceptance of an ideology. Faith is knowledge.

The paradox of this is that, somewhere along the way there must be a leap of something – I almost said 'faith' but that would be a tautology, a short in the circuit of reason. But then I know, too, that I cannot reason my way to certainty, or heaven, or the certainty of heaven. I cannot reason myself into the arms of Christ. There will always be a gap between my train of thought and my sense of a destination. The question is: do I take this gap as absolute, in the sense that my capacity to think in a straight line of logic is unable to cross it; or do I simply come to rest alongside it and wait for something to happen? My life has been not a line but a circuitous journey, which brings me back to where I began. After all my voyaging, I lie down in the spot on which I was baptised, the spot on which I cried and kicked at the coldness of the water.

For all the difficulties and horrors associated with this, the fact is that Ireland has long been a Catholic society, which means that it depends for its very life on the tradition, however imperfect, that we know as Catholicism. The language we depend on to perceive ourselves in our totality is therefore a language forged in the culture of Catholicism. We, as Christians, are bequeathed a belief that the Mystery, in a disposition of mercy, became flesh and presented Himself as the answer to death and despair. It is all but impossible, in conventional discourse, to separate this from the debris of piety and power-play and see it for what it is: our most vital guiding idea, the source of the hope-beyond-hope that, as human beings, we most desperately crave and depend on.

Catholicism, then, comes after the fact of my religion. I am not religious because I am a Catholic, but Catholic because I am religious. My need for religion is like my need for air, and comes from approximately the same region of my body: my heart, nestling beside my lungs.

Religion has to do with my natural structure, my createdness/creature-ness, my intrinsic desires, my dependence, my mortality, and my relationship with reality, pregnant with evidence of the Mystery that defines me. I call myself a Christian because for me this Mystery has at its centre the Presence of Christ, Lord of History. I am not an incidental phenomenon, randomly arrived and soon to depart, but an intrinsic part of infinite reality, my identity unbounded by the three-dimensional impediments or the laws and principles that govern this physical realm. That I am part of infinite time and space is a description of my very nature.

There is a hope inside me that is bigger than what the world thinks of as me, that overwhelms me with confidence and optimism and that rests its heavy expectation upon the light that it has placed just beyond my sight, beyond the horizon of human understanding. My desire tells me of the promise Christ made, a promise that something is always coming, something is always happening, something is always waiting for me just as I am always waiting for it. Nothing I can see, hear, touch or smell comes near to satisfying this desire.

Catholicism comes into this because I was born a Catholic and, after years of running away, I decided that the specificity of this cultural experience is vital to my sense of Christ, the Mystery incarnate. Because there is this distance, this disproportionality, between what I hope for and what I can find in this dimension, I have in the past tended to shift around the place, mooching for a correspondence. Belatedly, it came to me: the optimal position resides in what is, in the specificity of what is there, which implicitly has been given for a reason. Our culture seduces us to think of what might be elsewhere, or different, or other. But the Other is already here, where we are, right now.

Our cultures do not understand what freedom is, defining it as the ability to do as we please, blind to man's experience which consistently reveals that this avenue of exploration leads ultimately to disgust and disaster. Real freedom resides beyond our reach, like a shape floating in the corner of the eye. Only in repose do we begin to discern its shape.

For all kinds of reasons to do with such corrupted notions of both religion and freedom, our cultures have been led to believe that religion is something imposed, and therefore something that can be discarded at will, in order to be more 'free'. This is impossible, because religion is an original essence of the human being. You can, of course, claim you have 'moved beyond it', as I did for nearly twenty years, but this won't change your fundamental structure. Religion is not a choice, but a fact. We may choose to identify ourselves outside the embrace of formal religion, but this changes nothing. Our natures remain.

Even if it were possible to shake off this essence, it would be an act of self-destruction. I am not a Hindu or a Buddhist. If you have a path, why waste time looking for one? I see no point in fighting the Catholic Church any more than I might think it a good idea to fight the air or kick a tree. Neither do I see the church as a refuge or a club, or a political party, still less a source of moral guidance. The church is a place I look to in order to maintain a structured engagement with the Mystery and also in my need for a source of reflective experience of the human condition.

Belonging to the church doesn't for me relate to any social or political circumstance, but to my fundamental humanity and destiny, to my relationship with reality and with Infinity, which is just another word for Mystery. This, not Catholicism *per se*, is my religious identity.

There is another virus in our culture today, equally deadly to the human spirit, which separates believing from knowing. This became manifest in the idea that religion comprises the action of going into some room, even a very big room, getting on your knees, scrunching up your brain in an attempt to 'believe' something, and then entering a hostile world holding this quality of 'faith' in front like a shield. But faith is not an irrational leap in the dark; it is the reasonable response to the real.

Reality is God-given. It therefore cannot be hostile to God, except in a superficial sense usually arising from the operation of man-made elements of reality. For example, modern man's inability to accept the limits of his own structure has created conditions of thought in our cultures which are hostile to the idea of a God. But reality *per se* is neither antagonistic nor neutral towards someone seeking to connect with the infinite dimension of being. If I stay for long enough in reality with the questions that come teeming from my heart, the answers become visible. Reality cannot, by definition, be other than sympathetic to my essential condition, which is religious.

Faith, then, is the force that animates my total humanity, that allows me to stand up straight against gravity and wait in hope for what is promised. 'Believing' doesn't come into it. Faith is know-ledge, which derives from experience of the promise with which reality is pregnant. Faith is no more than honesty before reality. What do I see? Where did it come from? And then, where did I come from? What or who made me? What makes me now, in this moment, if I do not make myself? Sooner or later, the true intelli-gence arrives at God, because God is what intelligence derives from.

Religion involves not some esoteric engagement with the mystical, but the prosaic process of going into the great outdoors knowing what I am engaged in and open to seeing what is there. I cannot 'believe' in God by looking at reality – I can only know that He is. This is a reasonable inference – the only reasonable one – from reality and my deepest experience of it.

I cannot merely hope. That alone would not sustain me. Hope must be connected to the proceses of reason, or it cannot survive. Hope without reason is like a bucket with a hole in the bottom. It holds nothing.

What is hope anyway? Hope is the force within me that keeps me going, the light that must never go out or else I'm halfway to being dead.

What then? Knowledge. I don't 'believe'. I know. I know there is a force that equates to my concept of creation, and I am happy to call this God. I know there is a Beyond, which I am happy to call heaven. I know Jesus came from this Beyond and I feel fairly sure He was who He told us He was. He didn't lie about anything else.

He wasn't confused about anything else. His words remain, every one, as clear and vital as in the moments he uttered them. In the 'modern' world, with its sense of perpetually 'going forward', all this seems increasingly implausible. But if it is, any use of my deeper intelligence must alert me to the problems with the thought process which have arrived at this sense of implausibility, because nothing else I have heard has seemed to offer the answers this story does.

Such thinking seems an affront to 'rationality'. Perhaps it is. But the false rationality our cultures conventionally employ present us with a false choice: belief in things that are demonstrable only, or superstition. The problem is that believing only in what is demonstrable leaves vast gaps in my knowledge and self-understanding. And no matter how much I 'know', in 'rational' terms, there is still the Mystery, not least the mystery of myself. I can sit here writing and take myself for granted: a machine-like entity performing the obvious and banal task of making marks on a page. Or I can detach myself from this, and indeed from what I think of as myself, and observe the astonishing nature of what is happening. I step outside my body and contemplate myself. Who is this strange but familiar figure crouched over this white machine? Where did he come from to arrive here. Why? No matter how often these questions are rubbished or otherwise disposed of, they remain as the core and most vital thoughts of my being. No matter how much I distract myself or bury myself in the logics of the man-made world, they continue to jump up into my consciousness when I least expect it.

Either God made the world or He did not make the world. There are no other possibilities. If I decide He did not make the world, I have to come up with a better explanation, and this has for millennia taxed more practised minds than mine. I need, just to exist, a working hypothesis of reality in its totality, and only the God hypothesis gives me that. Without the concept of God, then, I am disconnected from reality, from my infinite circuitry, and am, by definition, unfree.

If I know, which I do, that there is more to reality than what I see, hear and touch, I need some affirmation, some structural entity that will make that relationship real. In the culture that I live in, this means the Christian proposal.

The Christian event is not a story, not history, not a morality tale, but an event of this very moment. The Resurrection happens moment to moment before our eyes, but in our pessimism we look and see nothing but randomness. Christianity cannot really be transmitted by theologians, only by witnesses who see clearly and describe what is there.

This is where Catholicism figures in my life. The church is where I go to be educated about my deeper structure and nature, and where I find companionship for the journey towards my destination. The Church fails me most of the time, as I fail myself most of the time, but without it I might be alone in a culture that denies my nature at every turn. The trouble is: if I am disposed to place my faith in the Great Hope, then the shopkeepers and innkeepers and prostitutes have a problem selling me things that may momentarily strike me as the answer to the question my humanity exudes.

Most people cannot even approach this fundamental truth about themselves because the initial access from our culture needs to be achieved through language, which has been booby-trapped by a ideological war waged on the one hand by a faction too 'modern' and 'intelligent' to give any credence to the idea that that man is fundamentally religious, and on the other by those calling themselves religious-minded, who have fuelled what is called secularism by holding faith up as a moral shield against the world. Between these two warring sides most of us have to find the true essence of our humanity.

So it is good and useful to have a club to go to. It gives me, sometimes, a sense of other people struggling with the same things, although sometimes it pushes me towards a short circuit and I resist that with every atom of my being. I will be standing or sitting there trying to imagine myself in my infinite dimension, and someone will utter something that doesn't ring true, or which sounds like a platitude, or smacks of trying to control other people's lives by foisting upon them some half-baked idea of what they should or should not be doing in the middle of the night. It is in moments like this, more than in any moments of introspection, that I am seized by doubt, by a feeling that, if the consolation of religion did not already exist, we would have to invent it.

The writer I love more than any other is Franz Kafka. The most beautiful book I have read is *The Trial*, the first sentence of which reads: 'Somebody must have been telling lies about Josef K. because, without having done anything wrong, he was arrested one fine morning'. These twenty-one words prefigure not just the novel, but an entire age, prophesying the era of the ism, in which guilt or innocence could no longer be decided on facts, but became a matter of ideological conformity. I think of Kafka as an Angel of Mystery, a strange, unearthly spectre come to make us shudder at what we take for granted and give us new words to understand the space between us and the Mystery. Josef K., the protagonist of *The Trial*, is Kafka, but also me and perhaps also you. Imbued with a craving for reason and justice, he inhabits a world in which such concepts provoke hilarity and suspicion. In the end he is brought to face the inevitability of his error: the absence of reason is itself reasonable; his insistence, in this dimension, on the existence of justice is absurd. In a time when we are more and more subject to rule by a nightmare of senselessness – bureaucracy, arbitrary power, political correctness, tribunals – the character of Josef K. embodies the spirit of an age in which nobody can any longer claim to be innocent because anyone may be deemed guilty at any time.

Don Giussani, in his book *The Risk of Education*, quotes from Kafka's *The Silence of Mermaids, Posthumous writings and fragments, 1917–1924*: 'There is a point of arrival but no way to get there.'

This is what it adds up to. I see the path. It makes sense from my starting point, which is my desire that there be a destination and that it be the one that will finally quieten the crying inside me. Because I desire it so much, it cannot fail to exist, because otherwise this world and my place in it represent a betrayal of my desire such as appears to be unprecedented. And so I could not trust my desires to tell me anything else. I could not be sure that I am hungry or lonely or tired, for fear that my desires, again, were misleading me.

I have a burning desire for an absent good whose shape I can apprehend from the knot of desire within me. I am a black hole into which the heavens have imploded, filling me with their expectation but denying me their pleasures. When I go through the process we call death, the heavens will unleash themselves from my belly and I will be free once again.

Meanwhile, I walk in a kind of daze, seeking the destination that all the while is inside me, because this is my only sense of what a journey is. In a mist beyond me I make out the shape of the destination, but the path seems to break down some way ahead. For the moment I can keep on walking, but perhaps there will be a time, in the future, when I will encounter a ravine. I may have to jump it. I don't know. But for now I keep on walking. From time to time I glimpse the path entering the gates of the castle which I recognise as my destination. Will the path break down before I get there, or after that? I don't know. I keep walking. I see someone rushing past, making for the same place. The gate ahead appears to open. I hurry onwards, but the gate seems no closer.

This is faith. Perhaps tomorrow there will be no path, but today there is. This is hope.

Without this there is only consolation, the drowning out of the distant howling of the wind in the abyss. Entertainment, art, what is called 'nature', all these can provide such consolation. And so can religion, presented just a semitone off-key.

The word 'consolation' itself already implies a lie: something dreamed up to compensate for the loss of the true prize. If faith is consolation, it is a lie, perhaps a greater lie than the pessimism it seeks to supplant, because instead of turning away from hope, it mocks and parodies hope to its face, patronising it to death.

Imagine yourself in an old, disused building, perhaps the ruin of a church. You are looking around when you hear a noise overhead. You look up and see, flying among the rafters, a bird. He has blundered in from outside, perhaps through a broken window, and now cannot get out. You watch him for a while. Sometimes, he flies about, seemingly without a pattern, swooping low into the belly of the building. Sometimes he rests, looking about him curiously. Sometimes he tries to get back outside, making lunges at the light he sees blinking through cracks in the roof. Then he reverts to flying. In the end he gets away, perhaps through an open door, and is gone.

This is the way for a human life in our culture. We watch each other come and go, but nothing makes sense. There is no pattern to be seen in the lives of others, or even in our own, other than an alternation of swooping and the crazed search for escape. In the end we seem to disappear as pointlessly as we appear to have arrived.

This is not the truth about us, but it is what our culture has decided and what it whispers to us every waking moment. This is a problem of knowledge.

It seems strange, in the midst of the information age, to be talking about knowledge as a 'problem'. We are bombarded with information: 24-hour news, and instant access to facts on the internet. Never in the history of the planet was so much knowledge available to mankind. True knowledge, though, is not just fact, but fact accompanied by meaning. It arrives into a context where it fills a waiting gap, and there is a 'ping!' of recognition as the knowledge goes to its place in the working hypothesis of an evolving self-understanding. This is largely absent from our information age. Because we have forbidden ourselves a total hypothesis, we learn things without ever knowing them. Something may be absorbed, understood and recorded, but its meaning is held in abeyance, as though we are waiting for the primary facts to be decided upon before we know what to do with this new information. We 'know' many things, but we do not know what they mean, where they fit in our reasons. We therefore merely use fragments to fill the void with rationalisations of our pessimism.

This process may not have been the occurrence of a single moment. Perhaps it started with the Enlightenment, perhaps it began at the moment when human culture started to whip itself up to a speed for the first time faster than the speed at which the species itself was developing. Perhaps it happened with the invention of television or the development of the mass media society.

However or whenever it began to happen, it is as if our sense of knowledge has flipped over, that having pursued an understanding of the world from the point of total unknowing, we have, on the basis of a few modest insights into the way reality works, inferred from these understandings that total understanding would soon be ours. On the collateral of a little knowledge, we have taken out a mortgage on all possible knowledge and, in effect, decided that we already, in a certain sense, 'know' everything.

We caught a glimpse of the possibility of the total mastery of reality through knowledge. It was not that we really 'knew' everything, or even imagined we did, but that our demeanour started to imply that we had. Knowledge had been devolved to human ownership. The Mystery was no longer 'The Mystery' but was redefined as the Unknown, which implied that it was potentially within the control of man, in the same way as The Future had become Going Forward. In this demeanour, everything that remains unknowable is an affront to our sense of ourselves.

Man's sense of his own place within reality changed: although his knowledge of things had grown only marginally, he was already, in his own mind, at the centre of his own existence, seeking dominion over everything. Because he had eliminated from his thinking the idea of a creator, he sought meaning now not from some coherent chronology of order that centred on his own existence, but randomly in a reality that seemed to have no purpose. His search was defined therefore not by a quest for a greater understanding of his own place in reality – a matter already decided – but by curiosity of a narrow and almost abstracted type.

Man became more and more successful at discovering things, but less so at understanding the meaning of his own life. Because the acquisition of knowledge was no longer a matter of understanding his relationship to the Mystery, but of building on his growing sense of his own potential omnipotence, the sense of exultation that knowledge had once bestowed began to wane. There was all this information, but it did not necessarily fit into any pattern that could be acknowledged. It was tentative, provisional. The fields of knowledge had become fragmented and disconnected from one another and from any overall pattern that could be described or defined. Man was waiting to break the codes of the universe, and expected a breakthrough any day now. His sense of suspension was merely a symptom of his impending omnipotence, and so could be lived with for a while.

But, implicit in the whole exercise was a weakening of man's sense of his own meaning, and therefore of his motivation, his will to live.

In pursuit of the freedom to break the laws that had governed him, but which he had become convinced were arbitrary and gratuitous, he had struck out in great waves of adventuring. But, having untied himself from the taut entanglement with infinity, his freedom resulted not in a greater autonomy but in the slackness and wriggling of a worm cut in two. No longer stretched between the non-existent poles of Eternity and Infinity, the freedom he found gave him nowhere to go but, rather, imprisoned him within the narrow dimensions of time and space. He turned inwards to the core of his own mind, but here found that, though his thoughts seemed to mimic the vastness of the universe, these were but abstractions and games, without an end, without a purpose, a fizzling of energy that died in time. Man, 'free' at last, could not think of anything he really wanted to do with himself. His freedom bored him because it had no purpose outside itself.

It is as though modern man has lost some essential element of his own being, as if some vital part of his mechanism had fallen out and had not been missed. And, without this part, nothing made sense, and the more information he gleaned, the less sense it all made. Having pulled down the heavens and erected a ceiling of his own, man walked about with a kind of stoop, his own sense of pointlessness bearing down on him. His children grew like flowers in a chimney, somehow undernourished, seeing something up above them – a movement, a flash – that drew their attention, but pessimistic as to its capacity to answer their needs. In the end it seemed to have gone away, and soon they would go too.

In *The Salt of the Earth*, a book-length interview with Cardinal Ratzinger by Peter Seewald, published originally in German in 1996, Seewald asks his subject about the idea that it might ever again be considered 'modern' to live the Catholic faith, 'even if, when examined closely, it actually appears as the most non-conforming, wide awake and radical lifestyle that could be imagined in the present circumstances'.

It is hard to imagine any proposition seeming less plausible to our present culture, which perceives all religion as imposing on freedom, and Catholicism as especially 'reactionary' in this regard.

Ratzinger responded: 'Many consider the Church to be an outdated and fossilized system which has become constantly more isolated and inflexible, creating around itself a defensive shell which is crushing its own life. Such is the impression of a large number. Not many manage to perceive that, on the contrary, it holds something surprisingly new for them, something daring and generous which entails a rupture with the routine habits of life. However, it is precisely those who have had to endure the full brunt of modernity who discover this.'

It is an interesting phrase: 'those who have had to endure the full brunt of modernity'. Only when we have explored to our fullest satisfaction the option of freedom as presented to us in conventional culture can we turn, usually in considerable pain, to look at the laws that make our experiences inevitable, and this, we tend to find, broadly corresponds with what the Church has been saying. I do not say this to vindicate the Church, nor do I say it with any sense of satisfaction. It just happens to be observably true. There is a significant part of my being that still wishes it otherwise, that still wishes the Church wrong about everything.

I am sometimes inclined to venture out again, just to see if perhaps I have been doing things wrongly or misunderstanding something fundamental about myself, to see if perhaps I might be able to find what I am looking for in the places my instincts lead me to. When, from time to time, I do this, the outcome is always the same as before. I make another tick in my notebook and hope that I am one tock closer to a final understanding.

It is not that I have grown tired and wish to submit myself to some authority that will take away my choice and freedom and quieten my desiring. I am not a good penitent. I feel no sense of smugness or *schadenfreude* to find myself in the company of virtuous people. I am turned off by a strain in almost all organised religions, and strikingly in the more traditionalist strains of Irish Catholicism, which seem to glory in the vindication of seeing people brought to their knees. I have no sense of being a prodigal son come home to be feasted. I shudder a little when someone congratulates me for 'returning to the faith'. I have returned noplace, except closer to an understanding of myself.

I desire my choices and freedoms as much as I ever did. But I have started to see something about how they work, these choices, freedoms and desires.

And the point is not that they get me into trouble, though they do all the time. The point is not that I need to lock these choices and freedoms and desires away from myself, because I am not balanced enough, or mature enough, to be sensible about them, although there is enough accumulated wreckage around me to suggest that as a plausible way of putting it. I have discovered that there is nothing wrong with having choices, freedoms and desires. They are the breath within me. My problem has been with what they mean, where they go, what I think they are for. When I pursue my desire in a particular direction and chase it as far as I can, the pain I invariably find myself entering is not a symptom of an angry God's wish to punish me but of the fact that, in searching for something in the wrong place, I have become lost in a fog.

I shout out no Hallelujah! I do not beat my breast. Instead I look in on myself in puzzlement and frustration, like a mechanic peering into an engine, his ear down, listening for a clue concerning some elusive stutter. What matters here is not the idea of repentence, but of understanding. What matters is that my experience whispers to me, again and again and again, that there is a way of living that, understanding the nature and limits of human desire, and harbouring no sense of superiority or smugness, derives from a pattern in human experiences that is consistent and ineluctable and in total harmony with everything I really, truly, am.